To: Patri

Clay Henry

Self Exposed

Self Exposed

Uncovering Dynamics of the Spiritual Self

Clay A. Henry

WinePressPublishing
Your Book, Defined. Since 1991.

WinePress Publishing (PO Box 428, Enumclaw, WA 98022) functions only as book publisher. As such, the ultimate design, content, editorial accuracy, and views expressed or implied in this work are those of the author.

ISBN 13: 978-1-4141-1717-1
ISBN 10: 1-4141-1717-5
Library of Congress Catalog Card Number: 2010900918

Throughout the book, the author avoids the single use of one gender category (i.e., masculine). Various combinations of pronouns—his or her, his and her, etc.—are all intended to include both genders without diminishing or enhancing the importance of either sex.

Contents

Preface: Where I'm Coming From. xi

Acknowledgments. xxiii

1. May I Help You...? 1
2. ... Survey the Barriers of Christian Spirituality? 9
3. ... Better Understand Self? *Part 1*. 27
4. ... Better Understand Self? *Part 2*. 39
5. ... Relate Self-Denial to Followers of Christ? *Part 1* 53
6. ... Relate Self-Denial to Followers of Christ? *Part 2* 71
7. ...Relate the Cross to Followers of Christ? *Part 1*. 83
8. ... Relate the Cross to Followers of Christ? *Part 2*. 97
9. ... Relate the Cross to Followers of Christ? *Part 3* 113
10. ... Relate the Cross to Followers of Christ? *Part 4* 129
11. ... Envision a Fulfilling Life? *Life* 143
12. ... Envision a Fulfilling Life? *Spiritual Maturity* 161
13. ... Envision a Fulfilling Life? *Deliverance from
    the Power of Sin and Self*. 175
14. ... Envision a Fulfilling Life? *Troubles* 189
15. ... Envision a Fulfilling Life? *The False Self*. 211
16. ... Envision a Fulfilling Life? *The True Self* 227

17. ... Envision a Fulfilling Life? *Marks of Spiritual Maturity* . . . 253
18. ...Envision a Fulfilling Life? *The Illuminated Self 1* 279
19. ..., Envision a Fulfilling Life? *The Illuminated Self 2* 299

Appendix A: Hyphenated Self-Terms 319
Appendix B: Scripture References to Self-Denial 325
Appendix C: Scriptures Containing Key Words 335
Appendix D: Models of Self. 337
Appendix E: Works of the Holy Spirit 339
Appendix F: What Christians May Know about Themselves . 341
Appendix G: List of Commonly Held Virtues. 345

Glossary. 347

Resources and Suggested Reading. 353

FIGURES

P.1.   An Inverse Relationship between Humility and Pride . . .xvi
P.2.   Spiritual Development by Addition of Virtues xvii
P.3.   The Illumination of a Believer's Self. xx
3.1.   Humankind's Pre- and Post-Fall Existence 35
3.2.   Distinguishing Features of Self-Circles. 38
4.1.   "Low," "No," and "High" Self-Esteem People. 46
5.1.   A Division of Self in Peter (1st Example) 63
5.2.   A Division of Self in Peter (2nd Example). 65
5.3.   A Division of Self in Peter (3rd Example) 66
5.4.   A Division of Self in Peter: (4th Example). 66
5.5.   A Division of Self in Peter: (5th Example). 67
5.6.   A Division of Self in Peter: (6th Example). 68
5.7.   A Division of Self in Peter: (7th Example). 69
8.1.   A Matrix of One's Responses to Jesus' Commands. 103
8.2.   The Effect of Sin on Self. 107
8.3.   The Effect of the Cross on the Defiled Self. 109
9.1.   The Effect of Justification on Self. 114
9.2.   A Christian's Realization of the Indwelling Nature of Sin . 117

9.3. The Justified Self Does not Equal a Sanctified Self 117
9.4. A Range of Selves having Relative Amounts
   of Two Natures 118
10.1. Mystical Identification with Christ's Passion 134
11.1. The Contrast between Temporal and
   Eternal Perspectives 157
12.1. A Plot of Spiritual Maturity vs. Time 163
12.2. A Faultless Progression of Spiritual Maturity 166
13.1. Mortification of Self-Life 178
13.2. An Exchange Christ's Humility for a
   Christian's Spiritual Pride 182
13.3. Mean Percentages of Subunit Amounts in the S-Factor . . 188
14.1. The Mortification of Self-Life 190
14.2. The Transformation of Rejection to Acceptance 195
16.1. The Mortification of a False Self 230
16.2. The Transformation of a False Self to a True Self 242
16.3. Plot of Altruistic Index vs. Selfish Index 250
17.1. The Transformation of Self-Life Results in
   Love to Others 268
17.2. An Expanded Matrix of One's Responses to
   Jesus' Commands 272
18.1. The Illumination of Christ's Self 284
18.2. Dispersion of Natural Light into a Spectrum of
   Visible Colors 292
19.1. The Transformation of a Mind from an
   Old Self to a New Self 300
19.2. Transmission of True Light Disperses the
   Virtues of Christ 308
19.3. The Illumination of a Believer's Self 310

Preface: Where I'm Coming From

AFTER BEING GAINFULLY employed most of our married life, my wife and I decided to enter into retirement a few years ago. During this time we became somewhat contemplative, pondering our lives to this point. In doing so we attempted to assess any notable achievements and failures. We understand that it is not uncommon for most seniors to look back to former years and begin to ask questions such as, "If we could relive our lives, would we make other choices or do things differently?" So in our case, these thoughtful moments not only involved some of the more gigantic decisions all humankind has to make, but especially included certain matters pertaining to our Christian beliefs. It also seemed normal for us to compare our evaluation to the views of what we assumed other believers of a similar age group might have had.

According to several published studies, the average church-goer in our nation grew up in the Christian faith, attended Sunday school or confirmation, diminished in the church activities as a teenager and young adult, yet attended church sporadically throughout his or her adult life. There also exists a similar group of Christians who, for whatever reason(s), have all but neglected any church affiliation. Both groups generally think of themselves as essentially no better or worse than others who also identify themselves as Christians. But the common threads that run in these individuals seem to be a lack of achievement in their spiritual lives with a less-than-complete degree of joyfulness, contentment, peacefulness, and lasting fulfillment. We recognize that all of these thoughts and emotions are meant to be realized by the attainable promises God made to all obedient followers of Jesus Christ.

We unabashedly admit that these same strands, that is, lacking spiritual achievement and completeness, also seem to be woven into our lives and we want to come to terms with them. So we particularly reflected on our past involvement in local churches during our earlier years. Throughout this thought-provoking process, we began to wonder whether we had been on the right track, or whether there was something to which we hadn't paid enough attention. It was such an issue to us that we fervently prayed to God for help and engaged in the reading of Scripture as we groped for answers to our predicament.

At that point my attention was directed to Matthew 16:24–25: "Then Jesus said to His disciples, 'If anyone wishes to come after Me, he must deny himself, and take up his cross and follow Me. For whoever wishes to save his life will lose it; but whoever loses his life for My sake will find it.'"

Even though I've heard and read these perplexing verses in this parable several times in the past, they were hard to understand, so I thought, *This passage is too taxing for me; it just does not make any common sense. I'll skip over it and maybe I'll understand it someday.* As it turned out, my comprehension of these verses was in the making.

What occurred was the beginning of an unexpected disclosure of knowledge that both my wife and me should have previously gained and applied from our participation in church activities. These two verses in Matthew (and repeated in the other gospels) were spoken by Jesus to His disciples and to any of His would-be followers shortly before the end of His earthly life. Specifically, His utterances were a paradoxical instruction that, in my opinion, contained at least four significant words: *self*, *deny*, *cross*, and *life*.

Jesus seemed to be speaking directly to us, and indeed saying, "Listen, Clay and Rose Marie, here is the necessary directive if you really want to be My followers. It will require a deliberate, well-thought-out choice for each of you. It's an option, and entirely up to you to decide which of the two roads to take."

In this last statement, we thought Jesus might be referring to His earlier teaching when He said, "The way is broad that leads to destruction,...and the way is narrow that leads to life" (Matthew 7:13–14). We were saying in effect to ourselves, "This sure sounds like we can't journey on both roads or skip back and forth between the two." It was only later that we discovered the roads were separate ways to follow Christ. Basically, our option centered on Christ's way or on our way. We hadn't realized the gravity of making a decision like this before: choosing a self-oriented approach or deciding to follow Jesus on His terms. If we chose Jesus' way, we knew one of the implications was to trust in Him and the Holy Spirit for continual guidance during our journey of faith. Yes, this directive of our Lord and our obedient response to it could well be a missing link each of us should have addressed and acted upon many years ago.

As a result of this spiritual insight, with the approval and endorsement of my wife, I initiated a comprehensive study on this particular command of our Lord to deny self and carry a cross. Using different translations of the Bible, in addition to reading commentaries, the writings of several historic and contemporary Christian authors, and engaging in dialogue with fellow Christians as reference material, I wrote this book.

Surprisingly, another event occurred, almost in concert with the "newness" of rereading and gaining a better understanding of the passages in Matthew. We were invited to participate in a biblical-related process called the Journeymen that was presented as a means of understanding the significance and the application of spiritual growth in a Christian's life. Again, because of our past activities in church, we were not totally ignorant of this term. As we progressed in this study, we soon discovered that in practical terms, believers who deliberately choose to follow Christ should not consider maturing in their faith an option, but a responsibility and a privilege that is clearly based upon Holy Scripture.

Could it be that we were living a lackluster type of Christian life and not experiencing the joy commonly associated with obedience to God's Word? It could be that we were somewhat "out of tune" and perhaps like those early Christians to whom the writer of Hebrews said, "For though by this time you ought to be teachers, you have need again for someone to teach you the elementary principles of the oracles of God, and you have come to need milk and not solid food" (Hebrews 5:12). The term *milk* likely refers to rudiments of religion as known from Old Testament teaching. Historically, for Christians, milk may simply mean a kernel of basic knowledge, such as the doctrine of justification, requiring little or no more than merely faith in the sacrificial death of Christ as a means of salvation.

After all those years of church involvement, and now in our seventies, what basic doctrine of God did we not get? The answer to all of these questions seemed to be that our spiritual growth had somehow become stunted earlier in our Christian walk, and consequently we had not achieved the maturity and accompanying joy we should have gained well before this time in our lives. Not long afterward, we began to believe that practicing a more Christ-oriented life was the second of the two major missing links in our lives—the first being a determined resolve to follow Him.

Regarding spirituality, and particularly spiritual growth, I must stress at the outset that I am addressing this subject not because we see ourselves in any way as perfect examples of maturity, but because we accept as true, along with many other Christian authorities, that this is one of the most lacking elements in the contemporary church. Furthermore, we understand that the qualities of spiritual maturity define the lives of individuals, of the church, and of society as a whole.

We now recognize the need for these qualities to be experienced and expressed in the lives of every believer. To emphasize this need, I wondered if the New Testament should have a subtitle that highlights spiritual maturity. Maybe it could be named "The Gospel of Jesus Christ and the Pathway to Spiritual Maturity." This suggested heading is offered in respect to the Holy Bible and is given only to call attention to the importance of spiritual maturity in the lives of all true believers. As you will see in later chapters, the term *spiritual maturity* could be replaced with words such as *holiness, sanctification, servanthood,* or *discipleship.*

In addition to placing an emphasis on spiritual maturity, I will attempt to identify some "mathematical" relationships, correlations, between various terms as well as to illustrate graphically selected aspects of spiritual maturity. Yes, you read correctly. I believe one can discern certain features and levels of spiritual growth, perhaps similar to measuring growth of children. Physically, one measures parameters of growth, weight, and height as a function of age. Obviously, semiquantitative parameters will be used as indicators of spiritual growth, much like the scientific methodology used for assessing less tangible qualities in modern behavioral and psychological evaluations. If nothing more, I trust they will aid readers to estimate personally their own level of spiritual growth and thereby help establish a vision of attaining even higher levels of maturity, often referred to as Christlikeness.

In attempts to examine the extent of spiritual growth of believers, I would like to be able to estimate like and unlike traits of human nature, such as measuring amounts of light as a function of darkness or degrees of heat in the presence of cold. Take, for example, the traits of humility (submissiveness) and pride (excessive arrogance). Most of us know that humility and pride are widely defined as opposites and therefore can be viewed as inversely related. If both of these traits were somehow measured in a large group of people who had varying quantities of each, the hypothetical data would indicate an inverse relationship between the two terms as represented by the darker line depicted in figure P.1 below.

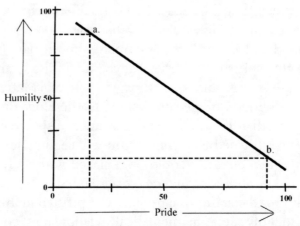

Figure P.1. An Inverse Relationship between Humility and Pride

Notice that at point *a* on the darker line, the humility of one individual is about 85 percent and pride is about 15 percent. Conversely, at point *b* in another person, humility is about 15 percent and pride is about 85 percent. If it was really possible to estimate these attributes, we could label a person's disposition as somewhat balanced between the two, or as predominantly humble or prideful. Obviously, the trait of humility would be an excellent indicator of spiritual growth in a Christian, whereas high levels of pride would not be expected from these results. Measurements of humility and pride would be unnecessary for Jesus, since He truthfully said, "I am gentle and humble in heart" (Matthew 11:29). We can confidently say that Christ is the only one whose humility value is 100 percent and pride assessment is zero percent.

The reader will find that I utilize several visual aids throughout this writing, such as figure P.1 above. I believe they are useful tools to help us better understand text or narration of speech, particularly when attempting to impart abstract ideas and concepts of spiritual matters.

Instead of trying to use numeral data as presented in the graphic above, another way to look at a person's spiritual growth is to view it in pictorial form. In 2 Peter 1:5–8 lists virtuous qualities or graces that will enhance the development of faith in believers: faith, knowledge, self-control, perseverance, godliness, brotherly love, and love. However, the names of these virtues are not necessarily the illustration of spirituality I have in mind; instead I will use simple circles.

For example, we can visualize spiritual maturity in an individual by drawing seven concentric circles that have the same outside circumference. As seen in figure P.2, the inner circles progressively become larger with each addition of another quality. Beginning with faith and ending with love, we can see how the successive addition of each virtuous quality to the preceding one will enlarge the inner circle at the expense of the darker outer part of the circle.

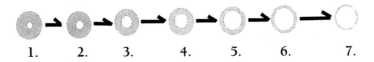

1.   2.   3.   4.   5.   6.   7.

Figure P.2. Spiritual Development by Addition of Virtues

I readily admit that this example of viewing spiritual maturity in figure P.2 is limited in so far as it does not provide any information about the time it takes or the means of bringing about these qualities. However, the purpose of these accumulations of Christian values is known. Peter tells us that the outcome of increasing development of spirituality in the lives of believers is to render believers useful and fruitful "in the true knowledge of our Lord Jesus Christ" (2 Peter 1:8).

The verse in which Jesus commands His followers to deny self and carry a cross contains the biblical truths relative to the concept of spiritual maturity in all believers. That is to say that what Jesus declared in these few words and the topic of spiritual growth are not mutually exclusive. As these directives are obeyed, I believe them to be linked together much like a master key that opens a door. When inserted into a previously unopened door of spiritual maturity, this proverbial key allows entry into a wonderment of new life, in which one admittedly experiences a measure of tension and discomfort along with increasing pleasures of joy, contentment, peace, and fulfillment. These latter qualities are the same elements many Christians apparently lack in their everyday lives.

To discern the qualities of self that promote or hinder spiritual maturity, we must look inside self. This need is somewhat illustrated in the photograph on the front cover of this book, which depicts a tree living above the ground with an illuminated mass of exposed roots deeply entrenched in the soil. The inherent composition and form of the earthly soil in which the normally unseen tree roots are embedded can represent the underlying nature of an inner self.

The inner self, like the makeup of soil, has a nature all its own that is spiritual and, like the living tree above ground, is rationally integrated in humankind's physical being. Biblically, we understand the origin of the internal self resulted from acts of disobedience to God. In some unknown manner, this nature is ancestral and able to propagate itself throughout history from generation to generation. When reading the Holy Bible, we find descriptive terms denoting this nature, terms such as selfish, prideful, evil, fleshly, darkened, defiled, and corrupt. Self, or at least a part of it, is generally characterized as a violation of moral laws and anything contrary to the character of a higher Being.

However, one does not require divine truths or any other religious writings to verify the existence of this often elusive unseen thing called self. It is self-exposing and self-evident throughout the world, apparent in all forms of the news media, and most of all from personal experiences of living in an imperfect world. Broken relationships, killings, wars, crimes, bigotry, and anger are only the beginning of thousands of examples that show us something is terribly wrong in the makeup of humankind.

Those who define humankind's nature as ungodly maintain that the outward sign of a person's wrongfulness is a direct reflection of his or her inner self—those elements that are counter to goodness. Therefore, the problem for those who seek righteousness for themselves and for others is twofold. First, how does one remove the wrongfulness of the inner self, and second, replace it with virtues of righteousness?

As a starting point, the answer to this all-important question can be derived by unpacking the title of this book, *Self Exposed: Uncovering Dynamics of the Spiritual Self.* In contrast to a static or unchanging condition, the spiritual self is dynamic. Quite often, such a state is characterized as an interactive system, especially one involving competing or conflicting forces. In this sense, the title of this book implies powerful forces exist within the inner self which are at odds with the other and constantly in quest of domination and control. Once this active dynamic between these spiritual forces is consciously realized, we can better approach the answer to the question stated above by achieving two major objectives of this writing.

One intention is to reveal interfering features of the ungodly power and to emphasize the imperative need to remove these hindrances. The second is to call attention to the provision of salvation that, by the grace of God and the finished work of Christ on Calvary's cross, Christians can detach these obstructions. As this provision is acted upon by followers of Christ, these barriers are overcome with the simultaneous development of virtuous characteristics.

I have selected portions of Ephesians and Hebrews in the New Testament to help emphasize both purposes of disclosing and removing the obstacles to Christian spiritual growth. Hopefully, these Scriptures can relate the soil and a tree's roots to an exposed self, and also show that the powerful illuminating light of Christ can help remove hindrances to spiritual maturity. The writers of Ephesians and Hebrews urge their readers "not to participate in the unfruitful deeds of darkness, but instead even *expose* them" (Ephesians 5:11, emphasis added) and to "See to it that…no *root* of bitterness springing up causes trouble, and by it many be defiled" (Hebrews 12:15, emphasis added); "all things become visible when *exposed* by light, for everything that becomes visible is light. For this reason it says, awake sleeper, and arise from the dead and Christ will *shine* on you" (Ephesians 5:13–14, emphasis added).

When these passages in Ephesians and Hebrews are knitted together, they are to be directed toward professing believers who, unwittingly or unknowingly, are sleepers, clouded in spiritual darkness, slumbering in their false security, and more spiritually dead than alive. Within the context of these verses, dozing persons are likely to continue to exhibit characteristics of immorality, impurity, and unfruitful deeds of darkness. They are told to awake and to arise, meaning that they need to be aware of their lostness and to come into the light of Jesus Christ. Everything is exposed by the light, illuminated by the light of the gospel. This good news tells us that Christ will enlighten the offspring of darkness to become children of light. These statements are in accord with all that is said elsewhere in the New Testament Scriptures, instructing reborn believers to grow spiritually and become set apart from the world.

"The Illumination of a Believer's Self" (fig. P.3) seen below is also shown on the front cover of this book among the normally unseen roots and surrounding soil. It represents a person who has heard the wake-up call of the gospel, is illuminated by the true

Figure P.3. The Illumination of a Believer's Self

light of God, and has removed significant portions of darkened obstacles. This drawing will be used in a later chapter to signify children of light who are becoming spiritually mature and to show their Christlikeness in a darkened world. Lastly, figure P.3 may also portray how those in God's family are to live righteous lives as stated by Jesus in His famous Sermon on the Mount. "You are the light of the world....Let your light shine before men in such a way that they may see your good works, and glorify your Father who is in heaven" (Matthew 5:14, 16).

My wife and I genuinely trust that the words that follow are in accordance with the truths revealed in Holy Scripture and the orthodox doctrines of the Christian church. It is also our earnest hope that you will find this book to be a significant help in your quest for a life of Christ-centered discipleship, and thereby reap increasing earthly pleasure in your heaven-bound journey. Come along on a mutually shared walk of faith based on the good news of the gospel. We can almost guarantee it will be an excursion into some unusual places where few have traveled before.

Acknowledgments

MY SINCERE THANKS go to those who in many ways assisted me in the writing of this book. Without their useful suggestions, editing and encouragement, I'm sure that I would have jettisoned this endeavor long ago.

Above all, I want to identify two women in my life who have profoundly contributed to my maturation in the Christian faith. In memory of my maternal grandmother, the first is Annie G. Thomas. As a child and through my early manhood, in her tender Christlike manner, she was the angel who helped guide me in my spiritual journey. The second is my devoted wife, Rose Marie Henry, a most special lady. She is steadfast in her trust and love of the Lord, an outstanding optimist and very supportive of my undertakings.

Chapter 1

May I Help You...?

Do not anxiously look about you, for I am your God. I will
strengthen you, surely I will help you.

—Isaiah 41:10

"MAY I HELP you find something?" Think for a moment about
how many times and under what circumstances you have
heard this question. In most cases, the person asking this question
perceived a need to assist another. The following story highlights
this question and is about three men, identified as A, B, and C,
who separately were shopping for the same advertised item in a
large department store.

Before they came to the store these three men were dissatisfied
with their lives. Each thought their spirits would be lifted if they
possessed a certain item that was happily owned by a few of their
acquaintances.

After arriving at the store, shopper A became frustrated as he
wandered up and down aisles and couldn't find the desired item.
Then unexpectedly, from behind him, a clerk asked, "May I help
you find something?" And after an exclamatory answer of "Yes, I'm
really lost!" the customer identified the item and responded to the
clerk's "Follow me." With his eyes firmly fixed on the clerk, he

trailed him to the shelf containing the desired item. He then discovered that there was not only one, but two items, each significantly differing in price. The reason for the great price differential was not immediately apparent to him. After the clerk explained reasons for the price difference and offered advice about which item might better suit his need, shopper A closely examined each of the two items, as to their construction, appearance, and durability. He then chose the most costly one, which had the greatest quality, thanked the clerk, paid the cashier, and left. Shopper A properly maintained and cherished his costly item with a great amount of joy, and it served him well during his entire lifetime. Moreover, several other individuals who saw the great satisfaction of customer A's purchase bought one for themselves.

Shopper B entered the store and he, too, was approached by a clerk who asked, "May I help you?" to which he quickly responded, "No, I am just looking around." After wandering aimlessly from aisle to aisle on several floors, he finally located the shelf containing the same two items sought by shopper A. After briefly listening to remarks offered by another clerk about the articles, he impolitely told him he did not need his help. Because the appearance of the two items was so similar, he finally chose the advertised item that was least expensive, paid for it, and left the store. B didn't care for this low-quality item, so it soon became useless, and B put it away with other discarded possessions in his attic.

The third man, C, also came to the department store looking for the advertised item, and a kind clerk asked him, "May I help you?" He abruptly and rudely said, "No, I don't need your help; I'll find it myself!" And indeed, this he did after meandering through the store. Shopper C listened for a short time to a store employee who described the two different items. He had serious misgivings about both of them, thinking that they were overpriced and would be of no use to him. He soon left with no intention to return.

This story illustrates five relevant points. The three men were lost in the department store (lostness), and an offer to help locate the item (guidance) was either accepted or rejected. After locating the items, a clerk provided pertinent information regarding the quality and cost of each item. Based upon these facts, the customers were provided with suggestions as to how well the item might meet their present and future needs (assessment). It was then that each decided to make the purchase or not (action), and the resultant level of satisfaction (happiness) was noted.

Relating A's actions in this tale to Christianity rests initially on a person's state of darkness and awareness of his or her lostness. Living without purpose or direction in an ungodly world many times motivates one to wake up. It is then that God's great summons of help will lead a person to accept the offer of redemption. This acceptance can be considered as an affirmation to the invitation made by Jesus to follow Him and this response entitles the person to be identified as a Christian.

However, the decision for attaining salvation is far more than just accepting the message of the gospel. Additional choices have to be made, some of which prove to be very difficult. In all cases, believers must recognize the need for help apart from themselves if they want to be followers of Christ throughout their lives. Subsequent to the act of becoming a believer of the gospel message, the topic of following Christ is the major avenue of thought that readers will find in this book.

The negative responses for help by both Customers B and C provide insights into their inner beings. Each relied on his own ability to locate the item and demonstrated a high degree of self-assertion and self-defiance. Perhaps each of them actually preferred to be lost, stubbornly so, which would suggest an obstinate, know-it-all attitude. Although Customer B's decision to buy the item was based primarily on cost, his purchase soon resulted in putting aside the product.

What is the relation of the behavior of Customer B—who, by his purchase implied an acceptance of the gospel message—to his initial reluctance to accept help? Here, I envision some believers maintain their self-dependency in their Christian faith and consequently are hesitant to receive freely offered help in their journeys of faith. The explanation for this unwillingness could be spiritual blindness, shallow knowledge of church doctrine, or possession of inaccurate preconceptions or inclinations about what it means to be a follower of Christ. Whatever the facts, the result was the same, namely, B gained little or no benefit from purchasing what he thought he wanted.

The New Testament book of Acts contains the account of the conversion and baptism of an Ethiopian to Christianity, aided by the preaching of apostle Philip (Acts 8:26–39). This narrative is especially engaging because it includes similarities to the tale of one of the department store shoppers. The five italicized terms below are selected features common to both stories.

The Ethiopian lacked understanding of the prophecy of Jesus in the Old Testament as he read Isaiah 53 (Acts 8:31). Philip was summoned by the Spirit to assist him (Acts 8:29) and asked, "Do you understand what you are reading?" (Acts 8:30). He responded by saying, "Well, how could I, unless someone guides me?" (Acts 8:31). The Ethiopian realized he was *lost*, as did one of the shoppers, and willingly accepted *guidance* from Philip, likewise offered by the store clerk.

Philip further expounded to him about the Messiah's redemptive work as prophesied by Isaiah. Reminiscent of the appraisal of items in the store by the shoppers, this careful *assessment* of scriptural truths (Acts 8:32) resulted in the Ethiopian making a heartfelt decision, saying, "I believe that Jesus Christ is the Son of God" (Acts 8:37). He immediately *acted* upon this belief by choosing water baptism to signify his identification with Christ (v. 38). Lastly, like the happiness of one shopper in purchasing the item, the Ethiopian continued his journey, *rejoicing* (Acts 8:39).

Like the guidance offered by Philip and the clerk, the design of this and remaining chapters is to offer help to those who are nonbelievers and to those who are already in their Christian journey of faith. But, as most know, God is really the Great Helper. Throughout the entire Bible, our creator God has revealed Himself, among other divine characteristics, as loving and forgiving, and is viewed by many believers throughout the centuries as the great Giver and Helper. In the New American Standard Bible, God is recorded as saying to Isaiah, "I will help you" (Isaiah 41:10). Yes, as many can attest, indeed God is the great Helper!

But to receive help, as in the Ethiopian's case, one must first admit to being lost and willing to accept guidance. Also, there must be a helper or a guide who leads and shows the way to another, as Philip proved to be to the Ethiopian and as God proved to be for Isaiah.

You may think that as the author of this book I am using the question "May I help you?" to assist you in your spiritual journey. If so, frame this question around the sacred words of Jesus Christ as found in Matthew 16:24–25: "If anyone wishes to come after Me, let him deny himself, and take up his cross and follow Me. For whoever wishes to save his life will lose it; but whoever loses his life for My sake will find it."

Regarding this text in Matthew and an almost identical one recorded in Luke 9:23–24, let us look at Peter as an example of one who displayed a wide range of loyalties toward Jesus. To some extent, he is the one to whom most of us can relate. Peter, by the way, was probably one of Jesus' dearest friends. For three years he closely followed Jesus, listened to His teachings, and witnessed with excitement a variety of Jesus' miracles. Peter likely believed Jesus possessed divine powers and indeed was the expected Messiah who would restore Israel and save the people.

When Jesus began to tell him and the other disciples He would suffer, be rejected, and be killed, Peter forcefully rebuked Jesus, essentially saying "No, Lord!" to such a forecast. It was then that Jesus instructed Peter and the other disciples to deny themselves and take up their crosses; then Jesus related these two commands to the saving and losing of life (Matthew 16:21–25). Rejection, suffering, dying, and self-denial were the last things these disciples wanted to hear about from the lips of the long-awaited Messiah.

It's totally understandable that we, like Peter, would react in the same way. Many of us would say, "Shouldn't religious faith make us acceptable and deliver us from suffering? Don't we just want to imitate and worship a God who shields us from adversity and protects us from harm?" All this business of denying ourselves and thereby giving up individual rights goes against every grain of common sense. Then to top it off, we, too, are instructed by Jesus to bear crosses! I have always been taught that Jesus is the one who died on a cross for our sins, and this one human act gave us salvation forever. Some might even say, "Yes, we understand Christ is our Savior, but what is this business of adding a title of 'Lord' to the name of Jesus Christ?" Yes, Peter's objection to Christ's words would likely be the same as ours, for we also possess a human nature with natural fondness of self-preservation and self-centeredness. Is there more to the gospel story than we have been told? And are there some things about ourselves that need to be exchanged, renovated, and transformed?

I maintain that there are clear scriptural answers to these and other related questions of which we may gain practical application by taking a closer look at the phrases *denying self*, *take up your cross*, *follow Me*, and sayings about saving and losing one's life. I will consistently refer to these words of Christ as they are found in all four of the Gospels in the New Testament. These passages of Scripture have substantially helped many of us in our spiritual journeys, and like those who have experienced a sense of joyfulness, I want to share my enthusiasm with others.

The sole motivation for the following pages is similar to that of the helpful clerk who modestly offered help to the wandering customers. He helped both in locating the item and by explaining further details concerning its use. I am asking this same question: "May I Help You?" At the same time I am offering assistance in discovering that something or, as we shall soon see, Someone. Perhaps you are looking for more pleasurable experiences or hoping to discover greater satisfaction in your spiritual life. Admittedly, many people in our culture are seeking all kinds of happiness, finding it, and enjoying it for the moment. But, at the same time, scores of these pleasure seekers admit there must be something more to life.

It is to that something or that Someone that we are devoting our primary attention here. Author Rick Warren addressed this same issue in his recent book *The Purpose Driven Life*. Among other considerations, he strongly suggested that the desire of people for a sustained, long-lasting, satisfying life here on this planet involves seeking, finding, and pursuing the will of God.

If the premise stated in the preface is correct, there are many Christians who also seem to be lost and need help to discern the will of God and to make progress in their spiritual maturity. Could it be that these particular Christians, for whatever reasons, are negligent in seeking, finding, and pursuing God's will?

At least in part, could you be one of these Christians? If so, this book is for you, and I sincerely ask the question posed above: "May I help you find something?" I am sure you may have already sensed that the something I am referring to is life, a new life with eternal dimensions, as amply described by Jesus Christ, the inspired writers of the New Testament, and leading authorities of Christian theology.

I am quick to add the other part of the question: "May I help you find that special Someone?" That Someone is none other than Jesus Christ. However, please know that I do not necessarily try to exclusively address this question to a particular denomination or brand of faith. I believe numerous people, ranging from unbelievers to those who claim advanced spiritual maturity, can gain additional insight into the doctrinal truths of the Bible.

In the preface I told you where I'm coming from, and in this chapter I'm giving hints to where we're going. You may already know our destination, but if you're unsure, recall Customer A. Not only did he verbally acknowledge being lost, but he willingly followed the clerk and had to make additional choices, all of which resulted in a great amount of satisfaction for himself as well as others who witnessed his pleasure.

Similarly, when the Christian finds a solution to an initial problem of lostness, further assessments await. Specifically, the believer must be mindful of potential benefits and difficulties that would come into play during his remaining earthly life. One also should realize there are costs, sometimes excessive costs, and therefore, one must decide if the price is worth entering into a new life with an expectation of gratifying outcomes. These and additional considerations will be presented in later chapters.

My role in this book is merely offering to be a guide. As previously stated, we should realize that the real Guide is none other than the Triune Godhead. I simply offer helpful advice for seeking, finding, and experiencing a meaningful and sanctified life here on earth. My intention is certainly not to dictate dogmatically a series of steps that lead to a magical state of euphoria, but to help escort you in your journey with Christ and thereby enable you to experience a more satisfying spiritual life.

... Survey the Barriers of Christian Spirituality?

I do believe. Help my unbelief.

—Mark 9:24

A S NOTED IN the preface and chapter 1, I believe the two verses (Matthew 16:24–25) spoken by Christ and the matter of spiritual maturity of Christians as presented throughout the New Testament appear to be unrelated. However, based on closer examination, I intend to show that they are directly linked to one another.

We now begin to consider some of the potential difficulties, either directly or indirectly associated with the understanding and application of Matthew 16:24–25. These barriers or potential obstacles will be arbitrarily classified under the titles of Cultural (Worldly), Church, and Christians. Keep in mind that these three categories are used as a means of grouping similar subjects within a title and are not rigid, as many times they will overlap.

CULTURAL OR WORLDLY INFLUENCES

Western societies and cultures vary, both in time and geography. It is not my purpose to detail or to categorize the variations in all of them. Therefore, I am identifying only a few of the more commonly mentioned systems of belief, philosophies, and ideologies in today's society. These structures may have the capacity to impact negatively and thereby bring about doubt in the minds of those who believe otherwise.

The culture in which we live might be viewed as the landscape of our environment. As in all natural habitats, there is the presence of harmful or noxious substances, and in our case, anti-Christian toxins. As believers in the Judeo-Christian tradition, we need to guard against poisonous practices, that is, the habits in our lives that pollute us. If we allow the culture to infringe upon our lives, it may influence us to make ungodly choices. So we must be aware of these venoms in order to maintain vigilance and discipline to avoid the many snares in our culture that may endanger us. In this regard, I see three common denominators of these cultural elements that stand in opposition to traditional views held by most Jews, Muslims, and Christians.

The first cultural standard is simply unbelief. Most nonbelievers cannot fathom a spiritual world, let alone a biblical worldview. Unbelief is deeply rooted in their minds by what they think to be the subjective or biased nature of a believer's faith. They seem to want to get answers from both religious conservatives and liberals in a way that comports with common sense, a way that fits with their knowledge of how the world works. In other words, these doubters demand irrefutable and objective proof of a God while they maintain a perpetual state of unbelief.

The second denominator is that many cultural systems have an active agenda against Christian communities because Christian beliefs are thought to intimidate and threaten them. Through such avenues as the arts, entertainment, media, and education, they vigorously promote their own beliefs in many menacing ways that are contrary to those held by most evangelical Christians.

The third factor is most clearly seen as social idealism, which claims that society should establish a standard model by which all people should hold fast. If citizens would only reject their notions of absolute truth and then integrate themselves in a model of communal or shared experimentation, the world would become a much better place. People unwilling to become absorbed into this social order are commonly identified as exclusive, dogmatic, intolerant, old-fashioned or fundamentalistic.

It may be useful to identify these three features by titles that are commonly used to describe these so-called philosophies. To repeat, there is a great deal of overlap between and among them. Such designations include naturalism, constructivism, relativism, individualism, materialism, secularism, consumerism, pragmatism, and lastly, worldly idolatry.

Naturalism

We can define naturalism as a belief in religious truth from nature alone, a belief that all religious truth is derived from nature and natural causes, and not from divine revelation. It is a doctrine that rejects spiritual explanations of the world; this system of thought discards all spiritual and supernatural explanations of the world and holds the premise that science and reason are the sole basis of what can be known. In its strictest sense, naturalism provides the basis of the evolutionary theory of the physical and biological world.

Constructivism, Relativism, and Individualism

The assertion that reality is something we construct and beliefs are merely the sum total of what we make of them is observed on many of our college campuses. Its supporters declare that truth and reality are simply made by individuals in dialogue with one another. It really does not matter what worldview a person chooses as long as one is chosen. There is no truth with a capital T, but only personal truths. To them, it is the journey that matters, not the destination; and there is no such thing as a final cause or answer.

It is becoming abundantly clear that the surging moral aspects of constructivism, relativism, and individualism in our boundary-less culture are eroding our value system. They reveal themselves most significantly in the breakdown of the family, which of course, most often affects children negatively. What's more, sleazy television, movies, and music poison the minds of young people, dulling their consciences. In addition, the curricula of most public schools do not allow the teaching of right from wrong, only tolerance. Therefore, these three *isms* of our culture tend to produce young people who seem to have either a limited or no moral compass.

Individualism is a term used to describe a moral, political, or social outlook that stresses human independence and the importance of individuality, self-reliance, and liberty. Individualists promote the unrestricted exercise of individual goals and desires. They oppose most external interference with an individual's choices. This resistance likely influenced early citizens of the United States who fled state and religious oppression in Europe to seek personal individuality and the protection of human rights, which later became popular with the framers of the U.S. Constitution and Bill of Rights.

It is easy to understand, then, the high regard of individuality many have, so much so that they also oppose the views of traditionalists, institutions of religion, or any other group possessing authority. According to individualists, such authority would only limit a person's choice of actions, especially when those actions do not violate the rights of other individuals. It is also understandable why people with this ingrained mind-set have little or no willingness to submit to the divine authority of God and Judeo-Christian beliefs.

Materialism, Secularism and Consumerism

In our capitalistic culture, physical images turn out to be materialistic. These worldly deities, along with a person's fixation on money, are also recognized as major barriers to spiritual maturity. Materialists' entire view of the universe, and the philosophy that emerges out of that outlook, depends upon the notion that the world one can see, hear, feel, touch, and smell is all there is. Materialists are opposed to a fairly new scientific endeavor of nature called Intelligent Design, which provides data that suggest a cause beyond what nature alone can explain. They also have an antispiritual attitude, which minimizes any worth of religious

12

beliefs, and they highly value the acquisition of material goods, sometimes defined as consumerism.

To people like the late Carl Sagan, a world-famous writer of the natural sciences, the whole future of humankind depends on being able to coax people away from their so-called irrational beliefs and to establish that there are no explanations of human nature that go beyond nature. This philosophy is akin to secularism, which promotes the exclusion of religion from public affairs. It is the belief that religion and religious bodies should have no part in political or civic affairs or in running public institutions, especially schools.

Materialists, secularists, and consumerists are combating the idea that the universe has meaning. Most of us have heard this thought disseminated before, but we don't always realize just how much it has infiltrated our culture and our lives. Generally, religious opponents of these *isms* say that such philosophies seek to give an entirely materialistic explanation of human intelligence, one that reduces it to a string of pointless physical causes. It tends to kill the soul, and in the process, reduces all of the evident genius of humanity to dust.

Pragmatism

Pragmatism is a practical approach to problems and affairs, in which any perceived truth is to be tested primarily by practical consequences of belief. Nobody will deny the development of a modern cultural attitude that is commonly called instant gratification. There are many examples about obtaining a desired item, whether material, psychological, or spiritual. Tangible results, particularly those that are immediate, are all that matter; quick proofs of present success and temporary satisfaction, indulgence, enjoyment, pleasure, and delight are the confirmations of pragmatism, giving hardly any thought to consequences.

There is a recognized element of society that operates as an approved source of solving human personal problems in our Western culture. Their acceptance is largely based on their integration into the scientific field of psychology. Their pragmatic approaches in solving personal problems of humans are largely grounded on behavior modification techniques that often disallow few if any biblical positions. These professionally trained individuals might be recognized in some of the phraseology used to treat patients, such as "Love yourself"; "think good thoughts about yourself"; "improve yourself"; "think positively"; "you are the key to your own future"; "no wonder you feel awful, considering how badly you were treated as a child." In the end, but not in all cases, these psychotherapies only tend to glorify self.

We even see American pragmatism spreading in the growing area of psychological counseling by laypeople, especially with the advent of counselors known as coaches, who give quick advice to anyone with a problem. When analyzing predicaments, many coaches use the common catch phrase "Whatever works for you." Using this abbreviated advice for the correction of an identified difficulty is labeled as either good or successful. But somehow truth and what is right never seem to enter into the real solution for the troubled individual who seeks resolution. This is but another example of expediency, where immediate results are justified without a regard to bringing about a complete problem correction.

Culture-Based Idolatry

We see in our Western culture an excessive quantity of alluring idols of all sorts. These idols are any cultural image, idea, or object that is worshiped, as opposed to the belief that there is only one God. Probably the greatest idol is that found in the entertainment industry. Modern people have become a parasite on the world, acquiring gratification from the environment, unable to live apart from the stimulation society affords. It hardly needs saying, but there are elements of goodness in many of these avenues of enjoyment. It is when one devotes excessive amounts of time to these pleasures, and particularly to those having immoral features, that idolatry comes sharply into focus (Tozer 1955, 31).

CHURCH

I need to briefly define *church*, for there are many ways the term is used. Some think of church as merely a building that houses attendees at various times of the week. Others immediately perceive the church to be an integral part of a larger organization identified as a denomination or as a universal church. These two examples barely touch on the many ways people identify the term. For the purpose of this writing, I simply define church as any organizational order that has a Christian doctrine that proclaims the gospel of Jesus Christ and the other writings as recorded in the Bible. In this regard, the church would have little or no trouble adopting a statement such as the Apostles' Creed as a part of its Christian doctrine. (See the glossary for a summary of terms used in orthodox Christianity.)

As strange as it may seem, there are certain aspects of the church itself that may be barriers to spiritual maturity. It seems that several Christian churches, especially those in the latter half of the twentieth century to the present, have neglected or at least marginalized the importance of some of the traditional doctrines of the church. We have experienced a period in which even some evangelical churches hardly dared to breathe a word of some doctrines because of the fear of being classified as holy rollers or self-haters. To maximize the importance of knowledge of these principles in the life of the believer, the church must assume a more responsible role for teaching time-honored scriptural doctrines.

Keep in mind that individual Christians have a responsibility to seek the truths of biblical doctrine and to apply the reality of these facts to their lives. However, I emphasize here that the church itself must take an equal or greater active role in presenting all of the major truths of Holy Writ. We will briefly focus on three areas that should be closely examined.

Authority of Scriptures

It has been suggested that the majority of the religious left and some evangelicals cannot tolerate the idea of the authority of Scripture, saying that truth is knowable only if we experience it. Charles Colson contends that if we weaken the Bible as our authority, we give up more than just some ancient set of dogmas and rules. Essentially, he believes that it leaves us rootless and drifting, ready to latch onto any fad. This conflict centers around authority—specifically, whether Christians are willing to acknowledge the Bible as the divine source of truth.

Validation from ourselves (self-validation) simply means we make up our own god. We Christians may interpret the Bible differently and we may apply it to life differently, but the Bible has to be the ultimate authority. Otherwise, we end up worshiping the goddess of tolerance and believing that broadmindedness takes precedence over truth.

Christian Education

There is an idea among some Christian educators (seminary faculty, pastors, teachers, and so forth) that although they endeavor to teach students traditional doctrines, somehow education appears tainted and deformed by the culture. While in training, many students declare their lives to be under the banner of Christ. Yet under the umbrella of Christian education, they continue to be exposed to lies, half-truths, and deceptions. Somehow the spirit of worldly philosophies, such as naturalism, creeps into their thinking. This should not be too surprising, since in our open society all of us are in contact with various *isms* and counter-Christian philosophies.

According to some in the field of Christian education, the major theme of Scripture is that the people of God should be holy, or more accurately stated, pursue holiness. Teachers must become bold in identifying sinful attitudes and practices, and be held responsible for instructing their students about these poisons that deprive them of exhibiting the glory of holiness in their lives.

It may be that although we are the most Christian-educated generation of believers who ever lived, it seems like there is a lack of heart knowledge in contrast to head knowledge. Some critical teachers of Christianity assert that we are learning a faith that is primarily information oriented, designed to help us be smarter. It is a learning that is focused more on content than on in-depth knowledge. As a result students become marginalized in our postmodern society, more self-centered, and what they learn has little impact on their lives and the lives of other believers.

Meanings of Salvation and Sanctification

One of the major tasks of the Christian church is to awaken individuals regarding their unholy existence in contrast to the holiness of God. As previously stated, they are told to stir, to break the surface of their spiritual consciousness, to come out of their catnaps, and to realize their depravity. This endeavor is especially important for new converts to the gospel message. Is it too broad of a statement to say that the majority of so-called Christians are like this? Their eyes are partially opened, but are they merely converted and not given clear guidance into further aspects of salvation the Bible clearly shows?

Salvation means a lot of different things. One foundational definition of salvation is that we are brought to the place where we are able to receive deliverance, a sovereign work of grace, a free gift from God on the authority of Jesus Christ, namely, forgiveness of sins. A significant sign that a person is saved is that he or she has received something from Jesus Christ. That something allows the new believer to live in a way that is objectively different than the person lived before.

For some converts, including some who have grown up in a church, believing in salvation these days has been reduced to a once-done act that requires no further attention. For these people, this act is an intellectual affirmation of Christ's atoning act, and thereby they receive salvation. Little more is required of the new believer by some church officials, except to attend services and provide charitable donations to the church.

This scenario can be labeled as a misguided doctrine of a divided Christ, namely, at one time Christ is a Savior and at another time He is Lord. In other words, a sinner may be saved by accepting Him as

17

Savior *without* yielding to Him as Lord. This manner of presenting salvation seems to be heretical, for hearers of this principle are permitted to accept one of Christ's offices and reject the other. So, it is obvious that such a deviation from traditional dogma will give new believers an incomplete view of their salvation. Yielding to His Lordship in the process of sanctification is an integral aspect of salvation, and this means we consciously are to allow Him to be the Lord of our lives.

The issue of the gospel of Jesus Christ and salvation comes into play with many churches that borrow methods from our society's pop culture. Some churches, including evangelical congregations, have planned their orders of worship following formats used in the world of secular entertainment. Most apparent is the use of contemporary Christian music and high-tech visual aids. Some skeptics of this approach have suggested that this is a way of enticing worshipers to continue to attend their services, hoping they become names and numbers on the church's "saved list." I am neither condemning nor condoning this progressive method. This is a deviation from traditional church services and as far as I know, has yet to be shown to have any significant merit in the long run.

CHRISTIANS

The New Testament addresses families and clusters of people as elements of the body of Christ or as the church. For the most part, however, more attention is directed to individuals. The following group of factors centers on individual believers in the Christian community. Each of these issues may have an impact on the understanding and behavior of the person, and could be a possible obstacle to his or her spiritual maturity.

Appearance of Duplicity

We have all heard criticisms leveled against Christians. The tone of these judgments usually deals with the appearance of hypocrisy or deceitfulness; critics say Christians act and speak two different ways.

A.W. Tozer, in his book *The Radical Cross*, states that this duplicity is a weakness of many Christians who feel too much at home in the world. In their effort to achieve restful peace in a society that is not reborn spiritually and not repentant, they have lost their pilgrim character and have become an essential part of the very moral order against which they are sent to protest.

This is a common finding by those looking from the outside in. Namely, the faith that many nonbelievers encounter in Christians appears shallow, sentimental, and ornamental. It does not compare very well when held up against the whole of the Christian intellectual tradition. From the earliest times until about the middle of the twentieth century, the old wooden cross was viewed by the majority of Christians as a symbol of death, sacrifice, and deliverance from worldliness. Now the "new" cross, often outwardly displayed as a pretty piece of art, may give the impression of showiness. If indeed this is the case, the practice of moderation should help overcome most objections of duplicity.

I'm not suggesting that Christians refrain from wearing shiny crosses. Instead, each professing Christian should evaluate his or her speech, actions, and behavior to reflect those desirable traits in the faithful people of God as directed in His Word. The outward manifestation of godly characteristics, such as humility and kindness, is a very good indication that their origin is inwardly motivated by saintly virtues.

Motives and Desires

A person may appear saintly by saying and doing the right thing, thus presenting as a legitimate imitator of Jesus. But appearances are one thing, and what is going on inside is another. Are the motives coinciding with the actions and deeds? If not, the individual's quality of motives might be in question. For example, the great weaknesses of the Pharisees lay in the quality of their motives. These leaders of religion in the time of Christ produced empty religious activities.

At the root of all true spiritual growth in Christians is a set of right and purified desires. If these desires are dominant and if these wishes are directed toward God and holiness, spiritual maturity will surely result. If one allows *unholy* desires to enter the heart, there is the great probability that growth in such a Christian's life will cease or at least slow considerably. I emphasize the word *unholy* because we must understand that these worldly desires come out of our selfish and prideful natures, and we are powerless on our own to do away with them.

Archbishop of Canterbury Rowan Williams believes that the notion that faith involves the purification of desire is deeply embedded not only in Christianity but also in other traditions. Thus, it is logical to conclude that a person of Christian faith, when aided by the power of the Holy Spirit, who possesses holy and ordered desires, can correctly seek out and further develop his or her character. When we want what God wants, then our desires are best ordered after God's purposes. This alignment is much more than theoretical and gives us a genuine sense of joyous well-being as we yield to God's will. All of this is foundational to the spiritual growth of a Christian.

Dualism of Spiritual Natures

I believe humans are dualistic. Although each person is uniquely one, having his or her own distinct personality, the individual exists in a state of two parts or two natures, known as dualism. Christianity and most other religious systems have some form of moral dualism that is eternally opposed by two coexisting spiritual principles.

One nature of a person is inherently egotistic, having little or no consideration of an authoritative being such as God. This self-orientated tendency is often defined as human nature, and further defined as the subconscious pull of definite attitudes of the mind. These attitudes or dispositions are established in us in varying degrees even as infants. Attitudes that revolve around self become normal. In other words, they become habitual. That is why so many authorities believe we were all born with a self-centered human nature—because it seems so natural and normal to be that way.

The opposing aspect of moral dualism is the spiritual nature within a person who yearns for something greater than just self. Centuries ago, a great French philosopher, Blaise Pascal, called this a God-shaped vacuum that we each have within us. This paraphrase of his statement further explains his assertion: "There is a vacuum within all of us that can be filled by God only." As the Bible says, God "has set eternity in the hearts of men" (Ecclesiastes 3:11). God put that perpetual vacuum in each of us, and we all have a soul that yearns for that someone or something. Most theologians believe God did this so we would have the capacity to seek Him, find Him, and come to know Him in an intimate and personal way.

When our desires do not yield some sort of significant meaning and contentment in our lives, we frequently experience feelings of unease, restlessness, boredom, anxiety, and dissatisfaction. If we do not find joy in our hearts from our personal relationships with God, in all likelihood we will seek it elsewhere. This gives rise to desiring and actually needing amusement and entertainment as sources of mental pleasure. Following and choosing an inordinate type of these pleasures is an excellent indicator that the human nature of self has commanding control over one's godly nature.

Knowledge of God, Jesus Christ, and the Holy Spirit

Although a lack of knowledge about the Holy Trinity can arise from the inadequate teachings of the church, each individual must be responsible to comprehend to some degree the unity of three persons in the one God. Such knowledge transcends finite understanding, yet is of great value as we are challenged almost daily with unworthy, secularized views of the Father, Son, and Holy Spirit. God has plainly revealed Himself in creation, in both the Old and New Testaments, and most thoroughly in the teachings, character, and life of Jesus Christ.

Not having a truthful view of God may well be one of the most important causes of spiritual immaturity. If we perceive Him only as a stern Father who expects much, excuses nothing, is highly temperamental and extremely hard to please, it is understandable that we would seriously question any divine love toward ourselves. Conversely, if we hold Him to be kind, understanding, and loving, our whole outlook on life would reflect that belief. This latter notion will help us generate a deeper relationship with Him, giving us a desire to live godly lives, which would elevate our level of Christian spirituality.

Some individuals perceive His Son, Jesus Christ, as a utility, performing minor miracles on behalf of anyone who calls upon Him. Christ then becomes useful to the world like the gods of paganism. This view, similar to having an incorrect view of God, is but an example of many other imagined and perverted notions. Again, any distorted views of Christ will greatly impair spiritual growth.

The Holy Spirit is typically identified as the third person of the Holy Trinity. Of the triad, the Holy Spirit is considered by many to be the least known and understood. A part of this problem stems again from a lack of sound doctrinal teaching on the part of the church. However, each Christian needs to continually seek a better understanding of the Holy Spirit. (Please see appendix E, which lists some of the characteristics of the Holy Spirit as they may apply to spiritual growth.)

Knowledge of God's Purpose(s)

If surveys were taken of people of faith who profess knowledge of God, asking them what ultimate purposes or plans He has for the salvation of humankind, answers would vary from person to person. Reasons for such variations would include their particular interpretations of the wording of questionnaires, the quality and quantity of instruction provided by the church, and their personal understanding of God's purposes. Many laypeople are confused by the several ways salvation is defined as God's purpose to be applied in everyday life.

Take the word *redemption*, for example. This is a glorious Christian word with a wealth of meanings. One of the most straightforward is that it refers to the divine purpose of salvation. The intention is simply to make us holy and restore us in the likeness of God. However, it seems that many times this function is glossed over, and the church seldom presents how this magnificent purpose is accomplished in the lives of believers.

Every now and then we find that some believers understand the purpose of salvation to be God's offer of a pardon, with the condition that a rebel intends to live a more Godlike life. But immediately, many questions arise, such as these: How can one stop being a rebel? How can God pardon a rebel who has not given up his rebellion? and, How do intentions bring about a reformation from rebellion to holiness and Godlikeness? These and a multitude of other related questions become a problem for the immature believer in the midst of theology where faith is emphasized alone, and where reformation of the person and the grace of God are seldom addressed. Thus one can readily see some of the unclear nuances of religious terminology that are confusing to many and therefore become obstacles to Christian maturity.

However, regardless of the fine distinctions made in God's purpose of salvation for humankind, I am totally convinced that the gospel, the good news of Jesus Christ, provides the transforming power and the provision for moral reformation to remold oneself into a new way of life. The New Testament also supplies a model after which the new life is to be fashioned, and that ideal representation centers on Jesus Christ and His finished work on the cross of Calvary. This statement, along with Jesus' commands for His followers to become disciples, is a major theme or definition of what it means to mature spiritually in Christ.

Meanings of Self-Denial and of Cross-Carrying

In the Gospels Jesus told His disciples to do certain things if they were to be His followers. As we now read those words of Jesus as presented in Matthew 16:24–25, namely to deny self and to carry our cross, it might very well be that some of us believe His commands were outlandish and lacked any common sense. Such standards appear to weigh us down and hang over us like a dark cloud or evade us as we struggle to keep our heads above water as we cope with life's daily demands. All of these apparently irrational principles, along with several of the barriers to spiritual maturity, are certainly a cumulative cause for some people not to enter into a deeper spiritual life, which by the way, may even include some unanticipated difficulties.

Having stated these seemingly bleak thoughts, I confidently believe both of Jesus' commands for self-denial and cross-carrying are of paramount importance to us in our walks of faith. If indeed these directives of Jesus are so essential, the church should regard them as such and explain them to the extent that believing members would understand and apply them in their spiritual journeys. So, if our understanding and application of these two commands of Jesus is incomplete, it is quite possible that our Christian experience will be also lacking and will not be in accord with those faithful followers of Christ as recorded in Scriptures and throughout church history.

Knowledge of True Self

To know who we really are is to recognize the essence of the spiritual aspects of our entire beings. Philosophers and seers have tried to describe the recognition of one's true self for thousands of years. For Christians, it is vitally important to recognize ourselves and be able to put into words this conscious awareness of who we are spiritually. In contrast to a false self, a true self has an advantage to enter into a personal relationship with Jesus Christ as he or she matures in the likeness of God.

This self-knowledge is derived from a level of understanding the Triune God and basking in the everlasting and unconditional love of God. God's love toward us calls forth our capacity to love God and neighbor. Without this healthy self-knowledge, we live without a sense of place, of true belonging in the world, or contentment with God, self, and others. Contentment is just one of the divine blessings and promises we have as believers, all of which are based upon our total identity with Christ. Other firsthand blessings include, but are not limited to, acceptance, security, assurance, confidence, and significance.

Some groups sincerely believe the troubled world in which we live is composed of distressed individuals who all possess a variety of mental health problems. Such groups are usually allied with those in the field of psychology. There is an ongoing debate about the role of psychology in Christianity. Some writers and theologians have criticized psychology for promoting a fake selfhood, being self-centered, humanistic, and ineffective. Others argue for the legitimate use of psychology, maintaining that it is a science and thus is legitimate. In our day, the concepts of self-image, self-esteem, and self-love have become a heated topic and the subject of much discussion.

My purpose is not to debate the use of psychology or Christianity as a means of enhancing the betterment of a self. It would seem that the behavioral sciences can substantially contribute toward this goal, especially in the area of severe mental health problems.

One of the early and cardinal signs of a self problem, whether it is psychological or spiritual in nature, is that the individual senses a lingering incompleteness or uneasiness. If this red or yellow flag is anywhere near reality, it just might be an indication that the person possesses that unfilled vacuum that is calling out to find that mysterious something or someone we spoke of earlier.

If you perceive this to describe you, it really might be a call or invitation for you to stop looking in the wrong places to discover the hidden richness of your true, authentic self. If you accept this invitation, I have some very good news for you. From my own experience, as limited as it is, I know you will find the true treasure right where it is supposed to be—in the Holy Word, in Christ's life, and in the voice of the Holy Spirit within you.

Jesus Christ says, "I stand at the door and knock; if anyone hears My voice and opens the door, I will come in to him" (Revelation 3:20). It is the same Jesus who says, "Seek and you will find" (Matthew 7:7), and "If anyone wishes to come after Me, let him deny himself, and take up his cross and follow Me" (Matthew 16:24). We also have the assurance that God is a "rewarder of those who seek Him" (Hebrews 11:6). Yes, there is a Caller, and there is one who is called. And the one who seeks and finds the Father and Son by responding in faith to the calling will most assuredly receive wonderful rewards.

When we accept this calling, we are promised joyful experiences that would more than offset any negativity associated with those strange and unfamiliar words of Jesus to deny self and to carry our cross. These two declarations remain a part of the true and inspired words of God for those who earnestly desire a vital relationship with God. For those who are developing a Christlike character and a true self, it is a prescription for holy living in the here and now as well as in eternity.

Chapter 3

... Better Understand
Self?

Part 1

BREAKING NEWS AND DEVELOPING STORY

In bold letters, a "breaking news" header appears on the television screen; the newscaster comes into view and says, "We interrupt the reading of *Self Exposed* to keep readers on top of the latest happenings in the world. This late-breaking news has just been released. An international research team announced today they have discovered what appears to be a new and unusual genetic substance."

Brief explanations are then given about the two chief genetic researchers who isolated this substance from a vast number of adults who live throughout the world. The newscaster then says, "As details come in, we'll keep you updated, so stay tuned to this channel for this developing story."

SELF: A GENERAL VIEW

WHAT IS A word that is familiar to everybody—the uneducated, the academicians, the citizens of all nations, the young and old alike? The word is *self*. You may wonder why I am making such a big issue of singling out a one-syllable word that is used almost daily by everyone. After all, many think *self* is readily understood by the masses. If that is really the case, it should be easy to define the term. Let's begin with a few definitions of self taken from several modern dictionaries. Self is commonly defined as:

1. a perceived personality: somebody's personality, or an aspect of somebody's personality, especially as observed by others.
2. a complete being: an inclusive and individual person, especially one that somebody recognizes as his or her own.
3. oneself: one's being, inner nature, ego, individual, person.
4. character: the sum of a person's traits, including one's disposition, nature, constitution, reputation, type, shape, quality, habit, appearance, and behavior.
5. a union of elements: a body of emotions, thoughts, and sensations that constitute the individuality and identity of a person.
6. the whole of what makes up the entity called "me," and is not a fully separate entity.

There is another starting place to understand self better, again found in the dictionaries, and it is clustered as self-fixated and hyphenated self- words. You will see a connection of the word *self* to various nouns, verbs, and adjectives that better describe the nature of a person regarding certain attributes. These qualities are further described in terms of one's disposition, conduct, attitudes, and manifestations of demeanor or countenance. Please see appendix A for a partial listing of hyphenated self- terms after you read the next paragraph.

Before referring to this addendum, may I offer you a bit of advice that may make this a little more entertaining than just a studious task? In past presentations of this topic, I gave copies of the self-fixated words to attendees and told them to concentrate only on the hyphenated words themselves and *not* on the definitions. Using this same approach, read each term and make a quick judgment about whether you think it is good, bad, or neutral by simply making some mark by each (maybe g, b, or i). There cannot be any other categories, such as, "well, it all depends." By the way, this is not a test of your knowledge; there are no wrong answers. The exercise is just a way to get your initial opinion. After you read the rest of this book you may want to repeat this task to see if your assessments are the same as before. You may be surprised!

In addition to using dictionaries to understand self, historical accounts reveal that several philosophical thinkers have attempted to understand self, including the famous assertion "Know thyself" from Plato. In more recent times, selfhood has become a central theory in psychology. Several noted pioneers have advanced a hypothesis of selfhood into clinical psychology, namely in the personality theories of such men as William James, Alfred Adler, Erich Fromm, Abraham Maslow, and Carl Rogers. One particular theory has been popularized by their many followers and it is known as complete autonomy. It is the view that all humans are capable of existing independently, a somewhat restricted version of selfhood. It is a uniquely Western approach to humanistic psychology, and this model of self and its several variations are employed constantly in areas such as modern psychotherapy, psychoanalysis, and self-help.

Probably one of the best known theories of complete autonomy, or total independence, in psychology was offered by Abraham Maslow. He contended that as humans meet basic needs, they seek to satisfy successively higher needs. This supposition later became known as Maslow's Hierarchy of Needs, with the highest being actualization. Once this peak is attained, one's experiences are alleged to be self-actualized, mature, healthy, and self-fulfilled.

According to this theory, people with low esteem need respect from others. They may seek fame or glory, which is dependent on others. However, high-esteem people have confidence, competence, and achievement, needing only one person, namely themselves. Excluding manipulative practices, everyone else is unimportant to one's own success. At this point in time, they are alleged to be authentic and ready for self-actualization.

However, not all psychologists agree as to the clinical value of Maslow's theory. Some argue that the preoccupation with independence is harmful in that it creates racial, sexual, and national divides and does not allow for observation of the "self-in-other" and "other-in-self." Others claim that it is linguistically impossible for an individual to talk about, explain, understand, or judge him- or herself, since it requires the self to understand its *self*. These intellectuals are mainly psychology researchers who propose that this limited version of selfhood is now employed as a technology that allows humans to buy into an invented and arguably false sense of self. So there is a question among psychologists themselves as to self being a core construct in psychotherapy and self-help.

In an endeavor to understand the essence of selfhood, some modern social scientists are attempting to make a distinction between *sincerity* and *authenticity*. They claim that an emphasis on the primacy of self, called authenticity, is linked to psychoanalysis and involves finding and expressing the inner self and judging all relationships in terms of it. They believe it dominates our way of viewing ourselves and our relationships, which breeds doubts, promotes distrust, and challenges overcoming prejudices. In contrast, these sociologists believe in a model of selfhood, labeled sincerity. This model seems more secular than that of authenticity and would require us to act and really be the way we naturally present ourselves to others without having to become concerned about the hidden depth of our spiritual natures, but to behave as if we had none.

It should not come as a surprise to anyone that self is the object of much attention in our culture. The preoccupation with self today is readily seen in slogans like "Be all you can be," at websites like www.self.com, and in many magazines and how-to-books. Many of these not only target the secular world but also the Christian community. These measures are aimed at directing us to more successful relationships, becoming more self-fulfilled people, realizing our potential, experiencing more thrills each day, pounding ourselves into shape, improving our diet, managing our money, and on and on it goes.

While many of these self-generated measures are important and have their places, they put emphasis on individuality more than on relating to a spiritual order. Simply put, it looks like our society is focused on making satisfaction alone its goal or its religion. If this ungodly influence is a reality in our culture, it is entirely possible that Christians, particularly those who are less mature in their faith, would be hindered in their spiritual growth, perhaps even to the point of abandonment.

So at this juncture, as we clearly see from the varied definitions of self cited at the beginning of the chapter and the lack of agreement among scientists in the fields of psychology and sociology, the concept of self is generally not easily grasped, but nonetheless becomes significant as we probe the idea of self from a biblical viewpoint.

Since introducing Christianity into our discussion of self and making an assertion that many aspects of our modern culture are counter to Christianity, the remainder of this chapter will be devoted to examining what the Bible and theologians have to say about self, either directly or implied. In addition, I invite you to assess these aspects of self in terms of how they positively or negatively impact spiritual maturity in the lives of Christians.

SELF: A BIBLICAL VIEW

It may be of interest to note the occurrences of the term *self* and hyphenated self- terms in the Bible. Only three times does the Old Testament (in the NASB) mention these terms. The New Testament contains nineteen hyphenated self- words. It also contains seven incidences of the word *self* and should be defined no differently than common definitions described at the beginning of this chapter.

Since the Bible is not a dictionary, we do not expect to find a lexicon-type of definition of self. But there is sort of a description of a true self quoted by Jesus when he was asked, "What is the greatest commandment of the Law?" His answer, taken from the Old Testament (Deuteronomy 6:5), did *not* use the word self. He answered, "You shall love the Lord your God with all your heart, and with all your soul, and with all your strength, and with all your mind" (Luke 10:27; Matthew 22:37).

In this famous commandment the words *heart*, *soul*, and *mind* have been singled out as distinct parts of one's self, both spiritually and psychologically. In addition, attempts have been made to relate these three words to other terms, such as one's will, affections, sensitivity, intellectual faculties, and consciousness. Narrations and graphic diagrams of these relationships are interesting, but in some cases can be difficult to understand. To illustrate the complexity of these undertakings, I have provided two graphics that were taken from publications in which the authors sectioned self in various levels and categories. (See appendix D.)

Since there is no uniform understanding of heart, soul, and mind, I believe these words signify one and the same thing in Luke and Matthew, that is, we are to love God with all of our ability and power. In essence, this command describes how one is to love God, namely with the totality of self. This view seems to be supported in Paul's prayer to believers: "May the God of peace Himself sanctify you entirely; and may your spirit and soul and body be preserved complete, without blame at the coming of our Lord Jesus Christ" (1 Thessalonians 5:23). In this passage, Paul is likely not referring to the parts of self, but representing the whole person.

In like manner, when we view self in terms of completeness and wholeness, we have the opportunity to simplify the way self is viewed. Ideally, to do this I think a sphere would best represent self. Since we are primarily focusing on the inner self, we have to look inside the sphere. In doing so, we readily find that our need is met with the use of a circle or disc, a geometric form that many ancient scholars believed to represent something intrinsically divine or complete.

As we mentally view a self as a circle, we can begin to describe certain inner features of self. One of those aspects within the depths of a person, or self, is simply human nature, or at least a part of it. According to C. S. Lewis, there is a law of human nature that humankind does not share with animals or vegetables or inorganic things. This so-called Law of Right and Wrong, Moral Law, or Rule of Decent Behavior, is one that a person could choose either to obey or not. This law tells us what human beings ought to do or not to do. It is a sort of inner voice that urges us to do right and makes us feel responsible, uncomfortable, and even guilty when we do wrong. Many would call this part of our nature a conscience, a sense of right and wrong, which, by the way, also could be added to our definitions of self.

We then might ask, where did this so-called Law of Human Nature come from? To answer this question, we would have to look into humanity's ancient religious and spiritual traditions. Most of these belief systems, such as Hinduism and Buddhism, acknowledge that humans possess elements of unnaturalness or irregularity. The major thrust of these beliefs is to change these dysfunctions, but they apparently provide little or no insight into the origins of these abnormalities.

However, according to Christian doctrine, the infinite, holy God of the Bible was the source of this Law of Human Nature in the beginnings of time. The Scriptures declare that God created human beings of both sexes having a free will, not as an exact duplicate of God, but in His image, meaning His representative likeness, or spiritual life (Genesis 1:26–27). We can recognize this creational act as forming a soul or spirit in Godlike humans, having a wholly Godlike self, which was in total accord with the Maker and possessing selected traits of moral identification with the Maker. Such a statement of identification is in accord with the person in the fine arts who wishes himself somehow reflected in and through the purity of his artwork.

As we know from the New Testament, this original life of humankind had an image consisting of righteousness, true holiness, and knowledge (Ephesians 4:24; Colossians 3:10). In addition, God has set eternity within us (Ecclesiastes 3:11). Many biblical authorities think the purpose of this grace is that all humankind will have a perpetual desire for fulfillment (love, joy, peace). Some simply call it wishing for happiness. Nonetheless, this longing can become a driving force for Christians as we mature spiritually in the here and now and look beyond our physical lives on earth.

Thus we can conclude that when God created humankind it was His chief aim to make humans partakers of His perfection by communicating to them a measure of His own goodness and purity.

However, the special relationship of each creature to holy God could only be one of complete subjection and dependence, thereby allowing humankind to personify God and manifest His goodness. This supernatural relationship between God and humankind would result in a Godlike life, a life not given only once, but continuously moment by moment.

However, this perfect harmonious relationship with God was short lived because man and woman yielded to the temptation of the evil one, Satan. Thereupon they acquired a much different human nature, an attitude of the mind that some say is chiefly characterized as pride. Though seriously defaced, we can envision that the divine image continues to exist in self as humankind's absolute capacity for goodness. If the Godly likeness in humans is a self-conscious, rational, and ethical personality, it cannot be a merely accidental or fleeting attribute, but is an essential principle of our being.

Before the fall, God called all of creation, including the making of humans, "good" and "very good" (Genesis 1:31). Then this goodness in man and woman changed, and the natural took on a much different nature in comparison to the former human nature. To call it tainted would be a gross understatement. It now exhibited traits of selfishness, pride, and self-serving, quite contrary to its previous state of innocence and harmonious relationship with God.

We—like Adam and Eve and everyone else, including Christians and non-Christians, except Jesus Christ, in spite of our good intentions—are under the power of the anti-God force Paul calls "sin" (Romans 3:9). Each one came into this world having inherited a tarnished self, an ungodly self that is infinitely different from that in the newly created humans, an unholy nature that drives us to be self-centered and self-seeking. Our perverted natures curb any means of reestablishing right relationships with a holy God on our own and even deprive us of the power to love God with all our hearts, souls, minds, and strength.

This spiritual catastrophe means that sin essentially invalidated the Godlike self in the human system. Our legacy or heritage from Adam substantially lost the image, or spiritual life, that was originally present in the first created humans. In spite of this dilemma, through the grace of God we nonetheless retained a small sliver of the image of God, which can reasonably be called one's conscience, the spiritual aspect of self or God's holiness.

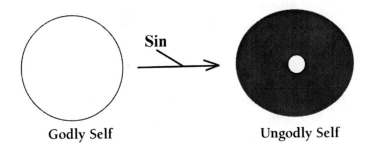

Godly Self   Ungodly Self

Figure 3.1. Humankind's Pre- and Post-Fall Existence

In this visualization, the godly self of humans prior to the fall consisted of the image of God. The innocence of a godly self is depicted on the left by a circle without any darkened area. Once the acts of disobedience occurred and sin entered, the godly self no longer existed as such, but was altered to a drastically different self, an immoral or ungodly self. The post-fall existence of humankind is illustrated on the right by the shaded circle that has a disposition of sin and a small inner circle that represents the goodness of God or the remnant of His image.

To help demonstrate that such a tarnished self resulted from the fall, consider some of the behavioral manifestations of Adam and Eve immediately after the entrance of sin in their lives as recorded in the third chapter of Genesis. The admission of nakedness (Genesis 3:7) mimics our common understanding of *self-awareness* and *self-consciousness*; they hid themselves from God (Genesis 3:8), suggesting *self-preservation* and *self-defense*; the man blamed both God and the woman and the woman blamed the serpent (Genesis 3:12–13), which likens to *self-justification*, *self-vindication*, and *self-defense*. And finally, the couple, having been warned by God that eating of the tree of knowledge of good and evil would result in death (Genesis 2:17), perhaps unwittingly thought God meant physical sorrow. Thus, they challenged God's warning, which can be viewed as *self-destruction* of their former created life of spiritual holiness. All of these self-fixated terms denote dispositions of the tragic internal effects of sin and would not be expected to describe an image and likeness of the righteous and holy God.

Before we start examining a few hyphenated self-terms more closely in the next chapter, let us acknowledge that the word *self* has the same meaning in the secular world as it does in the Bible. For example, Paul wrote in 2 Timothy 3:2, "Men will be lovers of self." In addition, he made a contrast between two types of self within an individual, distinguishing the previous with another. He said that "our old self was crucified" (Romans 6:6); "you lay aside the old self" (Ephesians 4:22); "put on the new self" (Ephesians 4:24); "[lay] aside the old self with its evil practices" (Colossians 3:9); and "put on the new self" (Colossians 3:10). So there is no biblical mysticism about the meaning of the word self—self is self.

This contrast of self made by Paul also can be viewed as existing simultaneously with two separate aspects, one outward and one inward. The outward self takes on the significance of the *things we do*. These are the external expressions or deeds of a person that can be observed by others; that is, our vocations, our positions of status, and our possessions of material things (houses, cars, clothes, etc.). If these expressions are offenses against humanity, they are condemnable by courts of justice or society. As a whole, they are variously labeled as crimes, human errors, weaknesses, faults, misjudgments, mistakes, or sins.

The inward self of each human that evidently is linked to the outer self, is much more complex and not easily discernable by the person or others. Its makeup includes our own "justified" feelings and our own rights, especially when we know we are "justified" (by the world's standards) in thinking and feeling the way we do. Unlike the outward self, the inward self uniquely identifies our personalities and character; in other words, the inner self reflects *who we are* at any given moment.

The inward self is our human nature itself, sometimes called personhood. It's a combination of inherited and acquired traits, our emotions, frustrations, hopes, desires, ambitions, expectations, and presumptions. These are attitudes of the mind, largely based upon our past experiences and belief systems (our reason, our senses, our self-image, our views, our worth, our likes and aversions).

Within the confines of the inward self is the legacy of our ancestry that began in the garden of Eden. This inheritance of our sinful nature centers on our innate self-orientation, self-reliance, self-love, and all of our natural habits. It is these characteristics, under the influence and controlling power of pride and selfishness, which make them inclined toward ungodly traits. Thus, the inward self actually has the capacity to rule us, often without our knowledge, and is the sum and substance upon which we build our lives. This is who *we really are*!

In our culture of materialism and secularism, there is an emphasis almost wholly upon doing, and an obvious center of attention on the external aspects of life. Conversely, little or no awareness is directed toward our true beings, or what and who we are. Herein lies a problem for the person who desires a deeper spiritual walk with Christ but hasn't spiritually matured over time or is unaware of the enemy residing within.

The problem of unawareness of what and who we are has been addressed by the cartoonist Walt Kelly, who has Pogo say, "We have met the enemy and he is us." This well-known statement has led many to acknowledge the location of the enemy, but Pogo's one-liner is not complete. More accurately, there is also an element within us that is at odds with this enemy and is on our side. The conflict between the two creates an antagonism between being and doing. The elements of being and doing within ourselves were meant to work together in unconscious harmony (in a perfect human nature), are (in a polluted self) often isolated from each other wholly or in part, and have a propensity actually to become hostile to each other.

I propose that we should carry this thought further by asserting that self, or more specifically an aspect of self, is comparable to a plant that has roots of unrighteousness and produces fruitless branches. I also suggest that this unrighteousness and unproductiveness in many believers illustrates the disharmony between the presence of the sinful nature of self and that of the holy nature of God. Finally, we should not consider this as a major problem of humankind that cannot be solved. The means to resolve this predicament will be presented in later chapters.

Because we have spoken so far of self in several ways, we need to establish a standard to identify readily the three major aspects of self used throughout the rest of this book. The concentric self-circles of the godly and ungodly self previously shown in figure 3.1 provide the basis to distinguish these features. In addition, the self-circle and the accompanying narration of its three features are provided below in figure 3.2.

Figure 3.2. Distinguishing Features of Self-Circles

- Self (in a normal font) in the arrow on the left refers to the total generic self, with no reference to parts or divisions. This common designation is visualized as the outer circumferences of the self-circle. Both the inner and outer self can apply to this convention.
- **Self** (in bold font) in the arrow on the right explicitly refers the darker portion of a self-circle. Up to this point, terms attached to this portion of self include an ungodly self, a disposition to sin, the old self, a tainted self, and the sinful nature of self.
- *Self* (italicized) explicitly refers to the light central portion of the self-circle. So far, these areas have been described in relation to a new self, God's image, His nature, and His goodness.

... Better Understand Self?

Part 2

SELF: A BIBLICAL VIEW

Self-Love

THE OBJECTIVE OF this chapter is to understand self better by examining biblical passages that specifically cite or imply instances associated with hyphenated "self" terminology. To begin, we need to look at what Jesus said about declaring our love for God as the greatest commandment in the law (Matthew 22:38). Christ used a form of self, *yourself*, in His next statement concerning the second greatest commandment: "You shall love your neighbor as yourself" (Matthew 22:39). As I understand from the literature, there are two basic schools of interpretation pertaining to the second important commandment.

One category of biblical scholars, identified by some as self-lovers, has connected the two words *love* and *yourself* into *self-love*. According to these intellectuals, there is a form of self-love that is a part of human nature and must be preserved and sanctified. This means that we must love ourselves; that is, we must have self-respect for our own natures and due concern for the welfare of our own souls and bodies. In this regard, self-love is thought to be a disposition essential to our nature, inseparable from our being, by which we desire to be happy. Some even suggest that love of self is a uniform wish of the soul to avoid all evil and to enjoy all good.

In keeping with this view, these same scholars say we therefore must love our neighbors as ourselves, as truly and sincerely as we love ourselves. In some cases we must give up part of ourselves for the good of our neighbors, and must make ourselves servants to the true welfare of others to the point of being willing to spend and be spent for them.

Lastly, this same group of thinkers believes that self-love should not be confused with any of the interpretations of selfishness. They state, and accurately so, that selfishness, an ungodly temperament, is always wrong. Self-interest focuses only on one's interests, gratification, and so forth, which are sought or indulged in at the expense, and to the injury, of others. It has been said, "So long as self-love does not degenerate into selfishness, it is quite compatible with true benevolence."

On the other hand, another school of Bible interpreters claim that the philosophy of self-love is likely to deteriorate into selfishness and that much of the version of self-love described above is not totally correct. They say Jesus gives only *two* great commandments: (1) Love God with all your heart, soul, and mind; (2) love your neighbor as yourself. There is no third command to love yourself. Thus, in this second commandment, Jesus is essentially saying that as you already love yourself, love God and your fellow human being. Within this frame of reference, think of the word *as* in the same way in which it is used in Ephesians 5:25, 28, and 33: "love your wives, just as Christ also loved" and "love their own wives as their own bodies" and "love his own wife even as himself." These statements may indicate a state of current existence, *not* a command to self-love. Jesus knows everyone possesses some level of love, that is, we love ourselves based on the virtuous character of others. Therefore, He simply commands us to love others with this same commitment.

This second group of Christian authorities further alleges that the pro-self-lovers use God's holy Word as a springboard to justify a lifelong process of self-love. It begins with the catch-phrase stated above in Matthew 22:39 and is repeated in Matthew 19:19, which says, "Honor your father and mother: and, you shall love your neighbor as yourself." However, the self-lovers together with some non-Christians quickly twist the meaning and context by asking, "How can you love your neighbor until you first learn how to love yourself?" Or, "The more you love yourself, the more you will become a positive person whom others will admire." This sets the stage for the promotion of self-improvement books, tapes, videos, seminars—all at a substantial profit for authors in our capitalistic society.

The latter group of biblical authorities also maintains that self-love, also termed narcissistic love, in some cases is the root of the greatest sins, and it must be put off and mortified. It is an aspect of sinful human nature and is primarily attributed to people who desire to gratify their carnal appetites and passions. This kind of self-love has been proclaimed as grievously destructive and dreadfully evil. Some authorities claim that it is not uncommon to imagine the existence of this type of self-love in nominal, secular Christians.

So it looks as though we have opposing views on the interpretation of self-love. The first group says the term *self-love* is basically used to denote an involuntary longing for goodwill or for well-being that activates every desire. In this sense, it has no moral quality, being neither good nor evil. It is also applied to a voluntary regard for the gratification of special desires, such as being happy. In this sense it is morally good or bad according to these desires.

The second group is sometimes called murderers of self and self-haters by the radical segment of the first faction. These so-called self-haters say self-love is viewed as a voluntary aspect of sinful human nature that is the opposite of altruism or self-denial, and hinders any substantial spiritual growth. In part, they base their views on 2 Timothy 3:2–4. In this passage of Scripture the apostle Paul aligns lovers of self with other people who exhibit detestable sins such as being slanderous, boastful, arrogant, unholy, abusive, and "lovers of pleasure rather than lovers of God."

Self-Esteem

Respecting oneself seems to be a reasonable personality trait that should be universally accepted in all societies. As I researched the term *self* in various web sites and publications, I was impressed with the numerous references to self, more than any other hyphenated term, that were connected to esteem and acceptance. This observation occurred in secular settings and, to my astonishment, was also predominant in Christian literature, teaching, and self-help instruction, as well as expressed by church leaders. For example, Robert H. Schuller, Sr. a famous proponent of positive thinking has highlighted self-confidence in his popular book *You Can Become the Person You Want to Be* and later espoused in *Theology of Self-Esteem*. I was somewhat surprised by this fact because as far as I know, the original manuscripts of the Bible do not mention self-esteem.

Since the Bible does not directly teach self-esteem as a virtue, help, or goal, I then undertook the task of seeking passages that could indirectly implicate it and thus explain why the subject is such a popular focus in Christian circles. I concentrated on passages that might infer something about self-esteem, such as respect, honor, and confidence. At the risk of being accused of taking verses out of context, I merely wish to list, with little or no commentary, the following nine passages and allow the reader the opportunity to evaluate any relation in Scripture to self-esteem.

- One should not "think more highly of himself than he ought to think" (Romans 12:3).
- "When they measure themselves by themselves or compare themselves by themselves, they are without understanding" (2 Corinthians 10:12).
- "If anyone thinks he is something when he is nothing, he deceives himself" (Galatians 6:3).
- "Regard one another as more important than yourselves" (Philippians 2:3).
- We "put no confidence in the flesh" (Philippians 3:3). Interestingly, in these several references regarding respect,

the apostle Paul does not warn against thinking too little of ourselves, which is quite contrary to the current sentiment of our society.)

- "So are the paths of all who forget God...whose confidence is fragile" (Job 8:13–14).
- "Do not throw away your confidence [in God], which has a great reward" (Hebrews 10:35).
- "they [the people in the island of Malta] also honored us with many marks of respect" (Acts 28:10).
- "Honor [respect] all people" (1 Peter 2:17).

It is important to note that the words *respect* and *honor*, as used in these and many other biblical passages, are not viewed as synonyms of self-esteem. I have found that respect and honor are not directed toward oneself, as would be the case with self-esteem, but always directed toward others. If the word *esteem* was substituted for honor and respect, examples of these biblical citations would include esteem of children to parents, younger to older, citizens to government, laypeople to spiritual leaders and clergy, and slaves to their masters. The Bible is very clear on the ordering of society because it helps maintain civility and provides the basis for a solid social structure.

There are several authorities, both secular and religious, who studied self-esteem as to its use and its effect in our society. Many conclude that the wide popularity of self-esteem, bolstered by numerous behavioral counselors, likely stems from the evolution and advancement of personality theories, such as that advanced by Maslow.

More than anywhere else, the issue of self-esteem has intensified with the youth in our culture. In recent times, there is a prevalent idea that praise is not just the best, but is the only motivator for children. American schools particularly emphasize self-esteem as the chief virtue, divorced from achievement or even effort.

Maureen Stout, author of *The Feel Good Curriculum*, pinpoints several destructive myths that have taken root in our educational system. Among other claims, the myths include the following: high expectations damage self-esteem; evaluation is punitive, stressful, and damaging to self-esteem; discipline is bad for self-esteem; effort is more important than achievement. Stout makes a strong case that the ideas that infect our public schools from kindergarten through college lead directly to preoccupation with self, detachment from one's community, cynicism, and a rejection of absolute truth.

Separate studies have shown that self-esteem can actually become self-delusion—a conviction that you are more popular, more capable, or more loved than is really the case. Such self-centered attitudes only tend to alienate other people. At the same time, in contradiction, the over-praised child can be addicted to approval from others.

Out of this philosophy of nurturing and glorifying self-esteem and praising children in the field of education, my wife and I, along with a few other grandparents, have witnessed some unusual attitudes in their now-parenting children. In the past, many parenting couples believed that children in their formative years should be guided by a set of values that provided sincere, specific praise when appropriate, along with constructive criticism and loving correction. But now we wonder if these grown siblings got the idea that they should greatly improve on the outdated parental guidance in which they were reared by incorporating principles of self-esteem in the upbringing of their own children.

Adoption of this cultural philosophy by some of these now young to middle-aged parents has taken an alarming step that tends to dismantle family relationships. For example, we are personally aware of several incidences where younger parents have viewed their own upbringing as too correction-oriented or over-disciplined by their own parents. Consequently, they have all but excluded any meaningful contact between the grandparents and their own children. Specifically, the grandchildren are either prohibited from visiting grandparents or the parents themselves must be present to chaperone any visitation.

The apparent rationale for these restrictions is that these parents now are afraid that one or both grandparents might impose some of their traditional childrearing techniques on their children and thereby interfere with their seemingly successful attempts to yield happy, high self-esteemed children.

Some believe the originator of the self-esteem movement is Satan, whose heart was lifted up because of his beauty, and who was obsessed with his own brightness (Ezekiel 28:17). This "ruler of this world" (John 12:31) has the power to enliven our egotistical human nature and deceives us with this inflated sense of self-importance.

According to several spiritually oriented writings, a vast number of Christians also have been deceived by the self-teachings of humanistic psychology. Rather than resist the enticements of the world, they became culture-bound. Not only do these believers not oppose the tidal wave of self-ism, they are riding the crest of self-esteem, self-acceptance, and self-love. Many times one can hardly tell the difference between the Christian and the non-Christian in the area of the self, except that a spiritually mature believer proclaims God as the main source for any of his or her self-esteem, self-acceptance, self-worth, and self-love.

So we are basically left with two questions about self-esteem. Is the problem one of low self-esteem or a barrage of self-centered thoughts rather than biblical, God-centered beliefs about who we really are and how we fit into the plan of God? Or, is the issue one of exalting and lifting up ourselves, or one of understanding and accepting God's grace and provision for us in Christ, which alone gives our lives true meaning and value?

I believe the combination of self-love and self-esteem has become a philosophically based, counterfeit religion, quite different from traditional Christian doctrine. In his day, Paul identified Judaizers as those who proclaimed a gospel contrary to the good news. He said they were to be accursed or devoted to destruction because they were wrongfully distorting the true gospel of Christ (Galatians 1:6–9). Perhaps Paul may have viewed the teachers and promoters of the modern self-love or self-esteem movement in the same manner as he scrutinized the Judaizers.

Several biblical authorities have cautioned fellow Christians about becoming imprisoned by false beliefs. In like manner, the apostle Paul says in Colossians 2:8, "See to it that no one takes you captive through philosophy and empty deception, according to the tradition of men, according to the elementary principles of the world, rather than according to Christ." Charles Colson has stated that when our lives are held captive by false ideas, or worldviews, our witness may become at best confusing, and at worst a mockery of the truth we claim to believe.

Perhaps the following figure (4.1) will be useful as I conclude the discussion of self-love and self-esteem. It is a categorical analysis of "low," "no," and "high" self-esteem individuals in regard to focus and consequences.

"Low" Self-Esteem	"No" Self-Esteem	"High" Self-Esteem
Self-degradation (false humility)	Little or no self-concern (true humility)	Self-aggrandizement (pride)
Focus: Self (self-hate)	Focus: God and others	Focus: Self (self-love)
Result: Fear and Hiding; "Low" self-image	Result: Worship God; biblical view of self;	Result: Pride; "Good" self-image
Destructive— serve self	Productive—serve God and others	Destructive— serve self

Figure 4.1. "Low," "No," and "High" Self-Esteem People

(Adapted from Brownback 1987)

The table indicates that a person who possesses little or no self-esteem is more apt to be humble, God focused, and servant oriented with a biblical view of self. Such individuals would likely differ from those having a low or high self-esteem.

Self-Denial

In the interest of brevity at this point, most of the following self-fixated terms will be noted only with limited references to Bible passages. In the next two chapters, we will closely examine several other directives of Christ regarding self-denial. Here I will briefly introduce the term self-denial. Jesus said to His disciples, "Let him deny himself" (Luke 9:23). Sometimes it is helpful to understand wording by stating its opposite. For example, "Let him deny himself" could be paraphrased, "Let him not accept himself," "Let him not affirm himself," "Let him not commend himself," "Let him not yield to himself," or "Let him not spare himself."

It is helpful to cite the views offered by the secular and religious communities regarding self-denial. My study of this term indicates a wide range of beliefs. For instance, the mildest view of self-denial would be to follow a New Year's resolution with intent to lose weight. The most extreme case would be to deny self by taking one's own life.

Self-Centeredness

"Now you can have real love for everyone because your souls have been cleansed from selfishness and hatred when you trusted Christ to save you; so see to it that you really do love each other warmly, with all your hearts" (1 Peter 1:22 TLB).

Sincere love involves selfless giving; a self-centered person is often bitter and cannot truly love others. God's love and forgiveness free you to take your eyes off yourself and to meet others' needs.

Self-Condemnation

David said, "I have sinned against the LORD" (2 Samuel 12:13). Remorse, repentance, or self-conviction in the Bible is generally viewed favorably, for it indicates a wrongdoing that requires correction. However, self-condemnation should never be a trait of true believers since "There is now no condemnation for those who are in Christ Jesus" (Romans 8:1).

Self-Control

"Gentleness, self-control; against such things there is no law" (Galatians 5:23). Self-control is sometimes rendered as temperance. Someone with this virtue conquers personal desires and passions, especially sensual appetites. Self-control is identified as one of the Christian graces and indicates a sober, temperate, calm, and composed approach to life, having mastered personal wishes and obsessions. The Bible cautions God's people to exercise self-control in their daily lives.

Self-Deception

"If anyone thinks himself to be religious, and yet does not bridle his tongue but deceives his own heart, this man's religion is worthless" (James 1:26) and "Let no man deceive himself" (1 Corinthians 3:18). Self-deception is viewed in the Bible unfavorably since it cons a person into think of himself as other than he really is. In addition it is usually accompanied by numerous unworthy acts.

Self-Delusion

"But they are altogether stupid and foolish in their discipline of delusion—their idol is wood!" (Jeremiah 10:8). The Bible is filled with indirect references of self-deception and self-delusion. Both terms are characteristics of the wicked, and are exhibited in thinking that one's own ways are right, they are better than others, and they may have peace while in sin.

Self-Exaltation

"Whoever exalts himself shall be humbled; and whoever humbles himself shall be exalted" (Matthew 23:12). Both Old and New Testaments provide many references to the opposition of those who boast and thereby manifest pride, selfishness, and self-righteousness.

Self-Examination

"Test yourselves to see if you are in the faith; examine yourselves!" (2 Corinthians 13:5). The Bible does make allowances for the examination of oneself. Some forms of meditation and self-examination can help determine whether godly or ungodly characteristics are truly present in the hearts of Christians. Thus, one has the capacity to uncover some aspects of his inner self. Lastly, it has been claimed that self-examination is not the same as self-introspection, for this term commonly denotes excessive seeking of a person's identity within him- or herself.

Self-Indulgence

"Woe to you, scribes and Pharisees, hypocrites! For you clean the outside of the cup and of the dish, but inside they are full of robbery and self-indulgence" (Matthew 23:25). Regarding excessive or unrestrained gratification of one's appetites and desires, the Scriptures clearly repudiate this self-fixated trait.

Self-Righteousness

"[The Pharisees] trusted in themselves that they were righteous, and viewed others with contempt" (Luke 18:9). "I tell you, this man [the tax collector] went to his house justified rather than the other [the Pharisee]; for everyone who exalts himself will be humbled, but he who humbles himself will be exalted" (Luke 18:14). The Pharisee in this parable did not go to the temple to pray to God but to announce to all within earshot how good he was. The tax collector went to the temple recognizing his sin and begging for mercy (Luke 18:13). Self-righteousness is dangerous. It leads to pride, causes a person to despise others, and hinders one from becoming spiritually mature.

Self-Rights

To my knowledge, self-rights is not a term that is cited in the Bible. It is, however, used in some theological circles to describe a certain virtue, character trait, or attitude of Christian servanthood. More specifically, it is a form of self-denial that discredits any natural right of a servant to his lord. For example, the servant is so subservient and obedient to God that even his independence and individuality is to be abolished in his total dedication to the Lord and His will. According to Oswald Chambers, one's human nature tends to desire certain rights to benefit and maintain oneself. Such rights are to be viewed neither as sin nor as spiritual, per se, but could be in opposition to our supernatural relationship to Jesus Christ.

Self-Surrender

There exists a struggle between the natural human impulses of self-seeking and the altruistic inclinations toward self-denial and self-surrender. All religions imply some conception of denial or surrender of self to deity, ranging in an ethical quality from a heathen fanaticism to the high spiritual quality of self-sacrifice.

Similar to self-rights, self-surrender is not directly described as such in the Bible. To surrender is to yield to the power and control of another. However, the Scriptures present the concept of unconditional self-surrender as among the noblest of human natural virtues. It is used by many Christian thinkers to describe the absolute surrender to Jesus Christ by His followers. They are to totally yield and submit to Him and to His will.

Self-Will

Self-will is found once in the Old Testament "In their self-will they lamed oxen" (Genesis 49:6). This is a description of those ancient Israelites who were headstrong, vindictive, and cruel as they conquered the Shechemites. Their evil dispositions were summed up as self-will and were demonstrated in the laming of captured oxen by cutting the leg tendons, an unmerciful act of destruction.

The idea of self-will is found twice in the New Testament. The first instance concerns some of the characteristics of church elders. Paul tells those in an early church that these overseers should not be self-willed. To be so may indicate an attitude of arrogance, overbearing, or pleasing oneself. In contrast, the elders are to be "hospitable, loving what is good, sensible, just, devout, self-controlled" (Titus 1:7–8).

The second mention of self-will regards false teachers. These people are described as "Daring, self-willed, they do not tremble when they revile angelic majesties" (2 Peter 2:10). Some theologians say self-will in these texts stands for a false pride, for obstinacy, for a persistent adherence to one's will or wish, especially in opposition to the dictates of wisdom or propriety or the wishes of others.

Self-Seeking

Self-seeking is a manifestation of behavior to secure an advantage over others, not in sharing or cooperating. We find the term *self-seeking* cited in 1 Corinthians 13:5, the famous chapter that describes what true love is and what it is not. Love is not several things, including self-seeking. Some translations translate the term "does not seek its own," meaning never looking for the welfare, comfort, security, and salvation of others. A self-seeking person is anxious only for his or her own happiness and cares not about others.

In this and the last chapter we examined an often vague but definable term *self*. I believe no single word or sentence could completely describe it. In the secular realm, any definition of self should include that it is an integral part of human nature, related to the character and behavior of each and every human being. Similarly, from a biblical viewpoint, self is functionally described by the deeds that reflect one's personality and character. Moreover, depending upon circumstances, the Scriptures reveal that the character and actions of a self at any time is either consistent with or contrary to the divine nature of God. This disclosure of variable character traits and deeds suggests that a dynamic state exists between one's godly and ungodly natures within the inner self.

If Christians are to become like God, and therefore take on the nature of God in this life, it is reasonable that they need to understand themselves and God. To understand themselves, they need to have a true concept of themselves, and this is developed only out of their knowledge of God, His creation, and His grace. Attempts to understand self better, and subsequently to become more Godlike, will become important as we further consider Christian spirituality.

When we build up ourselves without a biblical concept of self and God, we end up playing spiritual king-of-the-mountain and engage in promoting culturally driven personal agendas. In doing so, we often seek relief from a worldly view, position, power, and praise; those things are what we really should get from resting in God's grace, derived from His only begotten Son, Jesus Christ.

What awaits us is answering this question: How do we as Christians deal with those temperaments that are contrary to the divine nature of God during our journey of faith? I trust that the answer will be forthcoming as we delve into the words uttered by Jesus concerning those who wish to follow Him. Those individuals must deny themselves and take up their cross.

BREAKING NEWS AND DEVELOPING STORY

After local and national news, the words *Developing Story* appear on the television screen. In a few words, the newscaster reviews the breaking news story about the two molecular scientists who discovered what they call the S-Factor, a seemingly genetic element in body fluids taken from several hundred living people as well as biopsies obtained from deceased individuals.

Preliminary evidence suggested that the S-Factor was not associated with any diseases, either physical or metabolic. To discover other possible functions of the factor, they plan to evaluate the neurological and psychological makeup of the people tested. This approach seemed feasible, since larger concentrations of the S-Factor were found adjacent to nerve tissue, especially in samples recovered from the brains of autopsied people.

Chapter 5

... Relate Self-Denial to Followers of Christ?

Part 1

If anyone wishes to come after Me, he must deny himself.
—Matthew 16:24

WE NOW BEGIN to scrutinize the hyphenated term *self-denial*, the first key word given as a commandment by Jesus to those who desire to be His followers. In this and the next chapter several synonyms of self-denial will be identified, which many Bible scholars and commentators have used as substitutions for this term. In addition, we will further describe self-denial as it has been used in historical Christianity, applied in the context of Christ's teaching, observed in His life, and visually illustrated in His disciple Peter. Lastly, the reader is invited to peruse a list of Scripture references pertaining to self-denial in appendix B.

SELF-DENIAL

To deny, an action verb, implies to refuse, renounce, repudiate, give up, reject, abandon, forsake, disown, leave, release, hand over, give over possession or control, or stop holding on to someone or something. The term *self-denial* is often used in connection with a preference or tendency, such as restraining (oneself) from gratification of desires.

Throughout the ages many have used self-denial as a way of appeasement of a person to a higher authority or a means of self-control. In its simplest form, it can mean merely denying oneself certain bodily pleasures over a period of time, such as by abstaining from food and drink. One form of self-denial that developed quickly in the early centuries was the practice of virginity, thereby giving up the pleasures of sex. It can also be practiced by deliberately choosing an impoverished lifestyle, as the hermits in the fourth century did when they populated the deserts as their ways of doing penance.

In some of its more severe forms, it can actually mean inflicting pain and physical harm to oneself. In these instances, perhaps it is better to use the terms *asceticism* or *austerity* to describe a strenuous way of practicing self-discipline in order to promote self-control. Self-denial or voluntary suffering has been practiced in various ways and degrees by members of many religions and spiritual traditions.

My literary research indicates that Christian self-denial, although often misinterpreted, is relatively easy to understand by itself. However, there are several scripturally related consequences that are directly associated with self-denial that increase its complexity. One way to illustrate the aspects of this topic is to imagine self-denial as a cube. Etched on each of the six- surfaces is one of the following six terms: *surrender, abandonment, penance, abnegation, renunciation,* and *relinquishment.* When the cube is rolled, it matters not which side is on top because each of the terms can be related to self-denial and become explanatory of self-denial for the followers of Jesus Christ.

There is also a historical association of self-denial with another word: *mortification.* This term (as it is used in some translations of the New Testament) means to die, and therefore takes on the connotation of self-mortification. Mortification is no longer commonly used in modern English, except occasionally to express embarrassment or humiliation.

Some branches of the Christian church have institutionalized the practice of self-inflicted penance and mortification through their mandates on fasting and abstinence for specific days of the year. Through the centuries, many Christians, particularly in

Catholicism, have practiced corporal mortification. These voluntary, corporal penances are a way of imitating Jesus Christ, who voluntarily accepted the sufferings of His Passion and death on the cross at Calvary in order to redeem humankind.

As recorded in the annals of Christian history, the great saints and founders of Christian religious organizations led the way in this imitation of Christ. A few examples of these individuals include the following: Saint Jerome, a biblical scholar who translated the Bible into Latin (the Vulgate); Saint Francis of Assisi, who received the stigmata, that of painful wounds like those of Jesus Christ; St. Catherine of Siena, a Doctor of the Church, who was especially famous for fasting and living for long periods of time on nothing but the Blessed Sacrament; and St. Ignatius, who was praised in his Litany for being "constant in the practice of corporal penance." More recently, Mother Teresa of Calcutta practiced self-discipline as a form of self-denial and used the cilice (an article of clothing to induce discomfort or pain) as means of doing penance.

Pope Paul VI has stated, "Self-denial helps a person overcome both psychological and physical weakness, gives him energy, helps him grow in virtue and ultimately leads to salvation. It conquers the insidious demons of softness, pessimism and lukewarm faith that dominate the lives of so many today" (*Crisis Magazine*, July/August 2005).

Pope John Paul II is recorded as saying, "Suffering, more than anything else, makes the powers of the redemption present in the history of humanity. Before His disciples and others, Christ clearly demanded a moral nature that could be fulfilled only on the condition that they 'deny themselves.' The way that leads to the Kingdom of heaven is 'small and narrow,' and Christ contrasts it to the 'wide and broad' way that 'leads to destruction'" (Matthew 7:13–14).

Benedict XVI has declared that "Suffering is the inner side of love, and thus it is important to learn how to suffer," and Pope Paul VI has stated, "The necessity of mortification of the flesh is clearly revealed if we consider the fragility of our nature, in which, Adam's sin, flesh and spirit have contrasting desires. This exercise of bodily mortification—aims at the 'liberation' of man."

CHRIST'S LIFE OF SELF-DENIAL

In addition to those mentioned above, there are numerous examples in history of individuals who attempted to live a life of self-denial. To some degree several were only moderately successful in their attempts. Most would agree that only one person, Jesus Christ, was completely victorious in this regard. Christ is the ultimate model for typifying self-denial. This assertion is based upon the many scriptures in the New Testament that reveal multiple instances of self-denial in His teaching, manners, and actions throughout His entire life. This was particularly evident in His earthly ministry, in which He was totally subservient to God and obedient to His will.

It is on this last point that we should emphasize the importance of Christ's self-denial as it is related to His human heredity. This becomes clearer when we examine the two scriptural terms used to define Jesus Christ. One expression is "Son of God," which identifies His genetics from a divine source, as one of absolute holiness. Moreover, mysteriously coupled with the divine ancestry is the human element, totally without sin of any kind, describing Him as the "Son of Man." The incarnation of Jesus Christ having a combined nature of divinity and humanity has been and still is an enigma to many. The mystery of the personification of Christ possessing two natures cannot be totally explained but should be understood simply as God Incarnate. Paul gives us this same comprehension of the God-Man when he states, "For in Him [Christ] all the fullness of Deity dwells in bodily form" (Colossians 2:9).

In connection with self-denial, we need to remind ourselves that it is not the deity, but the humanity or bodily form of Christ to which we must direct our attention. For us to even begin to think about self-denial, we first should consider that all of Christ's conscious life of self-denial on earth centered on maintaining His sinless human nature. If this declaration is correct, we have a place to begin to not only identify with Him but to understand why He would say in Luke 9:23, "If anyone wishes to come after Me, let him *deny himself*" (emphasis added).

Paul also provides us with evidence that Christ's unselfish state is related to self-denial. In Philippians 2:5–11, Paul declares that Jesus humbled Himself and took upon Himself the form of a servant with an attitude of selfless humility, a quality the apostle says all believers should have. A true servant, totally bonded to his master, is characterized not as much as a person to be despised or to be insensitive to, but as one who willingly restrains his self-interests, relinquishes his personal rights, and totally submits himself without reservation.

Jesus, who had all the rights that belonged to the eternal Son of God, veiled His deity and gave up the exercise of these rights to manifest His divine prerogatives. In the Philippians passage noted above, Paul states that Jesus placed Himself as low as possible in emptying Himself, laying aside the emanation of His glory in being incarnate, taking upon Himself the human form and assuming the lowest innocent character. Through self-denial Jesus willingly took upon Himself the limitations and vulnerability of humanity.

As the Son of Man, having a complete human nature, albeit undefiled, He possessed, like us and all the rest of humanity, self. We then have to ask, "Why was it necessary for Jesus to deny Himself?" To answer this question, we should be reminded of His attitudes toward His Father and Himself. Regarding His stance toward His Father, His mind-set was an intimate, ongoing relationship that was clearly defined by His total obedience and subordination to God, yet, at the same time, maintaining complete oneness or unity with Him.

We further understand this attitude when we see that He viewed Himself as a true servant in this relationship. He used the words *not* and *nothing* in reference to Himself repeatedly in John's gospel (5:19, 30, 41; 6:38; 7:16, 28, 42; 14:10, 24). This disposition of nothingness was necessary so that any and all attractions within His human nature toward Himself were totally restrained. This servant-oriented attitude allowed His Father to do in Him what God pleased to do. The unique disposition of servanthood and nothingness was accomplished by Jesus throughout His earthly life, while at the same time preserving His sinless nature, even in the offensive environment that He faced almost daily.

An outstanding master ideally never gives instructions or tasks to his servants that he himself has not experienced or understood. So for Jesus, the Master of all masters, to direct His followers to deny self, we logically deduce that He fully and personally experienced events and situations necessitating self-denial.

His whole life was one of humiliation, poverty, and disgrace. He had nowhere to lay his head. He was a man of sorrows and acquainted with grief, did not appear with external pomp, nor any marks of distinction from other common men. In this context, from Scripture we can identify several troubles, circumstances, or incidents in which He indeed denied Himself.

Jesus met rejections from His fellow countrymen: "He came to His own, and those who were His own did not receive Him" (John 1:11), and when He identified Himself as a prophet, He declared that He "had no honor in his own country" (John 4:44). Those who witnessed or experienced most of His miracles rejected Him from the cities of Chorazin, Bethsaida, and Capernaum (Matthew 11:20–24). The hostile aggressiveness of the scribes and Pharisees and many temptations of Satan were trials that were unable to deter His oneness with His Father. The Bible tells us that Jesus was "tempted in all things as we are, yet without sin" (Hebrews 4:15).

Jesus was hated, but He hated no one; He was met by antagonism but did not respond in anger; and He was killed by jealousy, but He never envied nor hurt anyone. Instead He carried the stressful insults of anger, hatred, and jealousy throughout His earthly ministry. (We will discuss cross-carrying by Jesus' followers in subsequent chapters, but at this juncture we only want to consider that the carrying of these traumatic abuses by Christ may be a form of His self-denial and may possibly be a basis of His commands to carry crosses.)

The question at hand now is this: How was Jesus able to transform the aggressions of others into forgiveness and compassion? A few writers have suggested that Jesus was insensitive or numb to opposition by means of His divine nature. However, because Jesus was truly human and truly divine, I believe He would have felt emotion because of His humanity. Whatever else is offered as an explanation to this question must include an element of self-denial.

I believe He denied any tendency within His being to be resentful, revengeful, or retaliatory.

Again, we are speaking of the humanity of Christ, not His deity. If Christ had not laid aside His deity and had rather used supernatural powers to cope with the many troubles mentioned above, we would have great difficulty identifying with Him. He would be labeled as an imposter, a con, or a pretender. Instead, out of His full humanity, Jesus endured these mind-wrenching troubles, yet did not succumb and did not yield to the natural human disposition to sin. Therefore, He had the perfect right and authority to tell His followers not only to deny themselves but also to persevere under the tensions of temptations and trials.

In addition to the many negative accusations and ill treatment Jesus suffered, how did He handle achievement, such as the thirty-five separate miracles recorded in the four Gospels? Miraculously feeding thousands with a few fish and a few loaves of bread and healing the blind and others, provide ample proof of supernatural power to bring about many kinds of changes in people, and perform wonderful works.

If any of us were to achieve even one of these miracles, we would probably respond with self-adoration or self-glorification. Most likely, the buttons on our spiritual vests would fly off! However, we do not read anywhere of Jesus manifesting any prideful behavior associated with these supernatural events. As we survey each miracle Jesus performed, we see He either made no comment or fully credited God for these unnatural occurrences. Again, some might say He was just modest or insensitive. Or, could it be He rejected any selfish or prideful tendencies and exhibited the virtuous traits He attributed to Himself? "I am gentle and humble in heart," He said (Matthew 11:29).

Jesus experienced testing at the beginning of His earthly ministry, at which time He was severely tempted by Satan to disobey His Father. All three temptations were directed toward His human nature, and if He had yielded and not totally denied Himself, He would have manifested various degrees of self-gratification, self-display, and self-aggrandizement (Matthew 4:1–11).

We have scriptural evidence that Jesus experienced personal temptation before the climax of His earthly ministry. He told His disciples the time had come for which He had been working throughout His ministry—His death and resurrection. "The hour has come for the Son of Man to be glorified" (John 12:23). Then He freely admitted to them that part of His human nature was tempted to resist this painful experience: "Now My soul has become troubled; and what shall I say, 'Father, save me from this hour?'" (John 12:27). His agony proves the genuineness of His humanity. Jesus said no to His human desires in order to obey and glorify His Father (John 12:28).

But the lowest steps of His self-denial took place during the last days of His earthly life. The night before His crucifixion in the garden of Gethsemane His agony began to intensify, not only because of the foreknowledge of His forthcoming passion and death, but due to the fiery testing of His life as the Son of Man. On the side of the Mount of Olives, supreme testing took place. Jesus prayed, "My Father, if it is possible, let this cup pass from Me." These words suggest a vulnerability that is similar to ours, which could be the presence of a self-preserving aspect of His innate human nature. With the aid of the abiding Holy Spirit, which He possessed throughout His entire earthly ministry, He willingly and relevantly applied self-denial to counter this temptation and concluded His short prayer, "Yet not as I will, but as You will" (Matthew 26:39).

To further illustrate the unmatched extent of this testing, yet denying any human tendency to resist, the biblical text says, "While being reviled, He did not revile in return; while suffering, He uttered no threats, but kept entrusting Himself to Him [God]" (1 Peter 2:23). On the cross He was mocked by the people, chief priests, scribes, and elders; they repeatedly used the word *save* as they taunted Him: "*Save* Yourself. If You are the Son of God, come down from the cross;" and "He *saved* others; He cannot *save* Himself." The soldiers said, "If You are the King of the Jews, *save* yourself." The robbers said, "*Save* Yourself and us" (Matthew 27:40–44, Luke 23:35–39, emphasis added). You may sense a measure of unholy irony in this mockery of Jesus. His one and only objective at this time in His life was to save humankind, not Himself. Out of love for all humanity, He willingly surrendered any right to save Himself.

I believe the repeated use of the phrase "save yourself "was none other than an all-out assault orchestrated by Satan and directed at any susceptible aspect of Jesus' human nature. The personification of evil in these mockers was aimed directly toward the humanity of Jesus' self, namely those natural affinities of self-preservation, self-survival, self-glorification, and life itself. If the evil one had been successful, Jesus could have cried out for mercy, thereby rejecting God's will and ending His sinless and worthy existence.

But instead of denying God and His eternal purpose of redemption, Christ applied the same principle He had expressed to His disciples; that is, He denied Himself. Christ knew He had every entitlement, both from a divine view and a human view, to save Himself, but He had boundless love for His Father and humankind and allowed Himself to be killed (John 10:18).

There is a highlight placed upon the manner of His death, which encompassed all humbling circumstances possible. His death on the cross was cursed, painful, and shameful. It was a death accursed by the law, the death of a slave who was not a free man with rights to seek and choose independence, prominence, and self-will. Then there was the immeasurable anguish of the rejection by His Father and the mandatory separation from God because of the sins He bore. Such was the self-denial and total submission of our Lord and Savior.

Jesus' extreme anguish of separation and rejection by God may well underline His exclamation uttered from the cross: "My God, My God, why have You forsaken Me?" (Matthew 27:46; Mark 15:34). According to Richard John Neuhaus, this petition cannot be viewed as a final cry of desperation. In his book *Death on a Friday Afternoon: Meditations on the Last Words of Jesus from the Cross*, Neuhaus said Jesus' words were a cry of desertion from the abandoned One, a perfect surrender of Himself to the very end of His earthly life. Having no immoral nature of self, Jesus surrendered Himself totally to His Father God; He surrendered His will and thus lost (relinquished) control of His destiny to His Father.

Jesus expressed the agony of unmitigated sin. The very nature of sin, all the sins of humankind and the hell they deserve for eternity, were laid on Him. Every detail of His horrific abandonment declared the heinous character of sin. In the silence of heaven and darkness of these moments of His Passion, Jesus knew He was in the thralls of abandonment by God and in extreme of self-denial. At this point, Jesus descended into the essence of hell, the most extreme suffering ever experienced. Neuhaus claims Jesus' abandonment of self was uncompromised even under the ultimate test of being abandoned by the One to whom He appealed.

We as believers in Christ are admonished to abandon ourselves, to completely deny ourselves, to Jesus Christ and God. In later chapters, we will carefully look at the means by which self-denial is a prerequisite to living a joyful life of true spirituality.

SELF-DENIAL IN THE CONTEXT OF CHRIST'S STATEMENTS

"If anyone wishes to come after Me, he must *deny himself*, and take up his *cross* and *follow* Me. For whoever wishes to save his *life* shall lose it; but whoever loses his *life* for My sake will find it" (Matthew 16:24–25, emphasis added).

I want to point out that various combinations of these italicized words are recorded in all three of the Synoptic Gospels (Matthew 10:38–39; 16:24–25; Mark 8:34–35; Luke 9:23–24; 14:26–27; 17:33) and in the Gospel of John (12:25–26; see appendix C for details of these groupings). These statements were presented to Jesus' disciples as well as to the multitudes who gathered around Him on many occasions.

I mention these details to stress the common view of all four gospel writers regarding the multiplicity of this invitation in Christ's teachings and its universal inclusiveness to anyone who would come after Him. Therefore, it seems clear that great significance was attached to these words of Christ, not only to His contemporary disciples and others, but to subsequent hearers and readers. All have had the freedom to accept or reject His teaching.

It is also important to consider the context in which Christ delivered these words to His would-be followers. Using selected scriptures, particularly in Matthew, Mark, and Luke, we will examine the settings in which Jesus made these remarks. Doing so should help clarify the meaning of Christ's statements. We begin with a setting in which Peter, one of Christ's closest disciples, plays a pivotal role.

DENIALS OF PETER

There is a remarkable dialogue between the disciple Peter and Jesus immediately preceding Jesus' comments as recorded both in the gospels of Matthew and Mark. Following a bold affirmation by Peter that Jesus was the Christ, the Son of the living God, Jesus began telling His disciples of His impending sufferings and death. Thereupon, Peter strongly advised Jesus to spare Himself, and essentially gave a cold shoulder to Jesus' forecast of His passion by uttering, "God forbid it, Lord! This shall never happen to You."

In turn, Jesus firmly reprimanded him for these daring words and, referring to him as Satan, told him that he merely had an inflexible mind, "For you are not setting your mind on God's interests, but man's" (Matthew 16:23; Mark 8:33). The Amplified Bible says Peter was "minding what partakes not of the nature and quality of God, but of men."

It seems Jesus was actually describing Peter as having dual natures in his mind; a major part of him was involved with the wishes and wants of humankind (humanity) and a lesser part with God's desires. Such a division of self at the time Peter responded to Jesus' remarks concerning His death can be illustrated in the simplified drawing as shown in figure 5.1.

Figure 5.1. A Division of Self in Peter (1st Example)

Remember our standard visualization of describing self in a self-circle (fig. 3.2)? In the figure above, the outer circumference represents Peter's total self. The darkened area of the self-circle represents his remarks emanating from his humanistic self, and the smaller, inner white circle (*self*) denotes a feature of God's image within Peter.

In this case with Peter, the predominant controlling aspect of self was his world-mindedness, which restrained and hindered the influence of God-mindedness. Despite the daily tutoring by Jesus during a three-year period, Peter still exhibited a lack of self-denial, which is evidence that his unaltered or unregenerated self was the dominant part of his total self.

The duplicity in Peter is one of world-mindedness versus God-mindedness that oftentimes are incompatible with one another. Using Jesus' evaluation of Peter, these two ways of reasoning both compete for our wills. Most of us are aware of God's statement, "'For My thoughts are not your thoughts,…' declares the LORD" (Isaiah 55:8). Yet, Paul cautions believers, "Set your mind on the things above, not on the things that are on the earth" (Colossians 3:2).

So we see Peter in his self-will minding the things of this world, trusting his own understanding, and actually forbidding Christ to die. At this point in Christ's tutoring of the disciples, Peter's self-life was still very apparent, as evidenced by his self-assertiveness. He openly revealed himself (from whence the title of this book comes). Now we begin to see that Peter represents our own human natures, our common prejudices, our cultural standards, and our natural desires to achieve success and happiness.

This part of Peter's old self and also ours is the tendency to affirm ourselves (self-confidence or self-opinionated) and concentrate on what serves our own interests (self-centeredness), to accept conventional human wisdom (self-confidence), to question the validity of authority and credibility (self-independence), to avoid affliction (self-preservation), and perhaps unwittingly to accommodate ourselves (self-delusion) to a realm ruled by the prince of this world, Satan.

So, in His reprimand of Peter, Christ tells him and the other disciples that the Creator's desires should supersede those of the created and that each must deny himself if he wishes to come after the Lord.

It is not my intention or purpose to write a biography on the life of Peter. He is highlighted for the purpose of illustrating his wavering mind-set, as well as those of other followers of Jesus. To demonstrate this further, let's pick up the saga of Peter in the garden of Gethsemane. We note that Peter was the spokesman for the other disciples and fervently claimed, "Even though all may fall away because of You, I will never fall away" (Matthew 26:33). At this point, Peter's self-circle may have looked similar to figure 5.2.

Figure 5.2. A Division of Self in Peter (2nd Example)

The self-circle of Peter (and of the other disciples) shown in this figure is at the time they claimed total allegiance to Jesus. Such loyalty is evidenced by Peter's affirmation, "Even if I have to die with You, I will not deny You" (Matthew 26:35). Note the expansion of *self*, the inner circle, when compared to self in figure 5.1. Also note the diminishment of **self**, which when considered together, would lead one to believe Peter's words of allegiance were truthful.

However, Jesus knew this vow of Peter was impulsive and said, "Before a rooster crows, you will deny Me three times" (Matthew 26:34). During the hearing before the high priest, Peter then vigorously denied Jesus three times. In a very short time, Peter completely turned around from a solemn affirmation of devotion to an unashamed rejection and denial of the Son of God (Matthew 26:69–75). The dynamics of the spiritual self are evidenced by the rapid increase in Peter's **self** and decrease of *self* indicated in figure 5.3 when compared to figure 5.2.

Figure 5.3. A Division of Self in Peter (3rd Example)

We cannot provide a better example of one's natural self being exposed as we see it clearly manifested both as a result of fear and as a controlling power in Peter at this momentous occasion. Then, remembering Jesus' prediction and hearing the rooster, Peter experienced extreme remorse and guilt. Maybe he now began to realize he couldn't trust himself, or more likely, he really did not know himself.

Perhaps we, as Christians on this side of the cross, do not understand ourselves so well either. For more than a fleeting moment, ponder a couple of questions: "How well do I know myself?" and "Are there indications of self-life in me?" To answer these questions, imagine your own self-circle. Does it have both shaded and light areas, and do they remain constant throughout the day? Do they sometimes change like Peter's did?

Without revealing your answers to these questions, let's return to the story of Peter. After Christ's crucifixion and resurrection, we find Peter receiving instructions from Jesus and then questioning Him about John: "Lord, and what about this man?" Jesus gently rebukes him, saying, "What is that to you? You follow Me!" (John 21:20–22). Jesus perceives that Peter is attempting to take the focus

Figure 5.4. A Division of Self in Peter: (4th Example)

66

off himself, for his only duty is to follow Christ. It has always been a temptation of human nature to look at the duties or actions of others rather than one's own tasks.

This self-circle portrays Peter's attempt to take the spotlight off himself when Jesus told Peter to follow Him. Notice a prevalence of the inner white area (*self*), but a substantial amount of the dark self still remains.

We pick up Peter again in the book of Acts after he and the other disciples received the Holy Spirit at Pentecost. Peter is now a completely different person; he becomes a brilliant crusader of the gospel (Acts 2:14–47; see figure 5.5 below). To a significant degree, this transformation can be explained by the acquisition, power, and influence of the Holy Spirit in Peter. In part, the absence of the indwelling of the Holy Spirit in Peter during Jesus' trial may explain why Peter was unable to deny himself. Instead he not only denied Christ but also enhanced the agony of His Master. However, now he takes on a significant part of a godly self.

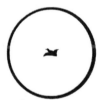

Figure 5.5. A Division of Self in Peter: (5th Example)

Note that *self* now contains a symbol of a dove, which represents the indwelling presence of the Holy Spirit: "Your body is a temple of the Holy Spirit who is in you" (1 Corinthians 6:19). This new self also includes the presence of the Spirit of Jesus Christ. "Christ is formed in you" (Galatians 4:19), and as followers of Christ, we mature to "the stature which belongs to the fullness of Christ" (Ephesians 4:13).

Despite preaching the gospel and effectively performing miracles, we again see the absence of self-denial, and perhaps the remnants of ignorance, in Peter. At this time, he was divinely shown that he possessed prejudice against non-Jews and that he should not exclude them from the grace of God (Acts 10:1–25). This episode simply illustrates that some bits and pieces of the self-life remained in Peter. Perhaps at this juncture in Peter's life, while still retaining the indwelling Holy Spirit and the Spirit of Jesus Christ, we can picture his self-circle as seen in figure 5.6.

Figure 5.6. A Division of Self in Peter: (6th Example)

At this time, the self-circle of Peter does not reflect his embracing of the full gospel message to all people, including non-Jewish believers. Such an attitude is represented by the somewhat enlarged but ever present **self** of Peter in the outer portion of the circle.

I suspect that the words of Jesus' commandment to deny himself and Peter's repeated denial of Jesus at His trial before Caiaphas and the Sanhedrin were conscious reminders in the apostle's mind about what denial really meant.

I also believe Peter further developed into a much different person than he was before those instances surrounding the Passion of Christ. There are scriptures that would lead us to think he gained a deeper and better knowledge of his true self in the latter part of his ministry. To justify this assertion about Peter's improved self-knowledge, we need to first look backward to Peter's negative response to the forecast of Jesus' death (see fig. 5.1). In His rebuke, Jesus told Peter that he was man-minded (a partaker of worldliness) instead of God-minded (a partaker of God's nature).

In these verses, Jesus may have stated the highest principle upon which all moral spirituality, true knowledge of God, and oneself is based; namely, there must be a change of one's inner self in which the worldly nature is replaced by a divine nature. We think Peter must have realized that he was becoming more

God-minded, because about thirty years later he told the early Christians that they too were blessed by escaping the evils of the world and were becoming sharers of God's desires, or "partakers of the divine nature" (2 Peter 1:4).

In addition, we find in 1 Peter 4:16 that this apostle told his faithful brethren they should not be surprised at the painful suffering and trials, "but to the degree that you share the sufferings of Christ, keep on rejoicing, so that also at the revelation of His glory, you may rejoice with exultation" (1 Peter 4:13). Instead of denying Christ in times of distress like he did at Jesus' trial, then experiencing deep sorrow and shame, Peter found joy in denying self with an expectation of even greater joyousness in the future.

Perhaps you are wondering what occurred in Peter's life that would explain his changes of character. We will address this subject later, but it must be apparent that there were many transitions between his old self and his new self. At the time Peter wrote the two letters mentioned above, he was a seasoned follower of Christ. His self-circle might have looked like figure 5.7.

Figure 5.7. A Division of Self in Peter (7th Example)

This figure depicts a proposed self-circle of Peter during latter part of his ministry before his death. The faint outer boundary of the circle indicates the very small but ever present self-life, while his new Christlike life is matured to its fullest extent.

So far, from our study of self-denial in the lives of Jesus Christ and Peter we can glean at least one major truth: The mind of Christ was solidly in the will of His Father, and conversely, Peter's mind vacillated widely between his own desires and those of God. It was only through many transformational episodes in Peter's life that, instead of having self-oriented desires and denying his Master as he did before, Peter's own self-denial was divinely translated into the mindfulness of God and Christ.

BREAKING NEWS AND DEVELOPING STORY

Anchor: "We have an update to our story about the discovery of a previously unknown substance identified as the S-Factor. Many people have called our station wanting to know what the S stands for.

"Our investigative team of reporters has found out that both researchers have last names beginning with the letter S: Drs. John Selford and Barbara Sinton. Unable to agree whose name should be first in future scientific publications stemming from this amazing finding, they simply are calling it the S-Factor. Stay tuned for more developments in this very unusual story."

Chapter 6

... Relate Self-Denial to Followers of Christ?

Part 2

SELF-DENIAL: IN CONTEXT

U PON THE EXAMINATION of passages that might aid our understanding of self-denial, we find some of Jesus' sayings that have confused and troubled readers of the Bible for centuries. It appears that many of Jesus' teachings are inconsistent with the values and vision of the world. For example, Jesus stated that He did not come to bring peace on earth but a sword (Matthew 10:34). This declaration can be taken to mean that Jesus has absolutely no illusions of the universal acceptance of God's plan to redeem humankind. He came not to bring temporal peace, outward prosperity, and power in the world, but to give His followers peace with God, peace in their consciences, and peace with their brethren. In God's kingdom, the peacemakers are called blessed (Matthew 5:9). However, in an ungodly world they will witness and experience the sword, a possible reference to the reality of opposition and persecution (Matthew 5:10–11).

Jesus fully recognized that peace cannot coexist in people who possess a predominately sinful nature of self. Since the fall, the makeup of humankind includes an attitude of rebellion against a holy God and antagonism toward faithful followers under His authority. Jesus did not intend to cause disagreement, but the natural reaction of many, especially unbelievers, is to oppose all who live out Christ's message. We see this resentment, ranging from the most subtle to that of active hostility in our present world.

In the same chapter of Matthew (10:35–37) and in Luke 14:26, Jesus said He came to set relatives against each other, even within a household. Also, any families who love each other more than they love Jesus are not worthy of following Him!

We may understand Christ's words to mean that faith in Him immediately introduces another noble feature, a higher loyalty into our lives. This allegiance reverses worldly priorities so that God takes first place even before family relationships. Family and social ties cannot stand in the way of faithfulness to Christ and righteous living. So if we are willing to accept the offer of Christ to be His follower and obey this directive of self-denial, we must realize that we may face difficulties in our relationships with friends and family. If we are not willing to obey Jesus and renounce some earthly friends, we have no true attachment to Him.

Jesus' primary consideration is our undivided identification with Him with no interfering allegiances. For the follower of Christ, this amounts to an unconditional association with self-denial and surrender to Christ. A. W. Tozer, in his book *The Radical Cross*, says that this was a divine requirement that deserved first place in the lives of Jesus' followers; for the true disciple, Christ comes even before life itself.

In Luke 14, Jesus says His followers should think very carefully before deciding to come after Him. He illustrates this advice with two parables. The first is the need to consider and calculate the cost of building a tower before undertaking its construction. This parable represents the nonsense of those who agree to be disciples of Christ without having considered the possible difficulties and the means to deal with them (Luke 14:28–31).

The second parable concerns a wise king who must bear in mind his resources and plan of attack before engaging in warfare against an opposing king and his stronger army. Failure to think this through seriously would likely result in a disaster (Luke 14:31–32).

What are the costs and necessary resources to believers who are noted in these verses? The answer largely comes from the following verse: "So then, none of you can be My disciple who does not give up all his own possessions" (Luke 14:33). The cost to be counted is a willingness to give up everything for Jesus. Not all those who associated with Jesus thought they were capable of giving up possessions and following Him. Many of the disciples and the multitudes who listened to Jesus withdrew from Him because they thought His teachings were too harsh and because they considered the costs too great to follow Him (John 6:60, 66).

Regarding the phrase "giving up" as used in Luke 14, we understand that the Greek word for "give up" when used for a person means to say farewell, and to renounce when it applies to things. To be preoccupied with things such as money or possessions is to miss the demands and joys of true discipleship. Oddly enough, however, many Christians parrot the secular culture and say this is the only way to true fulfillment and satisfaction. Jesus' point is that, as His disciples, we are to surrender to Him the title deed to all we possess. As previously stated, Jesus does not ask anyone to give anything up without having given it up Himself.

At this point, let us look even deeper into the meaning of self-denial. To do this, we must learn first what it is to deny another, and then we may better comprehend what it is to deny oneself. What, then, is it to deny another? Is it more than saying farewell? The person who denies another (for example, either a relative or stranger, should he see him down-trodden, restrained, poorly treated, or in pain) is not inclined to assist him, feels no remorse or shame for him, and is completely estranged from him. Therefore, one who truly denies another is not to make any attempt to save or spare that other individual, even from death.

From the Bible, we cite two examples of determinedly denying another person. In both of these cases the person is Jesus Christ. First, we are reminded that Peter repeatedly denied Jesus and made absolutely no attempt to spare Him from the torment leading up to His crucifixion. By denying Jesus, Peter was protecting himself. If he had aligned himself with Jesus, he might have put himself in jeopardy. But, by his denials, Peter spared himself. That is to say that Peter, one of Jesus' closest and most trusted friends, did not deny himself as Jesus had earlier commanded.

The second example took place at the cross of Calvary. Paul tells us that God the Father "did not spare His own Son" (Romans 8:32a) and thus totally denied Him. To some this appears to be extremely harsh and malicious. Paul immediately explains this divine act of denial by saying, [God] delivered Him over for us all" (Romans 8:32b). So what seemed to be cruel and unusual had a definite purpose to be served and it was directed toward all humankind.

Knowing what it is to deny another helps us to have a clearer understanding of Jesus' command to deny self. When we deny ourselves as Jesus told His followers to do, He would have us pay no attention to our own selves, so that whether experiencing troubles, anxieties, or persecution, we may not spare ourselves.

The denial of self can also go beyond having no consideration of self. Like the denial of another person mentioned above, self-denial can be taken to mean the death of an element of oneself. This would not be a physical component of self, but death of some attitude or disposition within the sinful nature of self that is opposing the godly nature of Christians. If God did not spare the perfection in His Son in order to produce imperfection on the cross, in turn, we should not spare our ungodly imperfections in order to become more Christlike. By now, it should be evident that denying oneself plays a vital role in the spiritual maturity of believers.

Self-Denial: Rights

Although not so evident many times, self-denial as practiced by Christians also has divine and eternal purposes, including the relinquishment of personal rights. To consider rights in the context of self-denial may seem a bit odd. Rights are a familiar topic throughout the world. We often hear a lot about rights in our democratic society. Think of all types of rights we witness on a daily basis: legal rights, human rights, animal rights, abortion rights, airline passenger rights, patient rights, collective bargaining rights, free speech rights—the list goes on and on.

In the United States Declaration of Independence, there is a high emphasis and value on liberty, both nationally and individually. The part of this monumental document that is of interest to us here is the portion that states, "...all men...endowed by their Creator with certain unalienable [nonreversible] rights [and] among these are life, liberty and the pursuit of happiness." It is regarding the last three words of this text that author Catherine Marshall expressed her wonder whether we are brainwashed with our national fixed idea of happiness and asked, "Have we made a god of happiness?" She then answers, "Perhaps our national preoccupation with happiness dates back from these words in the Declaration of Independence. I see more and more people interpret 'the pursuit of happiness' as a license to grab for power or money or physical pleasure. How arrogant and ungrateful we must seem to our Creator when we demand our rights" (*The Inspirational Writings of Catherine Marshall*, 348).

If we are truly and totally dependent on God's grace and mercy for all we have, we do not have the right to anything—not happiness or even life itself. Undoubtedly, this radical statement sounds irrational to unbelievers and many Christians as well. But as we begin living a life of faith and self-denial as followers of Jesus Christ, we must hold loosely to our personal rights and in particular, waive our rights in the surrender of our will to God. Not to do so is clearly obstinacy, that is, "I will not give up my right to myself!"

To better understand the relationship of self-denial to rights, we must identify what rights we are talking about and where they originated. According to Chuck Colson (who presents daily commentaries on "Breakpoint," a worldview ministry of Prison Fellowship Ministries), these rights are best called natural rights. He says, "They are derived initially as God-given rights in His creation of mankind as a part of selfhood, including the capacity to exercise his free will. At the heart of Christianity is the concept of free will. We can choose good and evil, and this lack of restriction is a God-given right."

These so-called natural rights continued after the fall, but they maliciously tend to become self-serving rather than God-serving. In essence, the rights are directed toward self; even to this day people say, "I have a right to myself," or "I can make my own choices," or "I have a right to determine what I desire, whether good, bad, or indifferent." These are dispositions or attitudes of self that define a person who has not denied him- or herself. From self-proclaimed individualism, this individual does not give up, surrender, and relinquish these rights to self.

Keep in mind that these rights stem from a non-denied, unaltered, and polluted self. Unfortunately, if believers focus too strongly on independence, it often will lead to selfishness and wrongful pride. These two qualities are the underlying features of our fallen human natures and, if taken to the point of demanding our natural rights, begin to not only harm us but others as well.

Self-denial also means to relinquish or do away with our right to ourselves. This definition is based upon the writings of Paul, where he states, we have "crucified the flesh with its passions and desires" (Galatians 5:24). I interpret Paul's words to mean the riddance of our ungodly obsessions and cravings. In his book *My Utmost for His Highest*, Oswald Chambers claims we must deal with this aspect of our natural lives, not only with our selfish pursuits, but especially with our selfhood or individuality. We must give up and relinquish our rights to ourselves, our natural independence and self-assertiveness, which are the two chief characteristics of individuality. From the natural viewpoint, there are things that are right, noble, and good. But in large part, these natural virtues can easily be hostile to God. Chambers continues, saying, "We tend to debate with the good. It is the good [in the self] that debates with the best [in the *self*], and is in opposition to the Gospel" (meditation for December 9).

We have already described self-denial in the life of Jesus Christ, but it was evident in His teaching as well. In the Sermon on the Mount, recorded in chapters 5–7 of Matthew's gospel, Jesus presented the way of righteous living and the promises of grace for those who become His followers and citizens in God's kingdom. Jesus focused on what the attitude of believers should be when they deal with evil individuals. He said, "But I say to you, do not resist an evil person; but whoever slaps you on your right cheek, turn the other to him also" (Matthew 5:38–42).

We have been conditioned by society to consider a man to be a coward if he turns the other cheek and refuses to fight. The world advocates retaliation, revenge, getting even, looking out for oneself, and protecting one's personal rights. But Jesus says we should set aside our personal rights for the sake of bearing witness to a changed life in God's kingdom. Jesus wants His followers to have an unselfish attitude that willingly follows the way of self-denial instead of the way of personal rights.

Consider the principle that labor should have its reward. This is not only a universal standard; it is a natural and personal right for every person to expect remuneration for his or her work. Paul and Barnabas had every right to be supported by fellow Christians. But they chose to waive their rights because if the gain was viewed to be wrong by some, it may have caused a hindrance to the gospel of Christ (1 Corinthians 9:12). Unquestionable as this right was in the case of Paul, he did not exercise it, but rather endured all kinds of hardships. He was willing to suffer anything rather than give his opponents the slightest pretext for their opposition to him.

In our journey of spiritual growth, are we willing to waive any of our personal rights for the sake of Christ and the furtherance of God's kingdom? Those who would be true disciples should think it through before aligning with the Savior. We must carefully count the costs of becoming Christ's disciples so we will know what we are getting into and won't be tempted to turn back when the going gets tough.

SELF-DENIAL: ABSTINENCE OR ASCETICISM

As most would suspect, there are extremes at both ends of the spectrum of Christian self-denial. On one side are examples of relative easy means of abstaining from common pleasures, luxuries, and desires. In this case, the abstinence is usually only periodic and is not carried out continuously. A specific instance would be the observation of Lent, where individuals are directed to wean from sin by creating the desire to do God's will and to make His kingdom more of a reality in their hearts. However, in some cases this could easily induce a sort of pride, an exaggerated self-satisfaction in approving one's self-control, making one a spiritual Little Jack Horner who says, "What a good boy am I."

The opposite extreme would be those who practice severe self-discipline and willingly include the incentive to endure bodily pain. Nowhere in biblical texts is found a commandment of this type of self-denial, which is called asceticism. In fact, Paul warned against using self-denial as a tool to rely on our own will. He labeled it will worship, a mode of adoration a person chooses independently of the revelation God has given. He called such teachings sacrilegious and having only the appearance of wisdom. It was a self-imposed religion that was neither profitable to the soul nor of any advantage to the body. In reality this religious conviction consisted of self-inflicted disciplines, having no value for countering the passions that surge in the flesh (see Colossians 2:20–23).

Within the context of describing true conditions of discipleship of Jesus' followers, I believe self-denial means much more than abstaining from certain luxuries and delight or engaging in the inducement of physical pain to oneself. The denial of self goes much deeper and in every situation demands a careful deliberate decision.

Self-Denial: A Yes-or-No Issue

Self-denial seems to be one of the two hardest terms a Christ follower must face (the other is cross-carrying). This is always the case because the opposition to self-denial is intrinsic to self, that is, to one's fallen human nature, the hallmark of which is selfishness. When faced with selfishness, one needs to say, "No, I will not follow the urgings of my self!

To those of us who are unwilling to obey Jesus' command of self-denial, the indwelling Holy Spirit may gently whisper, "Do you know the consequences of not denying yourself?" An honest answer to this probing question must be an admission that a refusal to deny self will hinder God's divine will for us to enter more fully into harmonious union with Him. This desired outcome is commonly called a personal relationship with God, which so many of us parrot in religious discussions of spiritual maturity.

To deny oneself also means to reject summarily any temptation or gratification in order to discover one's true self and God's interests better. It is a willingness to let go of selfish desires and refuse to respond to the promptings of the sinful nature within us. This creative attitude turns self-centeredness to God-centeredness. Self is no longer in charge; God is. This is the way we say yes to Jesus Christ.

SELF-DENIAL: SURRENDER AND SACRIFICE

Self-denial also means to sacrifice or give up something, such as the surrender or destruction of something that may be prized or desirable for the sake of a much more advantageous and higher claim. The self-serving spirit and mind-set of the world is opposed to the mind of a sacrificial servant. The apostle Paul was completely aware of this animosity toward Christians and told his fellow brethren not to conform themselves to the world, but to worship God as living sacrifices. Essential to that form of living is the need for daily renewing the mind in the truth of the Word. (See Romans 12:1–2.) Such surrender and sacrifice unsurprisingly form the foundation and wellspring for servant living, which is clearly God's will for all Christians.

In the realm of surrender and sacrifice, the Lord Jesus is our perfect example. First, being willing to sacrifice His position and privileges, He surrendered Himself to the Father's will. This also meant He was willing to serve and even suffer to fulfill the Father's plan of salvation for us. Therefore, since He served our needs as Redeemer and Advocate, we should be willing to serve, surrender, and sacrifice to meet the needs of others as a display of the mind of Christ (Philippians 2:3–5).

Jesus does not ask anyone to give anything up without having given it up himself. Jesus' view of denial was immediate and practical. It had to do with a transformation of the disciples' attitudes and dispositions (*Life Application Bible Commentary: Matthew*, Matthew 16:24 in Quickverse, 2005).

79

SELF-DENIAL: AN "INSIDE" ISSUE

It is crucially important that we become willing to deny ourselves, to set aside our justified feelings, our rights, our frustrations, offenses, and anything that is not of faith, and agree to do God's will. This is something we do on the inside. This internal denial of ourselves is often much harder to do than denying ourselves outwardly (our careers, positions of status, material things). However, the resolution of inward issues affects who we really are; it's our personhood and our emotions. It hurts to set ourselves aside, especially when we know we are justified by the world's standards in thinking and feeling the way we do.

No one in the world knows us and who we really are as God Himself knows us. He also knows the difficulties we face as we develop the attitude and need to deny ourselves. God wants to take us from a position of self-reliance to a position of total reliance upon Him. He wants us to learn to detach ourselves from all other supports and all other guidance so we can enjoy something that is immensely superior, a complete faith and trust in Him. When all of our trust and hope in earthly and created supports is gone, then we will have no other place to run, except to Him.

SELF-DENIAL: NOT AN END IN ITSELF

For the sake of Christ, self-denial in ourselves is not an end, but a means in the kingdom of God. An analogy can be found in education. We complete high school and even college not as an end in itself; it is a means to enhance our future lives. Likewise, self-denial is a way of experiencing the demands and joys of true discipleship.

Self-denial, unlike formal schooling, is not a one-time happening, but a continuing reduction of our assertive self (commonly known as ego) along with all of its associated elements of selfishness and pride. It takes place on the higher road of life. To a large measure, with the empowering presence of the Holy Spirit, self-denial provides the means by which the believer lives a Christlike life that bears the fruit of the Spirit—that is, love, joy, peace, patience, kindness, goodness, faithfulness, gentleness, self-control (Galatians 5:22–23).

BREAKING NEWS AND DEVELOPING STORY

Anchor (three days after the discovery of the S-Factor): "This may turn out to be one of the biggest stories of the year. It has generated interest in scientists around the globe, prompting some to apply to join the research team.

"We've just learned that the two senior researchers, Drs. Selford and Sinton, who together made this discovery, have reason to believe the biological matter may be associated with behavior patterns of the sampled people. Stay tuned as this story continues to develop."

Chapter 7

...Relate the Cross to Followers of Christ?

Part 1

If anyone wishes to come after Me, he must...take up his cross daily and follow Me.

—Luke 9:23

IREGRET THAT I had to make a division between the subjects of denying self and the carrying of a cross. Presented together, as they are found in context of Scriptures, may have been better. But because of their individual importance to discipleship and the following of Christ, the partition seemed necessary in order to focus on each subject separately. As we shall see, both of these topics are related.

How close is this relationship? Is it like that between cousins, parents and children, or man and wife? No, it's more like conjoined twins. I believe self-denial and cross-carrying are the two sides of a single coin. We view them separately, but they are inseparably connected. Throughout history, evangelical Christians have attached self-denial to taking up one's cross. In addition to other possible associations, this view produces a construct that implies that a deliberate rejection and denunciation of self can be accomplished by means of one's cross.

By way of introduction, let us understand what the cross was and what it generally meant to those living in and around Jerusalem at the time of Christ. A cross was a large stake used by the Romans of the first century as a means of torturing criminals and putting them to death. The stake likely was made from a wooden tree trunk with a cross piece secured near the top; thus, to the Romans it was a cross.

It was the Roman custom to compel those who were condemned to carry their crosses to the place of execution; when Simon carried the cross for Jesus, this phrase was illustrated. The criminal who received a sentence of crucifixion was nailed to the stake, and then the stake was set up vertically in the ground with the criminal suspended by the nails through the flesh of his hands and feet. The criminal was left hanging from the stake, experiencing hours of torture until he died. The cross was an instrument of death; therefore, a man with a cross no longer controlled his destiny, but lost control when he picked up the cross.

In the Old Testament there is no mention of crosses, but we find the word *tree* used extensively. In one instance, there is a suggestion that the wood of a tree might provide a veiled prophecy of a cross. At the town of Marah, as recorded in Exodus, a curse came upon the Israelites because of their bitterness and disobedience (Exodus 15:25–26). They cried out against Moses, who then sought advice from God. God showed Moses "a tree; and he threw it into the waters." The application of the tree to the waters lifted the curse, and the waters were made sweet. Some Bible authorities believe this miracle symbolized a lifting of a curse, similar to Christ being made a curse for us by hanging on a tree (cross).

In some translations of the Bible, we find in the writings of Peter, Paul, and Luke (the author of Acts) the word *tree* used in place of the cross. However, New Testament scriptures contain almost all references to a wooden cross in relation to the sacrificial death of Christ. Immediately preceding John 3:16— "For God so loved the world, that He gave His only begotten Son, that whoever believes in Him shall not perish, but have eternal life"—the apostle John provides an illustration of Christ's vicarious death on the cross and the necessity of personal faith for salvation (John 3:14–15). The example John uses here is of an Old Testament story in which the complaining Hebrew people died when bitten by fiery serpents. However, if they looked upon an elevated bronze serpent that was supported by a pole, likely made of wood, they would live (Numbers 21:5–9). The emphasis seems not to be on the means of lifting up something or someone on a wooden structure, but to focus on the supported object in the belief that it will bring life and not death.

To the Hebrews, crucifixion was not an ordained punishment, although the Jews were quite familiar with the Roman use of the cross. Late in Jesus' earthly ministry, He spoke to His disciples about carrying a cross, likely in reference to the cross He was to carry. This may well have been one of those sayings of Jesus that the disciples did not understand at first, but the meaning was revealed later (John 12:16). Perhaps we, like the early disciples, have the same difficulty understanding the words of Jesus about cross-carrying. So, here we are two thousand years later attempting to grasp insight into the meaning of carrying one's cross.

MEANINGS OF CROSS-CARRYING

To better understand the intent of the word *cross* used by Jesus in Luke 9:23, we will look at nine obvious features of cross-carrying. These aspects of cross-carrying are not just academic. Rather, they contain spiritual significance and application for followers of Jesus Christ. In other words, we may use them as criteria to justify and decide which of the meanings probably best match these features.

Then we will consider what the cross likely meant to Jesus Himself, followed by what cross-carrying brings about for us as those who desire to follow Jesus. Lastly, we will examine certain views and interpretations expressed by biblical authorities on this subject.

CROSS-CARRYING: EVIDENT FEATURES

1. As stated in an earlier chapter on self-denial, the demand to bear a cross is *universal*. Jesus gave this mandate not only

85

to His disciples, but to the crowds as well (Mark 8:34). Just like self-denial, the command to carry a cross is given to all who follow Christ, not to a select few who walked near to Christ.

2. This demand was *intense* in that no one could be considered His disciple and be creditable in any sense unless he or she bore a cross. This assertion is clearly validated by the words of Jesus: "Whoever does not carry his own cross and come after Me cannot be My disciple" (Luke 14:27); and "And he who does not take his cross and follow after Me is not worthy of Me" (Matthew 10:38).

3. Like the denial of self, to carry one's cross is totally *voluntary*. It is an open invitation to a person who sets his or her will to come after Jesus. Although the command to carry a cross is forceful, the Lord does not compel a cross upon anyone against his or her will. One has the freedom of choice to carry the cross or not; there is absolutely no compulsion. Similar to the intentional choice to submit to God's will and to sacrifice His life, Christ followed the path to Calvary. "No one has taken it [My life] away from Me, but I lay it down on My own initiative" (John 10:18). In no way will God withdraw His gift of freedom of choice; out of one's own desire, the believer must choose to take up and carry his cross.

4. The cross one carries is not the cross of Christ; only He was divinely ordained to be placed on the "Old Rugged Cross." Each believer is instructed to take up his or her very own cross, so the issue is one of *ownership*. That is, it's the believer's personal cross, and so it must be used for a distinct purpose for that person. There is the possibility that one's cross may be placed or allowed in his path by someone other than himself. It is supposed that the cross lies in his way, and it is prepared for him. If so, he is still instructed to pick it up and carry it as it becomes his own possession.

5. The cross is to be taken up *daily*. For the true believer to carry his or her cross is not a onetime experience but a lifelong assignment. The implication here is that the person is conscious of what he or she is carrying and in whatever he or she is doing or not doing, in any and all circumstances. For the true believer, carrying the cross is an ever present, lifelong, daily task. There is no hint that this cross will have finally fulfilled its purpose while the person is living on earth. Like self-denial, this means cross-carrying will be an ever-existing responsibility on the part of the believer.

6. Carrying a cross requires *input*, a contribution of power, energy and strength. This participating effort is necessary for it to bring about its effect on the person. A deliberate act and power are required, and sometimes the person requires assistance.

7. Cross-carrying is associated with suffering or pain. For the carrier, this *discomfort* can be physical or outward. The suffering may also be inward, such as experienced toward one's dignity, a humiliation, shame, or an embarrassment. Suffering, like Jesus experienced as He was forsaken by God on the cross, is expected when carrying the cross. To deny self and its natural human traits may be a part of the suffering endured.

8. Carrying a cross is intended to be *mortal*, but during the time it is carried, the cross and the carrier have not reached the place for death to occur. Every cross is an instrument of death. The bereavement on the cross is not one of a chronic nature, but achieved to end one's life, or a feature of life, in a relatively short time. It is deadly. The cross has one objective: It ruthlessly intends to bring death, and the person is fully aware of what lies ahead.

9. Carrying a cross can be viewed as an *anticipatory* act. This would be like a prelude to an incident or crisis experience that has a purpose to be fulfilled, perhaps as a result of the troubling situation. Regarding many of the negative

aspects of cross-carrying noted above, the attitude of expectancy could well extend beyond the bad with the belief of something good happening in the future—much like a woman anticipating giving birth, which includes elements of both pain and happiness. The anticipatory aspect of cross-carrying might well fit in with the virtue of hope.

Cross-Carrying: To Jesus Christ

In previous chapters, I mentioned that ideally, no leader should ever give tasks to his followers to accomplish that the leader did not experience or understand. So when Jesus gave a directive to carry a cross, He met both these requirements. Remember that Jesus gave His disciples and others the command to carry their crosses late in His ministry, before He physically took up His cross and ascended the path to Calvary. This raises the question of what prerogative Jesus had to make this command.

Probably the best answer is that we simply do not know. But there is the possibility that the shadow of the cross fell on Christ from the infinite past and was as real to Him from then on as it was when He carried the crude beam all the way to His sacrificial death. That is to say, Christ was knowledgeable about His future involvement with the cross since the foundation of the world.

To validate this claim, let's look at evidence of Christ's preexistence. We know something about His preincarnate life as suggested in several biblical accounts. In this regard, Jesus Christ the Messiah is referred to as the following: the One who will go forth from God, as the One who was from long ago, from the days of eternity (Micah 5:2); is and was the Word before time began (John 1:1) and became flesh (John 1:14); the I Am before Abraham was born (John 8:58); He is identified in the creation of all things in the world (Colossians 1:16); and more clearly, the Lamb was appointed to redeem humanity by His blood from the foundation of the world, that is, from creation (Revelation 13:8).

It is hard to believe that an all-knowing, all-powerful, preexistent Christ did not know of God's plan to redeem humankind only shortly before or even at His Incarnation. But if this really was the case, then God might have said, "Golly, these Hebrew people just can't obey My commandments alone, so I will send My only begotten Son to take care of them and all other people's sins on a cross and later send the Holy Spirit to help them to become more like Me."

No! Based on the Scriptures noted above, it is more likely that Christ knew the good news plan well enough from eternity past, to the extent that He was acutely aware of His destiny with two pieces of wood. Paved with difficulties and temptations, the daily path He took was straight and narrow that led Him ultimately to Calvary.

If indeed this line of reasoning is correct—that Christ was always overshadowed by the cross on which He was sacrificed at Calvary—we then can begin to envision what the cross meant to Jesus, especially during His ministry. When we look to Jesus to understand His word about the cross, we see immediately that the cross of Calvary was the very heart and summit of God's work in Him.

We are reminded that Jesus also willingly took upon Himself the vulnerability of humanity, which included any self-preserving aspect of His innate human nature. With the aid of the abiding power of the Holy Spirit, Jesus daily applied self-denial to counter any selfish desires such as self-preservation. It may be that His thinking about the cross also was a daily experience. How can we make this assertion? Everybody who is even remotely aware of Christianity knows that Jesus carried the physical cross only on the last day of His earthly life. Although there is no scripture indicating Jesus carried some hand-sized or imaginary cross, we believe God's plan of salvation from the beginnings of time always included a crude wooden device on which a third of the Godhead would be sacrificed for the salvation of humankind.

I can't help but wonder if the essence of the cross was deeply embedded in Jesus' mind, soul, and spirit. Never to the point of hysteria or lunacy, but in an anticipatory manner, the cross provided a constant reminder that it would be the only thing that held Him up on Calvary. He knew many would let Him down; because all the sin of the world would fall on Him, He would even be let down (denied, abandoned) by His heavenly Father. If successful in His divinely appointed work, He also knew that the cross's shadow would ultimately become the backdrop for illuminating His and God the Father's love for the world. It is in this scenario of maintaining a state of complete sinlessness and in repeated adversities that we can begin to see an association between self-denial and the cross, even before Jesus personally took up a physical cross.

The combination of Jesus' denial of self and His knowledge of the tree on which He was to die is evidence of the assertion we made earlier in this chapter; namely, self-denial and cross-carrying are inseparably connected. As the time shortened (from years to months) for Jesus to begin His intense suffering and take up His cross, we imagine His tensions and mental stress varied, yet increasingly heightened. Over time (from months to weeks to days and to hours) the growing anticipation of enduring the agonizing suffering became more of a challenge to Jesus to carry out fully His Father's will.

One key to Jesus' ability to take up the physical cross upon which He was to die was his knowledge of God's will for His life. During moments of extreme agony in the garden of Gethsemane, something extraordinary happened to Jesus: "His sweat became like drops of blood, falling down upon the ground" (Luke 22:44). In this extreme state, Jesus the spotless Lamb began to offer His body for the sin the world, saying prayerfully, "Yet not as I will, but as You will" (Matthew 26:39).

From this time forward, in total compliance to the will of the His Father and in complete subjection to Him, Christ voluntarily allowed Himself to be shamefully treated and beaten, and out of devotion to God and love for humankind, to be killed. In living out this radical obedience to the Father moment by moment, Jesus was able to embrace all types of crosses that earlier came to Him.

This line of reasoning may explain that His ability to take up His cross on that dreadful Friday afternoon was related to the many times He successfully managed to cope with His daily troubles (trials, temptations, and tribulations) in the past. It was as if the conquering of daily troubles provided the training ground needed to prepare Jesus better for His anticipated Passion. The oneness with His Father and His total self-control in conquering temptations and troubles made His earthly life possible to the very end.

In this regard it has been suggested that the only cross Jesus carried daily was His very own self-denial. So what Jesus may be saying to His disciples and to us is that cross-carrying is His illustration of self-denial, something He Himself successfully did every moment of His human existence to counter any tendency to yield to temptation or sway from the will of His Father.

Let us also consider the several times Jesus encountered sinful individuals and told them their sins were forgiven. For example, the paralytic sought out Jesus and was told, "Your sins are forgiven" (Mark 2:5; Luke 5:20). I think the Lord must have perceived an inward pain with this pardon of sins because He knew the only way He could forgive that man's sin was to bear it Himself. Viewing these acts of forgiveness as types of trouble, He must have tasted the agony of the cross whenever He forgave sin. He knew He would bear the punishment He had removed from that helpless soul. Time after time, Jesus showed the mercy and love of His Father while under the darkness of the cross.

We must also address one of the main outcomes of cross-carrying and the crucifixion of Christ. He must have been aware that the total plan of salvation included eternal life, a resurrected life totally shared with God Himself. The writer of Hebrews tells us that "Jesus, the author and perfecter of faith, who for the *joy* set before Him endured the cross, despising the shame, and has sat down at the right hand of the throne of God" (Hebrews 12:2, emphasis added).

CROSS-CARRYING: TO BELIEVERS

Obedience to God's Will

Remember that for Jesus, the cross was rooted in obedience to God's will. Simply put, our crosses may represent the will of God for us. Taking up our crosses can be viewed as acts of submission, willingness to pay the price and do whatever God asks. In this regard, taking up our crosses means to cease rebelling and submit to His rule over our lives. We take up our crosses when we make the same decision Jesus made: to do the will of God, daily, moment by moment, whatever the cost or wherever God's will may lead us.

Before taking up our crosses, however, we should know something about God's purpose and will for our lives. Without this knowledge, it would difficult to obey Him and carry out His desires. Someone has said, "The highest motive for obeying God is the desire to please Him." The question then arises, "How can we be obedient if we don't know what pleases God?" This question can easily be answered by using a concordance or online search engine. Simply find all the Bible verses that contain the words *please* and *pleasing* in reference to God. Your investigation will reveal that pleasing God is solidly connected to faithful obedience and sanctification.

From the several dozen Bible verses which have this word combination, a very revealing passage is found in a letter written to the church at Thessalonica. Paul tells the members that they knew God's commandments and were instructed "as to how you ought to walk and please God…For this is the will of God, your sanctification" (1 Thessalonians 4:1, 3). Here we find that sanctification is God's desire and the purpose of every believer. The word *sanctification* means holiness, purity of life, and particularly, detaching those vices that both dishonor the Christian and God.

Living a Life of Sacrificial Love

The New Testament consistently describes Christ's death in sacrificial terms. The writer of Hebrews portrays Christ as the sinless High Priest who offered Himself up as a sacrifice for sinners (Hebrews 7:27). Believers who reap the benefits of His sacrifice are to be living sacrifices. Accordingly, the same author also says believers should "continually offer up a sacrifice of praise to God, that is, the fruit of lips that give thanks to His name" (Hebrews 13:15). This directive acknowledges that the Jewish system of sacrifices was abolished except for praise for the gift of God's Son. It is one that includes adoration and prayer, as well as thanksgiving.

The author of Hebrews continues on the theme of sacrifices and pleasing God, saying, "And do not neglect doing good and sharing, for with such sacrifices God is pleased" (Hebrews 13:16). We must speak to the necessities of others; we should not be content to offer only the sacrifice of our lips, merely words, but also the sacrifice of good deeds. These would be our unselfish acts of kindness toward others, not depending upon the merit of our good actions or deeds, but on the knowledge that we are pleasing our heavenly Father.

Paul spoke of Christ's death as a sacrifice to God and as such a fragrant aroma (Ephesians 5:2), and also spoke of himself as a libation (drink) poured out (Philippians 2:17). So the Christian's life of sacrifice is the logical consequence of Christ's sacrificial death. In this regard, there is also a sense in which Christians must sacrifice their lives to God every day. This means a daily total sacrifice of self to do the will of Jesus. Submission to God means dying to one's own desires and will; it means to go wherever He calls us to go and to be to do whatever He calls one to be and do.

We are told to be willing participants of Christ's anguish and pain: "To the degree that you share the sufferings of Christ, keep on rejoicing" (1 Peter 4:13). Christ Himself endured sufferings. We are accepted as disciples as we deny ourselves, carry our crosses, and share in His afflictions. Suffering for Christ's sake should create rejoicing, because through suffering we Christians further identify with Him. The New Testament is clear that those who take part in the suffering of Christ will also take part in His glory when it is revealed. To experience rejoicing, we must remember the purpose of the sufferings, and not react like so many, who ask the perennial question, "Why me?"

Christians are to present their "bodies a living and holy sacrifice, acceptable to God, which is [our] spiritual service of worship" (Romans 12:1). Paul elaborates on this truth of a life of sacrifice by exhorting the believers to not conform to worldly standards but to be transformed into conduct of sacrificial living. The behavior he identifies is in many ways contrary to the selfish and prideful nature of humankind. He says that the model of sacrificial life should not exhibit self-importance (Romans 12:3), or self-worthiness more likely than the merit of your brothers in Christ (Romans 12:10). Both of these ungodly human traits are not to be personified in the sacrificial life of Christians.

All of these phrases are sacrificial and show that there must be a complete surrender of self—the body, the whole person, mind and flesh, to be given to God; we are to consider ourselves no more our own, but the property of our Maker. We are also told that as believers we are to separate ourselves from immorality (wickedness), for we are "a temple of the Holy Spirit," and we are not our own because we have been "bought with a price." Therefore, we are to glorify God in our bodies (1 Corinthians 6:19–20).

It would be a great travesty if we overlooked the topic of love in connection with suffering and cross-carrying. God is love, and we, as followers of Christ, are to likewise love others (1 John 4:7–21). The love we are talking about here is Christian love, technically known as *agape* love. All three persons of the Holy Trinity attest to agape love. God's love "has been poured out within our hearts through the Holy Spirit who was given to us" (Romans 5:5). Jesus taught and always exhibited this type of love toward others.

Two questions arise: "What is the usefulness of this love?" and "How do we get it?" As we understand, agape love is the giving of oneself, having an active interest in the true welfare of others that is not deterred even by hatred, cursing, and abuse. It is unlimited by results and is solely based upon the divine nature of the Godhead. It is characterized in the Bible as unselfishness and a willingness to sacrifice one's own wishes for those of others.

It is at this point that we turn to the connection between love and sacrifice. Simply put, sacrifice means surrender of something very precious for the one we love. Sacrifice is the active message of love and is the major source of our spiritual growth in love. It has been said that we sacrifice only to the degree to which we love. If indeed sacrifice is surrender and the previous statement is true, what is the highest and greatest surrender we can make? In other words, what is the most precious thing we have that we struggle against? In a word, it is **self**, that part of us that must be dethroned to allow the Creator of the world to rightfully be the Lord of our lives.

An Elaboration of Self-Denial

When Jesus told His disciples to take up and carry their crosses in conjunction with the commandment to deny self, He may have been simply using the term *cross* as a vivid illustration of self-renunciation. This is the opinion of Walter J. Chantry, author of the book *The Shadow of the Cross: Studies in Self-Denial.* He states that "Jesus' figure of bearing a cross is an elaboration of his demand for self-denial" (25). This would be the way our Lord emphasized His explicit demand of denying oneself and living a sacrificial life.

The amplification of denial of self by taking up and carrying crosses is an interesting concept. So would be the reverse; self-denial may be the vehicle that drives one to carry his or her cross, which in turn is applied to living a sacrificial life for the sake of Christ. Nonetheless, again it is easy to see the interconnection between denying oneself and carrying a cross.

OTHER VIEWS OF CROSS-CARRYING

Perhaps Jesus' command to His followers to carry a cross was, in part, a prophecy that foretold the manner of the death He was to die. Later, after Jesus ascended to heaven, the apostles received guidance from the Holy Spirit to understand the full meaning of His death and the cross. Although the statements concerning a person's own cross were veiled at the time Jesus made them, they became clearer as the prophecies contained in the statements were fulfilled; that is, when Jesus was tortured and put to death upon the cross that rightfully belonged to His followers.

Some commentators suggest that the cross Christ bore was not His own, but it was the symbol of the judgment for our sins. If our judgment of death is to be canceled in the substitutionary death of Jesus on His cross, we must take up our own crosses and acknowledge the righteous judgment against us. Thus, this act of cross-carrying allows us the privilege and honor to follow Him.

BREAKING NEWS AND DEVELOPING STORY

Anchor: "Because the S-Factor seems to be associated with personality traits, the genetic investigators have been joined by two other researchers.

"One is psychotheologist Dr. Jay Carataker, who has degrees in clinical psychology and systematic theology. He has previously devised sophisticated tests to determine selected moral and behavioral traits in people.

"The other researcher is world-renowned neuropsychiatrist Dr. Joyce Cibalo. Her specialty is in neurobiology, which focuses on the neurological basis of behavioral patterns.

"The team plans to further evaluate the S-Factor and selected aspects of character traits in the living subjects who were first studied. Stay tuned to this channel for the latest developments in this ongoing story."

Chapter 8

... Relate the Cross to Followers of Christ?

Part 2

IN ADDITION TO the most reasonable meanings of carrying one's cross, obedience to God's will, living a life of sacrifice, and its application of self-denial, let us consider some other nuances related to this concept. One major connotation is attached to the various trials, tribulations, and temptations believers experience during our Christian walk of faith. We can arbitrarily classify these as "troubles."

TROUBLES AS BAD THINGS

One may presume that taking up our cross means accepting stoically those external or internal bad things that may happen to us in life. For example, perhaps we are frustrated over continued struggles with a pattern of anger. We may conclude that anger is just part of our personality and equate this transgression to a cross we must accept. Our sin must never be considered to be our cross. Taking up our cross does not mean looking for some external trial to keep us from being too comfortable, or enduring bad things calmly, or putting up with our sin.

TROUBLES AS ANNOYANCES

This view is painted with a broad brush, relating the cross to any troubling circumstances or inconvenience in the lives of believers.

How do the majority of Christians, as well as non-Christians, describe the carrying of their crosses? They would probably say, "It's a burden I have to bear." Such a response has become no more than an English idiom, and is often used when speaking about a seemingly trivial yet troublesome responsibility that continues over an extended period. "I'm afraid my chores are just my cross to bear." Surely carrying a cross means far more than merely bearing up under the trying inconveniences of life.

But let us not be too critical of those who relate the cross to petty troubles, for this could just be a good mind-set to build upon as these believers gain further spiritual insight and as they mature spiritually during more severe troubling times. For example, there was a time not long ago that Christians were instructed to offer up daily hardships in the form of devotions. They were convinced that these daily hardships were annoyances, although seemly petty, that could somehow relate to Christ's great compassion and suffering. In this way these daily inconveniences acquired meaning and served to better identify believers with their Lord.

There is also a more important reason not to be judgmental toward those who might define cross-carrying as annoyances. In most cases, the observer does not completely know the details of another's burdens. For example, many individuals perform menial and commonplace tasks, either for themselves or others, with little or no earthly reward, such as house cleaning, cooking, and the like. These works have nothing to do with sin, but the menial tasks just may be a force to guide their minds moment by moment toward the cross of Christ and the great merits derived from His death and resurrection.

TROUBLES AS A PERSECUTIONS OR TRIBULATIONS

To follow Jesus, carrying your cross could mean literal death, whether by means of a cross or not. This was the case for most of His first disciples as they met cruel opposition to Christ's great commission to "Go therefore and make disciples of all nations...teaching them to observe all that I commanded you" (Matthew 28:19–20). Historical accounts have accurately documented that under Roman rule, persecution, including death, was the fate for countless thousands who refused to align themselves with other deities.

Jesus told His disciples, "In the world you have tribulation" (John 16:33). You may ask where these tribulations or troubles come from. Keep in mind that a wide variety of circumstances come into play as troubles occur. Tribulations or troubles have been described in at least three categories.

First, there are troubling afflictions that originate because God purposely allows them to come into lives of Christians as a consequence of following Christ (2 Corinthians 12:7–10). Christ said, "Blessed are you when people insult you and persecute you, and falsely say all kinds of evil against you because of Me. Rejoice and be glad for your reward in heaven is great" (Matthew 5:11–12). Carefully note the words "because of Me" or "for My sake" in passages such as this. In this sense, the cross is perceived to represent any and all providential sorrows, sufferings, persecutions for righteousness' sake and every major trouble that befalls us, either for doing well or for not doing ill.

According to J. I. Packer, for believers to carry their cross means we must renounce all expectations from society and learn to take it as a matter of course if others shun us and view us with contempt and disgust, as if we are out of tune with the world. He further states, "We, too, may often find ourselves treated in this fashion if we are loyal to the Lord Jesus Christ" (*Knowing God*, 245). This loyalty to Jesus Christ is putting the Lord first above self and even family (see Matthew 10:37; 19:29). This means taking up one's cross regardless of the cost (Matthew 10:38; 16:24; Luke 9:23).

Second, it is clear from both the Old and New Testaments that God brings chastisements (punishments) to His children in the form of trials, mainly because of their disobedience. In the book of Proverbs we see that we are not to "reject the discipline of the LORD...For whom the LORD loves He reproves" (Proverbs 3:11–12). We are also told not to regard lightly the discipline of the Lord and that this scolding is for those whom the Lord loves (Hebrews 12:5–6).

Third, tribulations may come about for both believers and non-Christians simply because we live in a fallen world. These types of troubles include accidents, bereavements, injuries, and so-called acts of God, such as floods and earthquakes (Romans 8:35–36).

TROUBLES AS DELIVERANCES

If we were to poll believers as to their views of living typical Christian lives we would likely find that most would want to be delivered *from* trouble. However, the Bible, including Jesus' teachings about self-denial and cross-carrying, says Christian living is deliverance *in* troubles. The dictionary tells us that deliverance means release, liberation, and rescue, freedom from something or someone, including oneself.

To illustrate this principle (God's method of deliverance), let us focus on the cross of Calvary and the torturous steps of Jesus as He carried the cross toward His destiny. Humanly speaking, due to extreme physical abuse and the heaviness of the cross, His strength was depleted before He reached His destination. He knew His Father's will for Him was to die *on* the cross not *under* it. Then Simon the Cyrene, through a providential plan, was forced to use his power to help carry the cross for Jesus (Matthew 27:32).

There is a lesson about deliverance for us here, as we have already established that mortal believers possess the exact humanity of Christ, and as such are also vulnerable as He was. But unlike Christ, we retain unconquered Adamlike instincts and are limited in our spiritual ability, power, and strength to overcome troubling circumstances by ourselves. We need help and we cry out, "God, help me!"

We recall that Jesus said, "Apart from Me you can do nothing" (John 15:5). In times of certain troubles, we realize that the cross we carry is anything associated with our being, including our defiled (corrupted) self. This is when we think we cannot go on, and if we have not already made significant progress in denying ourselves, we finally realize that we now need to renounce any remnant of our human nature that says, "I am self-dependent, self-sufficient, self-sustaining, and self-empowering."

In these straining times of troubles, who will appear to help us? Maybe it will be a Simon, a burden carrier. But the Helper we can truly count on for that power to deliver us *in* our trouble is the One who indwells us from the time we accepted the gospel invitation, namely the Holy Spirit. He and the Spirit of the living Christ in our being will freely give us the energizing power to overcome any and all trials.

TROUBLES AS TRIALS OF FAITH

It seems as though our Christian faith is challenged in many common-sense circumstances. Human wisdom and common sense are not faith. Instead, they are part and parcel of our human nature, self, that often challenges our faith. As a necessary component of our spiritual maturing process, our faith is tested through various forms of temptations and stormy trials. The apostle Peter reminds us that we are secure and protected by the power of God through faith: "even though now for a little while, if necessary, you have been distressed by various trials, so that the proof of your faith...may be found to result in praise and glory and honor at the revelation of Jesus Christ" (1 Peter 1:6–7). In contrast, conventional wisdom or common sense will never, by themselves, view trials as producing praise, glory, and honor of anything or anyone.

Previously I suggested that cross-carrying could be viewed as an anticipatory act, a prelude to an episode in which a purpose is to be fulfilled. In his epistle, James did not use the word *cross* in his discourse on trials, but he said there was a purpose for trials: "Consider it all joy, my brethren, when you encounter various trials, knowing that the testing of your faith produces endurance...that you may be perfect and complete" (James 1:2–4). It is clear from this text that trials have a divine purpose and that the intention is simply to allow the believer to become more perfect and complete. Perfection and completeness are only found in the person of Jesus Christ. As we journey in our faith walks, we are continually called to be more and more Christlike.

So is this the excellence and fullness James is talking about? Out of such testing of our faith, we receive a glimpse of God's master plan. For many mature Christians, trials are His way of answering the (all too often) "why" questions. Testing faith is God's way of continuing His good work (His work of grace) in us (see Philippians 1:6). It is His way of forcing us to make a choice in times of troubles. Before acting in trying situations, we can either focus on the stormy trial with fear—a major feature of our human nature—or spotlight Jesus Christ, allowing faith, a vital aspect in our spiritual makeup, to yield to its perfect result. The outcome of this latter choice is one of producing spiritual maturity and completeness, as well as a Christlike character, in the believer. This has to be the major answer to all questions about trials and tribulations.

TROUBLES AS BURDENS

When we are told to take up our cross and carry it, one thought that comes to mind is that the cross is heavy like the cross that Jesus carried the last day of His earthly life. It has been estimated that Jesus' cross weighed about eighty or ninety pounds. To carry something of this magnitude throughout each day can rightly be termed a burden. Some may recall a Scripture passage that addresses the issue of carrying a heavy yoke. It is one of the most beloved in the New Testament, Matthew 11:28–30. Here Jesus describes Himself as gentle and humble and offers an invitation to give rest to those who are tired of having to endure the heaviness of a load. Some biblical interpreters believe that a burden, a yoke, was the demanding discipline of following the law that was required by the Jewish religious leaders of that day. Others think it means the self or the ungodliness of a person. Instead, Jesus offers us His yoke, which, in His words, "is easy" and His "burden is light."

Among the Jews the word *yoke* signified not only that sort of neck-harness by which cattle drew wagons and plows, but also any kind of bond or obligation to perform some particular thing. To achieve rest, Christ's yoke could then refer to the obligation to receive Him as the Messiah, to believe the simple doctrine of the gospel, and to be and do all things conforming to His character, including His meekness and humility.

Thus the matter of burdens may involve a comparison between two ways one is to live. One is the rigid and weighty rule-keeping life that has the potential of deceitfulness, selfishness, and artificiality. The second is the undemanding and tolerable yoke, a cross. By comparison, the cross would be an easier and lighter burden than living under the rule of a performance-based acceptance and a prideful life. This would be the cross of faith or the necessity of believing in the promised Messiah. It would be a spiritual, divine cross, the obligation to live a spiritual life, a life of thanksgiving and gratitude to God.

Our discussion leads us now to three pertinent questions: (1) Am I willing to be obedient to the revealed will of God? (2) Do I read correctly that God's will for me is to deny myself, take up my cross, and follow Jesus Christ? and (3) In doing so, can I entrust myself to the loving care of God in any and all circumstances during my journey of faith?

The matrix of Jesus' commands shown below will not totally answer these three questions, but it shows the necessity of complying with both self denial and cross-carrying.

Jesus's Commands Mathew 16:24 Luke 9:23 Mark 8:34		A Follower of Christ
Deny Self	Carry Cross	
Yes	Yes	Yes
Yes	No	No
No	Yes	No
No	No	No

**Obedience of Jesus's Commands
Determines Who is a Follower of Christ**

Table 8.1. A Matrix of One's Responses to Jesus' Commands

Notice in this graphic that it is only when believers are obedient to both commands that we correctly follow Jesus Christ. The "yes" response is obedience and a "no" response is disobedience. At any point in time, when our reaction toward self-denial or cross-carrying is negative, it is very unlikely that we will truly follow Christ.

CROSS-CARRYING: ANY CONCLUSIONS?

Can we come to any settlement about a practical meaning of cross-carrying for the believer? We can actually own and carry our physical replicas of the cross as a necklace, in a purse, or tattooed on the skin. However, there is a more meaningful spiritual way to view our cross. In a large part, we gained this view based on the nine evident features of carrying a cross, derived primarily from Matthew 16:23 and Luke 9:25. In these passages, Jesus' forceful commandment indicates that the action of carrying a cross is voluntary, accomplished daily, personal, required energy, and involved discomfort with an anticipatory feature.

Without being dogmatic, I believe we carry our crosses symbolically in our minds, remembering when Jesus yielded His life on the cross of Calvary on our behalf. For the Christian, this is not an occasional or sporadic recall of a person suffering and dying two thousand years ago or a story we are reminded of just before Easter. Nor is it an absolute fixation on an event that mesmerizes a person to a point of uselessness, neurosis, or psychosis. Instead, it is a mandatory recollection of the atonement for all of humankind's evil.

Jesus Christ directed all Christians to focus on this historic act of unconditional love by participating in Communion. In these special occasions, our response in this sacrament is one of obedience to Jesus' directive of not forgetting Him: "Do this in remembrance of Me" (Luke 22:19). The emphasis here is not forgetting when, where, and how Jesus died, but instead remembering this pivotal event in a very personal manner. In fact, the willful act of remembering is referred to more than 250 times in the Bible, often associated with God's plea to remember how He has mercifully acted in the welfare of His chosen ones. Through Moses, God entreated the Israelites to not "forget the LORD your God who brought you out from the land of Egypt, out of the house of slavery" (Deuteronomy 8:14).

There is a kind of remembrance called a flashback. In stories and media, a flashback (also called analepsis) is an interjected scene that takes the narrative back in time from the current point in the story. In other words, a flashback is action that interrupts the here and now to show a significant incident that took place at an earlier time. Understanding the magnitude of the earlier happening, such as the deliverance of the Hebrews from Egyptian slavery, is necessary to cope better with and comprehend a present happening.

So what does flashback have to do with cross-carrying? Some Christian theologians believe God uses situations and circumstances in our lives to jumpstart our minds to remember Him. If a believer is experiencing pain, confusion, or anxiety, this cross he is currently bearing energizes his thoughts to flashback to the suffering and death of Jesus on His cross.

In addition to experiencing troubles and associating such difficulties with the Passion of Christ, another way to mentally view cross-carrying is during times of prayerful meditation apart from the business of our daily life. We can reflect on the mystery of Christ's Passion by merely associating our personal cross with the one on which Jesus suffered and died. This would necessarily include thoughts directed toward a merciful God and His beloved Son. As a result we would better understand and appreciate the oneness we have with Jesus Christ in the here and now. It has wisely been said that a flashback pulls the past into the present. In later chapters we will see the merits of this wisdom applied to Christian spiritual maturity.

THE CROSS AND "SELF"

We begin the last part of this chapter by addressing the significance of the cross as it applies to living a victorious life, which is what God wants for every follower. Having considered the meanings of cross-carrying as it applies to Jesus Christ and to the believer, we have identified the greatest importance of having no reservations to obey God willingly. The Christian's total obedience to God is characterized by a number of features, including oneness, identification, and love. Christ says, "If you love Me, you will keep My commandments" (John 14:15). The "Me" and "My" of this statement imply a singular love, for Christ has also said, "No one can serve two masters; for either he will hate the one and love the other, or he will be devoted to one and despise the other" (Matthew 6:24).

"IF YOU CHASE TWO RABBITS, BOTH WILL ESCAPE"

If a believer's relationship to God through Christ, and Him alone, is completely love based, he or she will do what God says without any hesitation. If the person is even slightly unwilling, he or she loves someone or something else that is in competition with God. While we are fully aware of worldly influences that constantly seek dominance in our lives, I believe the chief adversary is an inner thing, the **self**, the very target we want to uncover and expose. The one vital element of Christianity to counter this misplaced love is the cross. Our true love of God does not run parallel with an ungodly self; it intersects it on the cross of Calvary. So let us more fully examine some of the pertinent aspects of both the cross and of self.

You recall that in chapter 3 I introduced the thought of self within a simple circle. (See fig. 3.1.) Based on the story of the creation of Adam and Eve recorded in the first three chapters of Genesis, the first circle on the left was totally white to show the innocent state of humankind. The fall broke the harmonious relationship between the Creator and the creature. As a result of this great calamity, the self-circle on the right is darkened because of sin and thus was defiled (corrupted). This ruined relationship between God and humanity is so disastrous (tragic) that it is spoken of in Scripture as the opposite of life itself; namely, spiritual death and a curse. Based on New Testament Scriptures, this curse continues to exist in all unregenerated humankind to this day. (See fig. 8.2.)

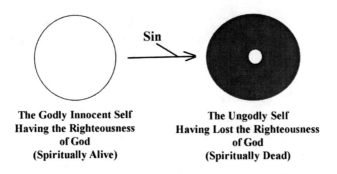

The Godly Innocent Self
Having the Righteousness
of God
(Spiritually Alive)

The Ungodly Self
Having Lost the Righteousness
of God
(Spiritually Dead)

Figure 8.2. The Effect of Sin on Self

The self-circles in this figure are identical to those in figure 3.1. In both cases, we see that the self-circles on the right are not totally dark; there remains a small but significant portion of the Creator, sometimes referred to as God's righteousness or holiness.

In this visual, the whitened portion of the godly innocent self-circle illustrates a default set. In the language of computer science, a default refers to a setting automatically assigned to a computer program or device by the manufacturer. In most cases, a consumer may change the default to a different setting and then may return to the initial default at any time.

There is an analogy between computer default settings in the pre- and post-fall states of humankind. Although specifically warned not to do so by God, the users (Adam and Eve) chose to customize their existence to a different setting. However, they were completely unable, even if they wanted to, to reverse their changed state to the original setting—from an ungodly defiled self to a godly innocent self, from being spiritually dead to spiritually alive, from being lost in the relationship to being found.

From this parallel, we picture the retention, however small, of the default setting in the fall, although tarnished and incomplete, as another example of the Creator's grace. By this divine gift of having an image of God, all humankind innately possesses some sense of morality, a sense of knowing right from wrong. Of greater significance, it allows a person to become alive spiritually and by faith to completely regain his or her original default setting, the righteousness of God. "For in it [the gospel] the righteousness of God is revealed from faith to faith; as it is written, 'But the righteous man shall live by faith'" (Romans 1:17).

In this all important verse, Paul is saying that in God's sight one can be in right standing only through faith. Most think the issue of faith and righteousness has its origin in the New Testament. However, the basis of righteous living by faith had its beginning in Abraham, the patriarch and ancestor of God's chosen people, for he "believed God, and it was credited to him as righteousness" (Romans 4:3). This assertion is a reference to Genesis 15:6, where Abraham trusted that the Lord would give him an offspring and thereby increase heirs to his lineage. Such a reckoning is essentially a verdict denoting the Lord's acceptance of Abraham.

If we know anything about the content of the Bible, we understand God's great desire is to have His people who live by faith obey His moral law, and to restore humankind in the image of His likeness, much like that in His newly created humans prior to the Fall. Also, if we are more than acquainted with the gospel and the rest of the New Testament, we know God provided a way for each individual to enter into His eternal kingdom (completely resetting the original default setting) by belief in the one great act of His Son, Jesus Christ, dying on a cross in our behalf (John 3:16).

We Christians respond in faith to these great truths, acknowledging our state of sinfulness (repentance) and belief in God's promises of forgiveness of sin and eternal life. Accompanying this conviction, we are changed. The Creator God planned to be the Father God and that His children (Christians) would attain the likeness of His Son, Jesus Christ. Paul wrote, "For whom He foreknew, He also predestined to become conformed to the image of His Son, so that He would be the firstborn among many brethren" (Romans 8:29); and "Therefore if anyone is in Christ, he is a new creature; the old things passed away; behold, new things have come" (2 Corinthians 5:17). These verses show there is a transformational phenomenon that takes place in a believer, which we commonly refer to as salvation, as illustrated in figure 8.3.

The Old Defiled Self
A Lost Self
Not Having the Righteousness
of God
(Spiritually Dead)

The New Uncorruped Self
A Found Self
Having the Righteousness
of God
(Spiritually Alive)

Figure 8.3. The Effect of the Cross on the Defiled Self

As we can see in this figure, a cross is included in the transition, and the background of the resultant self-circle becomes totally clean and white. This figure is clearly a reversal of the self-circle of Adam prior to the fall (see fig. 3.1) and of the effect of sin (see fig. 8.2). The self-circle on the left depicts the old defiled self, which has the likeness of fallen Adam but not of God. This self is not yet found, nor is it spiritually alive. However, the cross and all it represents renders the lostness and deadness of self null and void. In contrast to the old defiled self, the self-circle on the right illustrates the entry of the Holy Spirit as a bird, and the righteousness of God as annotated under the circle. This transformed self-circle represents a spiritually alive and found self.

These features are important because we also know that God's purpose in releasing our sins on the cross of Calvary was based upon His great desire that, with the assisting power of the indwelling Holy Spirit, we would allow Him to duplicate the likeness of Jesus Christ in our once-sinful lives. Christlikeness in Christians is simply the likeness of God manifested in the humanity of Christ: "And the Word [Jesus Christ] became flesh" (John 1:14); "He [Christ] is the image of the invisible God" (Colossians 1:15).

When comparing figures 8.2 and 8.3, we immediately see a reversal of selves taking place. Sin is absent in the new, innocent, and uncorrupted self, thereby restoring the right association between humans and their Creator; this brings back the default setting, that is, a complete Creator-creature relationship in every respect. These two figures, simple as they are, portray the major teaching of salvation within Christianity. If and when we believe this assertion is doctrinally accurate, we should permanently imprint this concept of salvation in our minds.

What we have said so far about salvation may be confusing to some. Here are the questions that must be answered in order to make sense of salvation:

1. If we already were granted the righteousness of God, why is it necessary to get any better than that?
2. If we are found and are spiritually alive, is this just another definition of salvation?
3. In the definition of salvation given above, what does the transformational phenomenon mean?
4. How is it possible to become Christlike if we already are Christlike?

Answers to these and other questions will follow in remaining chapters.

BREAKING NEWS AND DEVELOPING STORY

Anchor: "More, now, on the recent additions to the S-Factor research team. Psychotheologist Dr. Carataker has made a lifelong study of human spirituality and associated behavioral patterns. In these efforts, he uses both clinical and sophisticated scientific methods, such as detailed questionnaires, psychological testing, and so forth. His latest research is centered on detailing a number of opposing personality traits in young children, including altruism and selfishness.

"Dr. Cibalo, the neuropsychiatrist, is a leading researcher in neurobiology. She also has mastered many scientific techniques to explain the neural basis of normal and abnormal conduct. She uses several procedures, which include psychometric testing, brain scans, interviews, standardized measurement models, brain imaging technology, and measurements of blood flow to localized areas of the brain.

"These two individuals are expected to make a significant contribution to the overall efforts of the research team.

"Stay tuned as we bring you more details of this developing story."

Chapter 9

... Relate the Cross to Followers of Christ?

Part 3

T HE PREVIOUS CHAPTER focused on the cross as it may relate to both Jesus and to the spiritual status of believers. It ended with questions concerning salvation. Specifically, how are Christians to be spiritually transformed and thereby possess the divine image of God's Son? It should not be a surprise to any Christian that a discussion of Jesus and the cross must necessarily include the good news of the gospel.

For us to understand God's way of reproducing the likeness of Christ in us, as well as its implications of cross-carrying to the issues of spiritual maturity and living a Christlike life, we must review His plan of salvation. We also must come to know what was accomplished by Jesus' death. I admit that I cannot even begin to understand all of the implications of this mysterious subject. Yet most Bible scholars agree that the cross of Calvary is the starting point for all godly living and Christlikeness.

However, understanding and applying the facts of the cross can be extremely difficult for the believer who wishes to be a true follower of Jesus. Most doctrines of evangelical Christianity view justification and sanctification as dual aspects of salvation. Both are meaningful as they pertain to a relationship between God and Christians. The believer's knowledge of these major aspects of salvation gives the key to spiritually understanding these two apparently contradictory biblical themes: "life to death" and "death to life."

JUSTIFICATION: DELIVERANCE FROM THE PENALTY OF SIN

The first work of God's grace is generally referred to as justification or regeneration. Justification is the element of salvation that provides for divine forgiveness and deliverance from the penalty and punishment of sin. It states that Christ died in the place of sinners (substitution). A payment (ransom) was made for past, present, and future transgressions. Thus, sinners are released from all consequences of sin (redemption), and our state of alienation from God is changed so we might be saved (reconciliation). Accompanying justification is the entrance of the Holy Spirit into the lives of believers.

We are forgiven by means of justification because Christ died in our stead; that is, He died for us and makes possible the provision of forgiveness of our sins and the assurance of eternal life. We receive forgiveness and assurance when we by faith sincerely repent of our sins.

Justification is a judicial term and is further defined as imputed righteousness that puts us into a right relationship with our Creator, which is totally unlike our former sinful state. As seen in chapter 8, there is a miraculous conversion from a self wrongly related to God to a self who, in the view of God, is without any corruption or defilement. Under the title of justification, this mysterious alteration is illustrated again in figure 9.1 below.

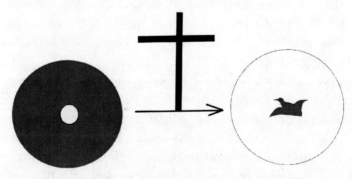

Figure 9.1. The Effect of Justification on Self

Through the years, in evangelical circles only the substitutionary feature of the gospel has been generally presented (justification), in which Christ was crucified on the cross for us and paid the punishment for sin. Unconverted persons were convicted of their sin and by means of faith received salvation. These truths are illustrated in figure 9.1 above. Notice that the arrow only points to the right, which indicates that justification is not reversible. Because of this fact, most of us first experienced salvation happily with the understanding that this was a gift from God and could not be taken from us. However, there may have been times when we were conscious of guilt about outward sins. Some offenses, such as theft, could be punishable by civil law, but, based on the principle of justification, all would be divinely forgiven through sincere repentance. All of these sins are easily apparent.

For those of us who may view sin as an ambiguous concept, I offer a few misnomers and suitable definitions in lay and scriptural language that should help lessen their vagueness. Popular euphemisms for sin include "an error in judgment," "a slip of the tongue," "an indiscretion," or "a moment of weakness." Sin is not a defect or an imperfection; it is a transgression of God's moral law, a disobedience of that law, a crime, a falling away or missing the right path, and lostness, either in a complete or partial state.

Sin is not just immorality or wrongdoing, but it is the nature of man's claim to his right to himself. In such a nature, self is put in the place of God with accompanying egotism, selfishness, and pride. Hence, sin is everything in the disposition, purpose, and conduct of God's moral creatures that is contrary to His nature and His expressed will (Romans 3:20; 4:14; 7:7; James 4:12, 17).

However, for the believer, Andrew Murray wrote, "there was likely little conviction of inward attitudes, such as pride, criticism of others, selfishness and arrogance" (*Absolute Surrender*, 39). I propose that these inward dispositions reside in self. As stated previously, I choose not to designate exact locations within self, such as the heart, spirit, soul, or body. However, I suggest, as others have, that the minds, hearts, and spirits of humans are more associated with self than any other, but these connections do not minimize the complexity of self. What we can say is that these attitudes of the self complex are internal and are less discernible by oneself and by others than dispositions that are manifested outwardly.

We know from our own experiences that many of our inward dispositions are not easily recognizable. But these temperaments can be exposed in individuals by supernatural means, namely through the Word of God and the penetration of God's Spirit to its innermost hidden depths of self. "For the word of God is living and active and sharper than any two-edged sword, and piercing as far as the division of soul and spirit, of both joints and marrow, and able to judge the thoughts and intentions of the heart" (Hebrews 4:12). And it may be that we see these attitudes in ourselves, as well as in others.

As we enter into relationships with God through justification, the first phase of salvation, there comes a point in time, or a growing awareness, in which we realize that there is a gap between how we are living and how we should be living. Some, however, merely accept this gap as normal and continue to live the rest of their lives this way.

The rest of us want to do what is right, but we lack the power to carry it out. We have known forgiveness of sins through justification, but we soon come to realize there is still an element of ungodliness and a moral depravity dwelling within us, an inward inclination and compulsion to sin. This perverse element of self in a believer certainly would counter any appearance of purity that Christ possesses.

Out of this self-realization, this personal experience, we need to reevaluate the concept of the changed self shown above in figure 9.1. Instead, as shown in figure 9.2, the resultant self-circle of a believer shows a degree of darkness. In addition, the arrow below the cross is pointed both toward the right and the left. Unlike the irrevocability noted in justification, this indicates that reversibility can take place between a self that is largely dominated by the old nature and a self significantly influenced by its new nature.

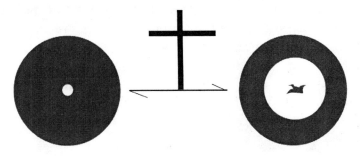

Figure 9.2. A Christian's Realization of the Indwelling Nature of Sin

We would likely conclude, perhaps to our astonishment, that after our commitment to Christ and His Spirit dwelling in us, in reality we do *not* possess a totally lily-white self-circle! If one has difficulty coming to this conclusion, I offer yet another way to view the inequality of a believer's salvation. In figure 9.3, note that the equal sign has a slash through it, meaning that there is a disparity between the justified and sanctified self.

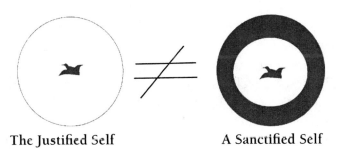

The Justified Self   **A Sanctified Self**

Figure 9.3. The Justified Self Does not Equal a Sanctified Self

In Christian salvation, we view self in two completely different ways: the justified self and a sanctified self. This figure shows that the justified self has no ungodly nature, yet a sanctified self contains both a godly part (the light central area) and, even with the indwelling Holy Spirit, a significant quantity of ungodliness (the outer darkened area).

Regarding the sanctified self, only God can truly distinguish between our two natures, the fleshly and the godly. As the all-knowing God, He also recognizes the relative amounts of each

117

and the relative impact one may have on the other. If we had this same capability and wanted to know these facts, we would know exactly our spiritual status at this very moment in time. Then we could easily select our sanctified spiritual condition from the range of "spiritual selves," all of which contain different elements of godliness and ungodliness as depicted in figure 9.4.

Figure 9.4. A Range of Selves having Relative Amounts of Two Natures

We now realize that we possess two natures. There is our old, natural self, also called *the old self, the flesh, or the old man (the darkened area)*; and our new, spiritual self, also *called the new self or the new man (the lighter area)*. The adjective *old* refers to all a person was before salvation, which is still referred to as old in contrast to the presence of the new life in Christ. According to figure 9.1, the regeneration of our spirit by God when He justifies us makes little or no change in our flesh! To resolve this predicament (see fig. 9.2), we need to eradicate, or tear down, the darkened carnality or fleshly aspect of our self.

At this point, I feel it necessary to clarify what is meant by the term *flesh*. In Scripture, flesh is sometimes referred to as physical ancestry or as physical existence, such as the biological body. However, the usage of flesh as the old self denotes an individual who is controlled by sin and selfish desires. It is symbolized by the darkened part of the self-circle. As Christians, we realize that these two spiritual entities, the godly and the fleshly, in a dynamic manner, forcefully struggle against each other inside of us. So the flesh is a self-trouble to both non-Christians and to Christians. Paul confirmed the existence of self-trouble in his inner person when he wrote, "Nothing good dwells in me, that is, in my flesh" (Romans 7:18). When speaking to His disciples, Jesus also authenticated this self-trouble when He stated that "the flesh profits nothing" (John 6:63).

So what can we further say about trouble with self? C. S. Lewis traced self back to Satan's lies that were put into our ancestors' heads when the Tempter said, "You will be like God" (Genesis 3:5). Lewis states,

> At the moment you have a self at all possessing a free will, there is a possibility of putting yourself first. In the heads of our remote ancestors was the idea that they could set up on their own as if they had created themselves—be their masters—invent some sort of happiness for themselves outside God, apart from God. And out of that hopeless attempt has come nearly all that we call human history—money, poverty, ambition, war, prostitution, classes, empires, slavery—the long terrible story of man trying to find something other than God which will make him happy. (Mere Christianity, 49)

Before conversion, there is only one ruling and reigning life in us, the old self-life or the old corrupt nature. It is corrupt because it was created in the image of the fallen Adam, rather than in the image of God (see Genesis 5:3). It is sin dwelling in our flesh and is a controlling authority that enslaves us. It's an energy force that resides in our incomplete regenerated bodies, whose whole intent and purpose is to cause us to veer off course and to miss the mark, the total conformity to the image of Christ. Satan uses this supremacy of sin as his tool. Every time we choose to follow what our flesh is saying rather than what God is prompting us to do, we ignore the indwelling of God's Spirit and become the Enemy's pawns.

Many Christian theologians have said and written a great deal about the fleshly side of human self, its origin and its main characteristics. A preponderance of them state that the origin of a polluted self occurred when the old serpent breathed his own satanic nature into the human nature of our first parents. This nature is identified as **self** and is viewed as lethal venom that possesses the capability of poisoning *self*. We can further develop our understanding of this adulterated part of self by identifying some of its traits.

One such hallmark of self is pride and its close associate, selfishness. Andrew Murray echoes the contention that the trademarks of self are pride and selfishness.

> All the wretchedness of which this world has been the scene, all its wars and bloodshed among the nations, all its selfishness, and suffering, all its ambitions and jealousies, all its broken hearts and embittered lives, and all its daily unhappiness have their origin in what this cursed, hellish pride, either our own or that of others, has brought us. (*Humility*, 8)

From this citation and multiple other comparable quotations, we conclude that self—or more correctly, its combined chief characteristics of pride and selfishness—is the taproot of all evil in our fallen states.

Nancy Missler takes a somewhat lighter view of the inner self in describing it as "the dark night of the spirit" (Koinonia House Outline website). She says we need to look at things we normally don't see as conflicts with the Lord, which, in her opinion, are not viewed as sins. These are attitudes, such as our reason, hopes, presumptions, affections, views, our narrow culture, creeds, church-ism, our senses, religious experiences, and our spiritual comforts. She further says,

> These seemingly natural ways come from our upbringing, from the influence of others in our life, from our preconceived value systems, from our habits and from our self-oriented thought processes. These attitudes are identified as 'flesh' and are impurities inside of us that rule us without our knowledge. They often feed our pride and our ego and our self-life.

Whether these impurities are justly labeled as sins, they are dispositions and belief systems God wants to expose and eliminate.

To be clear, we are not discussing sin in an academic or airy manner. This is personal. We are talking about your pride, bossiness, temper, self-centeredness, bent to be manipulative, lust for material things, arrogance and quarrelsomeness. Even when you do the right things for the wrong reasons, to impress people or purposely to gain the favor of others, it is a sin. I am talking about *you*:

- Mr. Choir Member: You dislike it when others are selected to sing solos because they are better vocalists. You think you could become the soloist if they would only quit. You also think the choir director is not fair in whom he chooses to sing solos. It is your attitude of jealousy and a chronic critical nature that enslaves you.
- Mrs. Busybody: You spend most of your time visiting with neighbors and other women in the church. You've managed to make most think of you as a gossiper or merely as an overly concerned person. But in reality, you are a manipulator and use your social skills to edify yourself. Your motives are self-seeking and you lack both a good self-image and a true value of self-worth.
- Miss Carnality: You believe you have no need for a spiritual life or spiritual development. You possess an inordinate amount of pride in your worldly viewpoint, belief of cultural tolerance, and rejection of absolute truths.
- Mr. Teenager: You believe you are invincible. You are ready to deal with whatever comes your way. You are sure that whatever it is, it won't be overwhelming. You are exceedingly self-confident and self-sufficient, both hallmarks of individualism.
- Doctor: You sometimes are addressed by others as Mister or Ms. and not as Doctor so-and-so. You think you're better than others because of your education and knowledge. You radiate self-esteem to others, which is nothing more than a mask behind which your low self-esteem is hidden.
- Professor: You conduct research for your living. You carefully plagiarized data from others to support your research findings. You are more than a literary thief, you are a first-class deceiver.
- Sir Anti-traditionalist: You believe all this renewal, self-denial, support group, cross-carrying business is for the

birds, not for you. You are not willing to accept another's concept of Christian doctrine, but only your own self-centered and self-dependent notions.

• Madam Positive Thinker: You claim biblical knowledge and believe you live a clean life, treat people fairly, and are generous to others. You believe you deserve to be happy and feel good in this life and receive bountiful fruits for your labors. That is the way it should be. Having been indoctrinated only with "God is love" theology, you are living in the illusion of grandeur, inwardly fearful of any crisis or bump in the road that would turn your world upside down.

THERE'S A WAR GOING ON IN THE CONFLICTED SELF!

Just because we as Christians are endowed with the image of God does not guarantee our ability to exhibit that image in our lives. Nor does it give us the assurance that we will become more spiritually mature and possess holiness. Why is this so? It is because we have conflicted selves. Conflict means a discord, contradiction, or tension. The tension is between our flesh (our old self, our polluted human nature) that pulls us one way and our spirit in conjunction with the Spirit of God (a supernatural holy nature) that pulls us the other direction. This is a dynamic battle that is fought in the realm of the mind. It pits two wills against one another in a maturing believer in Christ, the will of God versus the will of the corrupt self.

As stated above, this battle between our old self and our authentic self is waged in our minds. Romans 8:6 expresses the result of each of the conflicting mind-sets: "The mind set on the flesh is death, but the mind set on the Spirit is life and peace." This verse is saying that *if* we follow what the flesh, our carnality, is telling us to do, there will be a spiritual death within us (Galatians 5:16–17; James 1:14–15). In other words, God's Spirit will be blocked and whatever is produced will be worthless and fruitless.

Romans 8:7 goes on to say that "The mind set on the flesh is hostile toward God," which clearly means the flesh is opposed to God, and therefore, there is no chance of a harmonious and peaceful coexistence. Paul then concludes his thoughts on ungodly attitudes, saying, "Those who are in the flesh cannot please God" (Romans 8:8). *The Message* expresses verses 7–8 as follows: "Focusing on the self is the opposite of focusing on God. Anyone completely absorbed in self ignores God, ends up thinking more about self than God. That person ignores who God is and what he is doing. And God isn't pleased at being ignored."

Paul also warns his readers not to fulfill the desires of the flesh: "Walk by the Spirit, and you will not carry out the desire of the flesh" (Galatians 5:16), and expresses the war-like activity ongoing in self: "For the flesh sets its desire against the Spirit, and the Spirit against the flesh; for these are in opposition to one another, so that you may not do the things that you please" (Galatians 5:17; refer also to the list of the deeds of the flesh found in Galatians 5:19–21.) Paul's statements about this inward conflict clearly indicate that where these counteracting tendencies exist there is a warfare and disharmony, and we do not do what we otherwise would do.

Why is it so difficult to yield ourselves to the Spirit of God and allow His life and the life of Christ to come forth? It's hard because the flesh is *not* dead. A dynamic state exists between Spirit and flesh. Consider this warfare as two opposites: carnally minded versus spiritually minded. As depicted in figures 9.2 and 9.3, the carnality is still very much alive, and because of its governing authority, it constantly strives to express itself.

In addition to qualitative dimensions in the battle zone, there well may be a quantitative aspect. At any one time, something like a warring self will get its name from that which is most renowned or most striking. Referring back to figure 9.4, we can readily see a predominance of darkness in the circles on the left; therefore, we may correctly label these persons as controlled by flesh, not walking by the Spirit but carrying "out the desire of the flesh" (Galatians 5:16). Those circles of self on the right with more white than darkness indicate that these persons are more spiritually mature and walking by the Spirit.

Paul warns us about this conflict in Romans 7:15 when he says, "For what I am doing, I do not understand; for I am not practicing what I would like to do, but I am doing the very thing I hate." He goes on rather strongly to explain sin's power to derail him: "So now, no longer am I the one doing it, but sin which dwells in me. For I know that nothing good dwells in me, that is, in my flesh; for the willing is present in me, but the doing of the good is not" (Romans 7:17–18). These passages undoubtedly show the dualistic character of Paul. We, too, must realize that the Christian life can be one of antagonism and tension. It is especially a dilemma for the flesh-controlled believer who is not walking according to the Spirit. He requires a supernatural solution to walk in the holiness of God.

Paul feverishly acknowledged this perpetual struggle and the conflict within himself when he stated, *"But I see different law in the members of my body, waging war against the law of my mind and making me a prisoner of the law of sin which is in my members. Wretched man that I am! Who will set me free from the body of this death?"* (Romans 7:23–24). This is an impasse so catastrophic that Paul recognizes that someone other than himself must become the emancipator of his wretchedness (Romans 7:25).

What sort of salvation would we have if our heavenly Father simply saved us from the penalty of our sins and then left us on our own to deal with the power of sin? Many believers appear to feel this is about as far as He went, and they choose to live carnal or nominal Christian lives. Others are struggling to get on the best they can, yet are searching for solutions for deliverance.

SOLUTIONS TO THE NEED FOR A DELIVERANCE FROM SELF

It should be obvious that believers have a great need for deliverance from our old self in order to become more Christlike, spiritual, and mature in our faith. Let's look at a few of the many solutions that have been taught and practiced.

God-Reliant Passivity

It may be that some Christians think they merely chose to believe in Christ's atoning work on the cross of Calvary; consequently, God has chosen to act independently out of His gracious nature to eradicate any and all ungodly characteristics from them. This approach would mirror the understanding of justification that says our part of the atonement was based on our belief alone. In other words, there would be little or no effort on our parts; we could remain inert and apathetically let God do what He wanted to with the conflicting self. There seems to be no scriptural basis for this approach to suppress the power of an unprincipled self.

Self-Dependence

Have we sought out a form of activism, or self-reliant activities, to deliver us from the power of our ungodly natures of self and transform ourselves into Christlike followers? I imagine all of us have, but at some point we've concluded that the transformation didn't seem to work. Let's briefly look at a few of the many ways that are wholly or partially based upon our self-dependence, in which we have attempted to deal with the problem of self. The list includes self-denial or cross-carrying alone, intellectual knowledge of Christianity, special religious activities, confession of sin, non-Christian methods, and works through self-effort.

Self-Denial Alone or Cross-Carrying Alone

In the absence of cross-carrying, denying oneself alone is carried out by releasing certain desires and possessions for a time or even for all time. This kind of piety operates on the idea that the less we become, the more honored God will be. A.W. Tozer, author of *The Radical Cross*, believed that self-rejection alone was not workable because the old nature still thrives and will adjust under any conditions.

To many, this form of self-dependence may seem to be acceptable, since its common usage leads us to think of cross-carrying as a Christian thing to do. Like self-denial alone, God never wills us to fixate only on the crosses we carry daily. As commendable as cross-carrying may sound, it serves no purpose alone and should not be viewed as honoring God. As we will see later, cross-carrying provides an essential function in becoming more Christlike in our daily living.

Intellectual Knowledge of Christianity

We think education should work to subdue the old nature and bring it into line. Therefore we endorse good Christian training in the home, church, and non-public school. In this regard, head knowledge alone has been found wanting down through the ages.

Why can't we just study and enhance our cerebral knowledge of the scriptural passages that tell about our image of God, and then imitate Christ? Should that not be enough to reflect Christ in our lives? Well, unfortunately, learning selected Bible verses and being endowed with the image of God in our inner selves at our new birth does not guarantee our ability to manifest that image. In other words, being "born anew" by His Spirit does not assure us of being able to "walk by" His Spirit.

Special Religious Activities

Another failure of self-dependence has been the practice of attending special meetings, such as revivals and conferences, once or twice a year in the hope that something will change. Like New Year's resolutions, good religious intentions are admirable. Some of these distinctive spiritual actions work to a degree but usually are only transient. It might be of greater practicality for believers to gain personal spiritual insights on a daily basis rather than to depend on these intermittent activities.

Confession of Sins

Up-to-the-moment confession of sin and the resultant cleansing have also constituted a popular method to bring about these transformations. Many cite 1 John 1:9 as a basis of dealing with self: "If we confess our sins, He is faithful and righteous to forgive us our sins" Yes, our sins are dealt with by the atoning work of Christ, who procures our pardon, but the first part of this verse may be interpreted as having to do with sins already committed and not with the source (self) from which they emanate.

We need to admit there is a power within that draws us to sin, and when that spiritual force is in authority, we commit sins. We may seek and receive forgiveness, but then we sin again; life goes on in a vicious circle—sinning and being forgiven, then sinning again. Is this what grace is meant to be?

Having said all this about the first half of this verse, we are quick to point out the remaining portion of John's statement, "and to cleanse us from all unrighteousness" (1 John 1:9). The implication of the whole verse seems to be twofold, the first with forgiveness and the second with cleansing. If cleansing is taken to mean purifying the Christian, where cooperative actions between God and the believer take place, this is not self-dependence alone.

Non-Christian Methods

Many recognize humans as morally flawed, and in an effort to correct this situation they seek self-help aids and psychology-oriented religions to tone down their own natural egos and selfishness. As pointed out by Stephanie Forbes in her book *Help Your Self: Today's Obsession with Satan's Oldest Lies,* "Radical discipleship that denies the self stands in direct opposition to self-help's teaching, which insists that we must explore the self, find the self, and fulfill the self" (175). Here the emphasis is clearly on self, and it is an example of a self-dependent method that claims we can love God and others only when we learn to love self first. Many believe self-help techniques can overlook the very nature of self, and in doing so, seem to edify self and therefore are counterproductive.

Works through Self-Effort

Our works through self effort alone must depend upon the motives to carry them out. We may devise many ways to improve ourselves and to help others, but if these things come from carnal motives they will not satisfy the Lord, nor will they be judged to be worthy of a reward. God's pleasure or displeasure is established on *the source of the motivating power that produces the work.*

So overall, we conclude that self-dependent approaches in dealing with our old self are inadequate. We need to solve the problem of deliverance from the power of sin in a very personal and direct way by relying less and less on ourselves, and instead relying on God's omnipotence (all-powerfulness) as we become more God-dependent.

BREAKING NEWS AND DEVELOPING STORY

Anchor (two weeks after the initial discovery): "Chief investigators have released more information about their ongoing analysis of the S-Factor.

"The genetic scientists have further analyzed the factor obtained from a large number of adult human subjects and provided us with information about its molecular configuration. The substance is spherical in shape, and its total molecular mass is the same in all individuals studied thus far. In addition, the S-Factor is composed of chromosomes having normal nucleic acid sequences and encapsulated with yet unidentified proteins. We realize this is highly technical information, but it's what we have so far."

Chapter 10

... Relate the Cross to Followers of Christ?

Part 4

WHICH OF US does not know something of God-reliant passivity and self-dependence to subdue our rebellious selves, well intentioned as they may be? There is really only one way of deliverance: God's way to deal with the problem of self. Now just what is God's way? Following Christ by means of obeying His commands of self-denial and cross-carrying is the way that leads us time after time in wonderment to His finished work on the cross of Calvary. To comprehend God's divine plan, which includes provisions for His followers to conquer the problem of self by deliverance from its power, we are again drawn to the other aspect of Christian salvation, sanctification.

SANCTIFICATION: DELIVERANCE FROM THE POWER OF SIN AND SELF

To specifically know God's way of deliverance from sin's power, we must call special attention to the second facet of salvation generally known as sanctification, imparted righteousness, lordship, or cleansing of sin.

There is not a sharp demarcation between justification and sanctification. To help overcome this vagueness, one approach simply states that justification is a judicial term and primarily viewed as God's work alone. Technically, this view is known as monergism, which holds it as God's unaccompanied work only. In one sense, Sanctification is not monergistic but can be labeled synergistic. The term synergism, in its simplest form, insists that God performs action(s) leaving deliverance incomplete until individuals perform action(s) to complete salvation. More specifically, sanctification is an ongoing cooperative participation between what God has done and continues to do (His grace); out of the freedom of choice, the practicing God-dependent Christian faithfully exerts him- or herself in sustained obedience to His will. Obedience to God's will would fulfill the meaning of sanctification for the believer, which refers to the state or process of progressively being set apart and made holy.

We are reminded of Paul's realization of having opposing dual forces within himself, one of God and the other of sin. This is the dilemma mentioned in the previous chapter, and it is common to all sincere believers. Paul states that the problem is a state of living death, and in an anguished moment he asks for someone to set him free (Romans 7:24). Paul immediately provides an answer in the next verse: "Thanks be to God through Jesus Christ our Lord!" Through this stirring response and the many scriptural texts supporting the accomplishments of Christ, we come to the one and only way to be delivered from the power of sin and self: Christ's finished work on the cross!

In the need for deliverance from the sway of sin, we should see that Christ is our standard, or better yet, our gold standard. He is the paragon, the model of excellence that is revealed to us in our increasing knowledge of Him and our greater intimate relationships with Him. He is therefore our supreme example. This is what Peter, a mature apostle of faith, urged his fellow readers to realize: "You have been called for this purpose, since Christ also suffered for you, leaving you an example for you to follow in His steps" (1 Peter 2:21). We, like those early Christians, are to endure under hardships and realize that Christ is the ideal standard we are to duplicate.

To follow Christ and to hold Him as our gold standard means that we as Christians are to be coordinated, to be made like, to bring into agreement, to comply with, to agree, to be in accord with, to be submissive to, and to have the same dispositions, attitudes, goals, and thoughts as Jesus. A regenerated person, a born-again believer, is to become harmonious with Jesus. One can make the counterclaim that anything a repentant believer chooses to continually do that is not in harmony with or conforming to the Word of God is in a state of lostness, and rebellion against or denial of Jesus. If this revolt is persistent, the disharmony is correctly labeled a greater state of lostness, worldliness, carnality, and the dominance of an ungodly self in a nominal Christian.

But is it just a matter of merely imagining Christ will produce His likeness in our lives? In our pop culture, we see multiple examples of imitators of so-called model figures. Children and young adults often imitate musicians, sports figures, and movie stars by wearing similar clothing and acting like them in other ways. Even some religious followers mimic their leaders, such as the monks who wear robes and imitate certain gestures believed to have been practiced by Buddha when he was on earth.

Consider also the importance of perceived appearance, especially by people in Western cultures. People spend billions of dollars each year on clothing, cosmetics, and plastic surgery, all for the sake of looking like some esteemed idol and edifying themselves in the sight of others.

The answer to the question above about expecting Christ to manufacture His resemblance in our lives above is no. Becoming Christlike is not visualization, nor is it external. As we shall see, sanctification comes mainly by divine means and is God's way of removing the unrighteous aspects of self at the same time He imparts the very nature of Himself. This concept of becoming conformed to Jesus is frequently offensive to those living by worldly standards and is seldom taught in many Christian groups. Regardless of non-Christian views, the point of reference we as believers are to emulate is expounded and modeled by Christ Himself. Although under pressure from without and within, all of His human virtues—including love, humility, and patience—are not to be imagined, but received as gifts and manifested in everyday life.

131

We purposely return to the question about producing Christlikeness in our lives by imagining or imitating Christ. As strange as it may seem, we can help answer this question by examining the issue of identification. An insightful derivation of identification is provided by Eckhart Tolle in his book *A New Earth: Awaking to Your Life's Purpose*. He says the term "is derived from the Latin word, *idem*, meaning 'same' and *facere*, which means 'to make'" (35). He further explains that when one identifies with something, "one makes it the same." In doing so, one endows it with a sense of oneself and it becomes a part of one's identity.

One of the fundamental aspects of self is an unconscious force to identify, whether psychologically or spiritually, with something or someone else—an object such as a toy, or a person such as a celebrity or a parent. In all cases, however, the identification is viewed as a very close attachment to the object that creates a sense of delight, worth, and well-being.

As believers, who can truly create worth and wellness in us? Only the One who said, "I am the way, the truth, and the life" (John 14:6). So it is no wonder that we identify ourselves with Christ in the New Testament. Biblically speaking, when this happens, we are "in Christ."

According to the *Exhaustive Concordance of the NASB*, the expression "in Christ" is found eighty times in the New Testament, mainly written by the apostle Paul. It is found predominately in the context of a believer as a person who is identified as being in the Lord Jesus Christ. Several other scriptures indicate that Christ is in the believer, and this divine condition is often associated with sanctification. Without trying to rigidly define the terms "me in Christ" and "Christ in me," we can gain some understanding from Paul's dissimilarity of life and death in two different men, Adam and Christ. "As in Adam all die, so also in Christ all will be made alive" (1 Corinthians 15:22).

The names of Adam and Christ are more than designations of two humans; they represent two completely different realms of existence. Respectively, the domains are contrasted by death versus life, old order versus new order, old created humanity versus new created humanity, natural man versus spiritual man, old relationship versus new relationship and evil versus good.

This is understood best when we link Adam with a sinful nature and death, and contrast his being with Christ, who had a human nature like Adam but was totally without sin. From this truth, we see that the believer cannot be compatible with sin. He is no longer *in Adam* having an old sinful nature, but now *in Christ* possessing a new nature. Those who belong to Christ, that is, are *in Christ*, "have crucified the flesh with its passions and desires" (Galatians 5:24). For believers, the phrase "in Christ" is used to describe both justification and sanctification.

So we begin to better understand that the process of sanctification satisfies our need to be increasingly delivered from the power of sin and self. It is what God does in us with the aid of the Holy Spirit, by helping us to emphasize our identification with the Passion of Christ. Sanctification further enhances our relationship with Christ and has to do with our spirituality, character, and moral development, thereby exhibiting the fruit of that relationship. In this definition of sanctification, followers of Jesus Christ who live a life of faith see themselves spiritually and mystically identified with Christ.

At this point that we need to pause to briefly elaborate on the term *mystical* as it relates to the believer's identification with Christ. In general, we understand that mysticism is a method by which the finite, at least in part, arrives at a union with the infinite. There is a coming together of mortal with the immortal. For the Christian, the process centers on having a personal identification with God the Father and Jesus Christ. It aspires to apprehend and experience spiritual truths that are inaccessible to the believer merely through intellectual means.

Christian mysticism is traditionally practiced through disciplines such as prayer, meditation, contemplation, and various forms of self-denial. However, the major emphasis for Christian mysticism or spirituality concerns the transformation of the egotistic self to a Christlike self, whereby one develops more harmonious communion with God, others, and oneself. For Christians, this human potential is realized most perfectly in Christ, especially during Jesus' Passion. Three events of Christ's Passion are visualized in figure 10.1.

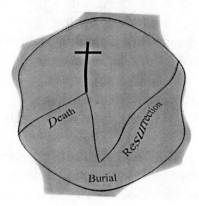

Figure 10.1. Mystical Identification with Christ's Passion

As we examine this figure, we can see that it represents three elements of Christ's Passion—His death, burial, and resurrection. When we completely identify ourselves with each of these essential truths supernaturally, yet in a most intimate manner, we can speak of them as a co-crucifixion, a co-burial, and a co-resurrection. These three major aspects of Christ's Passion are described by the apostle Paul in Romans 6:3–6.

1. The Co-Crucifixion of the Passion

Verse 3 says, "All of us who have been baptized into Christ Jesus have been baptized into His death." And verses 5–6: "For if we have become united with Him in the likeness of His death… knowing this, that our old self was crucified with Him, in order that our body of sin [the sinful impulses inherent in the flesh] might be done away with, so that we would no longer be slaves to sin" (that is, no longer under the enslavement of a sin nature and evil worldly powers).

In these quotations, we find the words *death* and *crucified*, each of which are connected to the believer and to Christ. Many

Christian theologians have contended that the union of these two terms results in the Christian's liberation from the sin nature.

2. The Co-Burial of the Passion

Romans 6:4 says, "We have been buried with Him through baptism into death." Paul's use of the word *baptism* in connection with Christ's death and burial likely symbolizes the external rite of the Christian's baptism experience, or the Holy Spirit's role in the rebirth of the believer through union with Christ. It not only portrays the purpose of atonement by delivering sinners from both sin's penalty and power, but also promises the accomplishment of that purpose in the person baptized, which is gaining Christ's virtues and eternal security. (These two accomplishments are seen in Galatians 3:27 and Colossians 3:3.) By the external rite of baptism, believers profess their full identification and union with Christ. In other words, in our new identity in Christ that has come by our faith, we died and were buried with Christ.

In addition, the co-crucifixion and co-burial allow the believer to identify with Christ so that we "might walk in newness of life" (Romans 6:4). The idea of purity is associated with that of newness in the Bible. When compared with what is natural and original, newness of life is a holy life that springs from a new source.

3. The Co-Resurrection of the Passion

Romans 6:5 says, "We shall also be in the likeness of His resurrection." Not only are we to have a new life through our co-crucifixion and co-burial with Christ, but we are also solidly linked to His resurrection. Regarding our identity with Christ's crucifixion and burial with His resurrection, author Chip Ingram states that Paul "is teaching us that we can never live the resurrected life until we understand and accept that we already died with Christ" (*The Miracle of Life Change: How God Transforms His Children*, 69). This claim, along with writings of many others, indicates that these first few verses of Romans 6 apply to our sanctification.

135

Yes, we can be eternally grateful for God's grace that states that the death of Christ made the reigning power of the sin nature (**self**; see Romans 6:1–10) ineffective, thus making it possible to live a holy life through the reigning power of the Holy Spirit. As our Representative, He took us with Him to the cross, and there He died *as us*. We all died together with Christ, and the glorious consequence is that we are delivered from the ungodly self.

Why is it so difficult to yield ourselves to the Spirit of God and to allow His life and the life of Christ to come forth? It's hard because even though our flesh, that is the power of sin's hold on the flesh, has been *positionally* crucified with Christ at our new birth (see figures 9.2 and 9.3), it's not dead. This revelation is needed to initiate and carry on the process of sanctification in the believer's life. It is exactly the place and time to engage ourselves cooperatively with our Lord in order to overcome sin's power to reign in us. This is where we welcome the gracious gift of the Spirit, knowing we now possess the divine power to deliver us from the bondage of **self**.

This means that we can become victorious in this spiritual warfare because God's Spirit and the Spirit of Christ in our new created state are now the overcoming power forces to do so. If we choose to obey, trust, and follow God—*regardless of how we feel or what we think*— we can, in His strength and power, overcome whatever the flesh is urging us to do. This practice may be called putting off the old man, and can be visualized (see fig. 9.4) as an orderly progression toward godliness and Christlikeness. As we shall see in subsequent chapters, each stage of dispelling the flesh is associated with our co-crucifixion, co-burial and co-resurrection with Christ.

Paul knew what choices he had to make to continually free himself from this hostility and to walk humbly so Christ's life might show forth. He expressed it this way: "We are afflicted in every way, but not crushed; perplexed, but not despairing; persecuted, but not forsaken; struck down, but not destroyed; *always carrying about in the body the dying of Jesus, so that the life of Jesus also may be manifested in our body*" (2 Corinthians 4:8–10, emphasis

... Relate the Cross to Followers of Christ? *Part 4*

added). In the cause of the gospel, we, like Paul, may face all sorts of troubling situations. Like Christ, we, too, carry a cross and, if need be, are prepared to make sacrifices to demonstrate the very character of God.

We must understand this perpetual struggle of flesh against spirit and pride against humility, as well as know how to overcome it so we, like Paul, can reflect Christ's image and not our own. We need to carefully examine Romans 6:11, where Paul says, "Even so consider yourselves to be dead to sin, but alive to God in Christ Jesus." "Consider" means much more than think about or ponder this. It means to seriously reckon or calculate, as if you are a bookkeeper and you are adding up numbers or the true facts of what has just been stated. When combined with faith, it is the truth of this reckoning ourselves to be dead to sin that allows us to be "alive to God [living in unbroken fellowship with Him] in Christ Jesus" (Romans 6:11 AMP).

The result of this reckoning of faith is that we live life in Christ and not alive to sin! It is that part of sanctification in which we voluntarily choose to act out of our faith and believe that we mysteriously died with Christ on the cross of Calvary; in doing so there is a divine separation of sin from our being. To be sure, the process of reckoning ourselves dead to sin is not something we can easily do. It becomes easier when we find ourselves in less self-dependent and more God-dependent circumstances.

What has died, whether whole or in part, is that aspect of self that pertains to our sin natures. It is the flesh, the **self**, that effectively hinders our spiritual progress. One may ask what happens to that dead ungodly flesh. It is buried, as was Christ when He took upon Himself the sins of the world. According to Oswald Chambers, we cannot go through our journey of faith without having a "white funeral," that is, a burial of the old life. Our identification with Christ is so real that we can envision laying the old life to rest. Obviously, this would be the burial element of Christ's Passion as depicted in figure 10.1 and subsequently expressed as a co-burial.

Paul tells us, "If you are living according to the flesh, you must die; but if by the Spirit you are putting to death [mortifying, KJV] the deeds of the body, you will live" (Romans 8:13). The issue of mortification in this verse has been addressed by Puritan John Owen, one of the greatest of the English theologians who lived in the seventeenth century and wrote an extensive treatise titled *Of the Mortification of Sin in Believers*. For Owen, two main theses arose out of Paul's words in Romans 8:13:

1. The choicest believers, who are assuredly freed from the condemning power of sin, ought yet to make it their business all their days to mortify the indwelling power of sin [of **self**].
2. The vigor, power, and comfort of our spiritual lives depend on the mortification of the deeds of the flesh by the Holy Spirit.

Not only does Romans 8:13 tell us the Holy Spirit's role in connection to the "white funeral," but because of our intense identity with Christ, it also promises us life—a new kind of life. So we do not just hope death and burial of self is followed by rebirth into regeneration, but we exercise faith and expect the blood of Christ and the power of the Holy Spirit to make real what our faith has reckoned, a resurrected life.

Remember the four questions in the traditional spiritual titled "Were You There?":

"Were you there when they crucified my Lord?"

"Were you there when they nailed Him to the tree?"

"Were you there when they laid Him in the tomb?"

"Were you there when He rose up from the grave?"

Obviously, we were not there in the physical sense, but, in a historical setting, did not He take all our transgressions upon Himself that we could be rightly related to God? Another lyric writer of "Must Jesus Bear the Cross Alone" asks the question, "Must Jesus bear the cross alone, and all the world go free?" He pointedly answers, "No, there's a cross for everyone, and there's a cross for me."

Paul, in Galatians 2:20, states, "I have been crucified with Christ." Students of biblical Greek say this phrase indicates the present consequence of a past action. In effect, the apostle said, "I was crucified with Christ [at the time and place He was crucified] with the present result that I am now still crucified." This phrase in the first part of verse 20 is also similar to a flashback. As stated in chapter 8, a flashback is an action that interrupts the here and now to show a significant incident that took place at an earlier time. For Paul, this is not a casual recall or a wandering thought. It is brought about at times of unsettling tensions within his inner self to a place in time where he was completely identified with his Savior.

Regarding the outcomes of identification with Jesus' encounter with the cross, Paul, in Ephesians 4:24, exhorts us to "put on the new self, which in the likeness of God has been created in righteousness and holiness of the truth." Colossians 3:10 urges the same: "put on the new self who is being renewed to a true knowledge according to the image of the One who created him." Paul is referring to the creation of Christ's life (His love and power) that resides in our hearts (if we are spiritually born again) and that we are daily, in faith, to "put on" the virtuous life of Christ. Living by the faith of the Son of God means to continually make *faith choices* that allow Christ's life to come forth from our hearts, regardless of how we naturally think or feel.

We have also considered that the crosses we are to carry might well serve the purpose of crucifying and bringing about the death to self. It's a matter of allowing our crosses to symbolically relate to the cross upon which Christ died. This might well be one of the best ways to identify ourselves in Christ, so we can vicariously die along with Him and thereby die to self. As was stated in the preface, a choice has to be made. Even as believers, it seems Jesus was telling my wife and me, "It's an option, and entirely up to you to decide which of the two roads to take." We came to understand that one of these roads was to follow our worldly inclinations and desires (the way of self). The other path was to follow Christ, on which the shadow of the cross fell.

But this is where the battle continues, for many of us refuse to identify with the death of Jesus Christ. We tend to say, "This part of the good news is too strict; surely God does not require this of us."

Yet, I believe this condition is precisely necessary in the sanctification process. It is in this state that the Great Exchange is made. We are one with Christ, and His perfect qualities are unconditionally given to us by God's grace. The very nature of Christ and His way of thinking become ours. The holiness of Jesus is developing in us, which then becomes outwardly manifested in our lives.

What are we giving up in this exchange? Part of our self-life is mortified in Christ Jesus as God intended. "But by His doing you are in Christ Jesus, who became to us...sanctification" (1 Corinthians 1:30).

Another way to look at this analogy is to envision that the cross on which Jesus died was really the cross that we in our unredeemed state deserved to die upon because of our rebellious, sinful natures. The old rugged cross had the inscription on a sign, THIS IS JESUS, THE KING OF THE JEWS. Each one of us should have been on our cross with a sign inscribed, THIS IS [insert your name], THE KING OF HIMSELF. But, glory be to God, in our redeemed states we still can have the privilege to vicariously carry our crosses in faith to the time and place of Christ's sacrifice on Calvary to realize the slaying of the residual old self.

Individually, we all could say along with Paul, "I am crucified with Christ." The statement can be a considered realization of an interior crucifixion and a burial of self, which specifically includes what Paul calls "the deeds of the body" (Romans 8:13). Such actions may be expressions of one's disposition, such as, but not limited to, the hyphenated self- terms of self-love, self-confidence, self-reliance, self-trust, self-will, self-pity, self-grasping, self-interest, self-seeking, self-preservation, and self-esteem. Many of these terms are often not conscious to us, but God knows about them, and He knows the quenching effects they have on His Spirit and His life in us.

Therefore, God wants us to see these self-edifying traits in ourselves. He wants self to be exposed, and in accord to the terminology used in this book, this means bringing to light both dimensions of self—**self** and *self*. In order to accomplish this, God begins to uncover things He knows about in our lives, but that we, in our false selves, desperately want kept hidden and covered. Thus, Paul told the believers in Corinth to scrutinize themselves, "Test yourselves to see if you are in the faith; examine yourselves!" (2 Corinthians 13:5). We, too, are directed to examine ourselves. God not only wants to reveal things about Himself as He does in the Bible, He also wants to show us things about ourselves. *Until we see ourselves through God's eyes, we really don't know ourselves.*

God wants to take all of us from positions of self-reliance to positions of total reliance upon Him, from self-centeredness to God-centeredness. He wants us to learn to detach ourselves from all other supports and all other guidance, so that we can enjoy something that is immensely superior—complete faith and trust in Him. When all of our trust and hope in earthly and humanly created supports has been taken away, we will have no other place to run, except to Him. And this is where we find peace and contentment.

BREAKING NEWS AND DEVELOPING STORY

Anchor: "More on the development of the S-Factor. Let's listen now to Dr. Selford, one of the discoverers of the factor."

The view switches from the anchorperson to an illustration, and Dr. Selford says, "The circle seen here represents a two-dimensional molecule of the S-Factor, showing it contains two subunits, tentatively identified only as a and b. Dr. Sinton and I are in the process of separating these subunits and measuring the amounts of each."

The newscaster concludes, "I am sure we will learn more about this unusual factor, so watch this channel for future information as this story develops."

Chapter 11

... Envision a Fulfilling Life?

Life

"For whoever wishes to save his life shall lose it; but whoever loses his life for My sake shall find it."
—Matthew 16:25

IN THIS CHAPTER, we will center our attention on some of the paradoxical statements of Jesus (referenced in appendix C). In each of these passages, we find various combinations of the words *deny*, *self*, *cross*, *life*, and *follow*. The grouping of these terms suggests that these passages are interconnected. This interrelationship, along with other scriptures, provides us with a broader context in which we may better gain insight into Christ's two instructions to deny self and carry a cross. Because the word *life* is used by Jesus in all the passages listed in appendix C, it is the focus of this chapter and we will seek its meaning as it pertains to following our Savior.

LIFE: "GET A LIFE"

Some time ago, my wife and I were having our evening meal with a couple who also reside in our retirement community. As usual, the conversation centered on health, weather, and grandchildren. The subject then turned to which television shows the four of us preferred. We mentioned two of our favorite game shows, *Jeopardy* and *Wheel of Fortune*. To our astonishment, the wife of the other couple said in a rather critical loud voice, "Get a life!"

The next few days we pondered her evaluation of our choice of evening entertainment. Was her comment more than something offered in jest? Did it infer that in some way our lives were less meaningful than they should be? Did we really need to change by watching more enlightening evening shows or even not viewing television at all? The comment about getting a life disturbed us somewhat.

Then it occurred to us that it is not unusual for people to have differing viewpoints about how others live life. The real reason for telling this story now is to use this common saying of "getting a life" in our current culture as an introduction to one of the greatest, yet probably most misunderstood statements made by our Savior, Jesus Christ, in Matthew 16:25. A Christian will "get a life" through self-denial, taking up his or her cross, and following Him. I think this approach will usher in a new kind of existence that profoundly differs from the life we may naturally think we lead.

LIFE: INSIGHTS ON THE MEANING OF LIFE

One of the major themes of both the Old and New Testaments is reconciliation, which pertains to God's great desire to restore all creation to Himself. Another theme is life, a word that appears more than seven hundred times in the Bible.

Two of the most common definitions attached to human life are as follows: life is the vital principle that gives physical vitality and existence, and life is associated with the period of one's existence, that is, a lifetime while on earth. In both a general and spiritual sense, life means the sum total of our highest interests and activities as we vitally relate with others and a Higher Being. For Christians, the prevailing references are those activities that are our expressions of fellowship with others and the Holy Trinity. This relationship is often referred to as eternal life, "that whoever believes in Him shall not perish, but have eternal life" (John 3:16).

The nearest approach to a definition of eternal life is found in John 17:3, which is Jesus' own description of eternal life: "This is eternal life, that they [believers] may know You, the only true God, and Jesus Christ whom You have sent." Jesus' concept of perpetual living for believers is their personal knowledge of God the Father and His Son. Jesus calls this divine truth eternal life and we can build upon Jesus' description of eternal life and say that in its totality, it is a relationship with Him who is the source of life. Eternal life is not something we exclusively have within us, but it is a shared communion and fellowship with God through Christ.

In the epistles of John, the apostle continued to connect the possession of eternal life with Jesus Christ. Wanting to assure early Christians of having eternal life, John wrote, "These things I have written to you who believe in the name of the Son of God, so that you may know that you have eternal life" (1 John 5:13). One of "these things" John is referring to is verse 11: "God has given us eternal life, and this life is in His Son [Jesus Christ]." Here we see that God has designed everlasting life for us in His eternal purpose and in His Son. From Christ life is communicated to us both here on earth and in heaven.

In Matthew, Mark, and Luke, Jesus teaches the reality of eternal life as a present possession that reaches beyond the limits of time. Therefore, eternal life implies the immortality of the soul and the resurrection of the body. It must not be confused with mere everlasting existence, which is also true of the unsaved. It involves the endless continuance and perfection of blessedness and communion with God that is entered into by the regenerated, the spiritually born-again believers. The surest way to find and experience eternal life is to have total confidence in God and to diligently obey Christ's command, "Follow Me."

Some may wonder about this last description of life. It is based largely upon the truth of having Christ in us. The Son of God's birth in humanity on earth is analogous to the rebirth of every believer. This is to say that the holy nature of the Son of God has been born into human life, sometimes referred to as incarnation life.

145

We then allow His nature, consisting of His virtuous dispositions, to be exhibited in us.

Could it be that possessing the Spirit of Christ in us and manifesting His nature in our lives is wholly God's will being fulfilled? Could it be that our ultimate destiny on earth is living an incarnated life? I will attempt to answer these questions in succeeding chapters.

The apostle Paul referred to eternal life many times, and his use of the term agrees with the teaching in the Gospels, and no doubt was largely based upon it. According to Paul, eternal life is imparted to us through the Holy Spirit (Romans 8:2, 6, 9–10; 2 Corinthians 2:16; 3:6; Galatians 6:8). Eternal life may be taken hold of in this earthy life (1 Timothy 6:12, 19) and is the end or reward of a sanctified life (Romans 6:22). It is a prize to those who patiently seek it (Romans 2:7) and will be received in all its fullness in glory (Romans 2:7; 2 Corinthians 5:4).

These and several additional scriptures provide some insight on the meanings of true life and a blessed life. However, as we attempt to more fully grasp an understanding of this type of perpetual life, we should not become too rigid in saying what it is and is not. Perhaps, as has been suggested by several early Christian saints, we should simply view our lives as spiritual journeys on earth having no other goal than joy, which is easily understood by all. But even then, some of us are challenged by what is meant by joyousness and whether the experience is intended while we live on earth or is held in reserve for heaven.

Pope Benedict XVI emphasizes that eternal life is really an unknown thing that should be viewed as the true hope. It is "a living hope through the resurrection of Jesus Christ...to obtain an inheritance...reserved in heaven" (1 Peter 1:3–4). In this sense, in his Encyclical Letter *Saved In Hope* (*Spe Salvi*, 34), the pope states that "eternal life is not an unending succession of days in the calendar, but more like a supreme moment of satisfaction... like plunging into the oceans of infinitive love...in which we are simply overwhelmed with joy." Here again we see that a significant part of eternal life is linked to an experience of joy.

There are many assertions that eternal life is not only a living hope of a glorified existence, but a joyous reality in the here and now. Here is a question to be answered: Are we, as faithful followers of Christ, ever given the opportunity to experience this type of joy on earth? Based upon several testimonials from other people, and in some instances my own, I believe that, as rare as they may be, an extraordinary joy is derived from acts of unconditional giving. In my case, the actions were always related to occasions when, without wanting or expecting anything in return, I responded and provided assistance to others who needed help. This almost unexplainable feeling was short lived but nonetheless real.

I wonder if you have had similar emotions when meeting the needs of others. If so, maybe those experiences were intended to be divine gifts from God. By our unselfish acts, He wants us to have a momentary foretaste of eternal life as it will exist in heaven!

LIFE: JESUS' PARADOXICAL STATEMENTS

Saving by Losing (Matthew 16:25a)

"Then Jesus said to His disciples, 'If anyone wishes to come after Me, he must deny himself, and take up his cross and follow Me. *For whoever wishes to save his life will lose it*'" (Matthew 16:24–25a, emphasis added).

Jesus spoke of life in many of His seemingly contradicting stories. In these paradoxical sayings, He described life as being found or lost, saved or lost, hated or loved, gained or forfeited. It appears that there is no middle ground between these opposites; it is only one way or the other. Jesus uses pairs of these contrasting words within each parable to describe how opposite ways life may be viewed and lived.

The wording in the beginning of verse 25, "anyone wishes," is similar to verse 24, "whoever wishes." This is a universal invitation that is open to all. An individual has an option and is not to be forced into this decision by Jesus or some other person.

Then, having stated the commandments of self-denial, cross-carrying, and following Jesus in verse 24, He begins to explain how these directives would relate to His disciples in terms of life itself.

It appears from the onset that submission or disobedience to the three demands would have far-reaching consequences that would unalterably affect the life of each of them.

Upon first reading, most would interpret the word *life* as one's biological or physical life. This would be a reasonable understanding, since history reveals that many believers met the end of life in the early part of the first century because of their unyielding Christian faith. However, the significance of such paradoxical sayings in the first part of the verse depends on which of the multiple meanings Jesus attached to the word *life*.

It has been proposed that meanings of *life* are very likely descriptions of existence that contrast between the lower and higher, the natural and supernatural, and the temporal and eternal. It should be noted that the Greek word for life can be translated to mean the soul, as it is used twice in verse 26. It is my understanding that the soul is the spiritual or immaterial part of humans, designed by our Creator God for everlasting existence. Along with many biblical commentators and authors, I believe that within the context of Jesus' paradoxical narratives I am justified to include the term *self* as part of the meanings of life and soul.

Oehler described the distinction between spirit and soul this way: "Man is not spirit, but has it: he is *soul*. In the soul, which sprang from the spirit and exists continually through it, lies his personality, his self, his ego" (*Old Testament Theology*, vol. 1, 217). The soul or self, therefore, is a human being's individual possession, that which distinguishes one person from another and from all other animate nature.

There is a similarity between Jesus' wording in our passage and His statement made in Luke: "Whoever seeks to keep his life will lose it" (Luke 17:33a). Many construe these two verses in the following manner. Whosoever wishes to save or keep his or her life (soul, self) in this earthly existence, either by renunciation of Christ and the gospel message or by shunning his or her cross, shall lose it in another. I have found that this interpretation of Jesus' statements is profound and difficult to grasp at first. Therefore, I want to offer a few thoughts on saving and losing one's life.

We begin to understand who and what Jesus is referring to in these paradoxes recorded in Matthew 16:25a and Luke 17:33a. The person could be one who highly cherishes his life and wishes to safeguard his temporal life, which will come short of eternal life; that is, he will lose it. He has no inclination to deny himself or carry a cross, but desires to retain all the natural tendencies or dispositions of his human nature. The law of self-preservation is very compelling, but in the end it will prove to be self-destructive. Someone has said, "A life saved is for the moment, but a life lost is for eternity." These interpretations of saving and losing clearly show how necessary it is to renounce oneself and take up one's cross.

To understand more fully this portion of the twenty-fifth verse—"whoever wishes to save his life will lose it"—we must also clarify what is meant by the words *lose* and *lost*. Semantically, to lose is to bring about a loss and a lost is not to be found. Some of the best examples of lostness (or being lost) are seen in chapter 15 of Luke's gospel. This chapter includes seven instances of someone or something lost, the most popular of which is the story of the prodigal son (Luke 15:11–32).

This story and the other passages in which Jesus uses life reveal one of the great outcomes of lostness is being found. There is sometimes repentance and always joy in being found, in those who brought about this finding, those who knew the lost one, the heavenly hosts, and most importantly, God and the one found. No wonder we have so many great hymns that speak of a state of lostness followed by joyfulness, such as "Jesus is Calling," "Softly and Tenderly," and "Turn Your Eyes upon Jesus." These familiar songs are invitations to know and experience the joy of finding the Savior of humankind.

Most think of being lost in terms of destined to doom, or as a result of lostness, existing eternally in a place of no return. Many biblical authorities understand being lost as a condition of the soul. In its most strict sense, it is best described as being out of place or having no use or worth. The person is not where he or she should be and, in this context, is lost to God. One reason individuals are lost to God is because they mistake themselves for God and falsely believe they are in charge and in control of their lives.

Stated in a similar way, they are lost to themselves because of self-deception. In this illusionary condition that they acquired from their Adamic heredity, they maintain a belief (or, at least, the acknowledgment of that belief) contrary to strong evidence derived from New Testament teachings. Thus, they are motivated by desires and emotions that favor the acquisition and hold to that belief. Simply stated, in the spiritual realm, they willingly and stubbornly submit their existence to their lower fleshly natures instead of subordinating themselves to the higher order of divine life in God.

Finding by Losing (Matthew 16:25b)

Jesus said to His disciples, "For whoever wishes to save his life will lose it; *but whoever loses his life for My sake will find it*" (Matthew 16:25, emphasis added).

The views of life previously described (a lower and a higher, the natural and the spiritual, the temporal and eternal) can be expanded to include contrasts between saving oneself and spending or giving oneself. I wonder how many people consider what saving one's life meant to Jesus Christ.

In chapter 5, we looked at the repeated taunts directed toward our Savior to save Himself from death on the cross (Matthew 27:40–44; Luke 23:35–39). The same Greek terms translated *save* in all these passages is used in verse 25a. At the time Jesus gave these instructions, I propose that He anticipated the scornful attempts to terrorize Him to the point of aborting His earthly destiny. Furthermore, I suggest that the personification of evil in these mockers was aimed directly toward the human nature of Jesus, namely that part in Him (and us) with the natural affinities of self-preservation, self-survival, self-glorification, and life itself.

Had He succumbed to the temptations to save Himself in any way, the perfect person would have become imperfect, and He would have been an unacceptable sacrifice for the atonement of the sins of humankind. He would still die and be buried, but there would be no resurrection from the dead and no ascension back to His Father. However, we should rejoice in the knowledge that through the power of the Holy Spirit and Christ's total self-denial of these inherent attractions, evil temptations were thwarted, resulting in the salvation of millions who have faithfully responded to the gospel message.

So what is the practical message of Matthew 16:25b and Luke 17:33b: "and whoever loses his life will preserve it?" Those who make a committed decision to follow Jesus, knowing full well that suffering, trials, and tribulations may be consequences of following Him, will faithfully endure them because they will discover new and fulfilling lives that they will possess and safeguard for eternity. They have not caved in to the excessive desires of the flesh but denied them as their Master commanded.

Speaking of the flesh, there is another aspect of losing life for the sake of Jesus so it can be saved. It is possible that it would be an advantage for the believer to relinquish, give up, or let go of something in his life. It might be best if one loses the lower and natural for the higher and the supernatural. Such losses may be the result of self-denial and correctly labeled losing or being liberated from the bondage of selfishness and pride.

In addition to self-denial, these faithful followers of Christ have taken up their crosses, knowing full well the likelihood of sacrificial experiences ahead. Similar to the path taken by Christ toward Calvary, what awaits them is something exceedingly greater and more rewarding than any passing temptation, trial, or tribulation. It is the joyous knowledge of resurrection from a lower to a higher life, from the natural to the supernatural life, from the temporal to the eternal life, all promised by God and Jesus Christ.

It is significant to note that Jesus uses the phrase "will find it" in contrast to losing life. The word *find* brings to mind discovering or detecting something that was lost or misplaced. The word *it* could simply mean life. Notice the verb *will* is a promise made by Jesus. So the interpretation here is this: Whoever loses his life for My sake is guaranteed to discover life. At this point, I believe "life" means living a joyous life with God or living in God's kingdom.

The famous French theologian and philosopher Albert Schweitzer must have shared this same sentiment. In his autobiography he wrote, "Many a time already had I tried to settle what meaning lay hidden for me in the saying of Jesus! 'Whosoever would save his life shall lose it, and whosoever shall lose his life for My sake and the Gospel's shall save it.' Now the answer is found. In addition to the outward, I now had an inward happiness" (*Out of My Life and Thought, An Autobiography*, 84–85). As many know, Schweitzer uncompromisingly promoted the will to live and respect for life, and personally led a life of service to others. Perhaps his inward happiness was finding an answer to the *it* of Jesus' sayings and happily applying this discovery to his vocation of advancing his goodwill to others.

In this regard, it is no wonder Jesus compares the kingdom of heaven to finding "a treasure hidden in the field…and from joy over it he goes and sells all that he has and buys that field" (Matthew 13:44) and finding "one pearl of great value, he went and sold all that he had and bought it" (Matthew 13:46). We, too, can expect to come upon and discover extraordinarily great treasures, such as gifts of grace from God, during our journeys of following Jesus. These gifts are free and worth everything we have. Later I will further identify the many nuances associated with the joyful discovery of a holy life in God's kingdom.

Living by Dying (John 12:24)

The views of life previously described as a lower and a higher, the natural and the supernatural, the temporal and eternal, also can be expanded to include contrasts between life and death. In John 12:24, we discover another paradoxical rule of death and life. Near the end of His earthly ministry, Jesus said, "Truly, truly, I say to you, unless a grain of wheat falls into the earth and dies, it remains alone; but if it dies, it bears much fruit."

In the *Message*, this verse is rendered, "Listen carefully: Unless a grain of wheat is buried in the ground, dead to the world, it is never any more than a grain of wheat. But if it is buried, it sprouts and reproduces itself many times over." In this short allegory Jesus uses an agricultural truth to illustrate a paradoxical principle that

His death will precede life instead of the conventional wisdom that dictates life always ends with death. Our Lord compares Himself to a grain of wheat, His death to a grain sown in the ground, and His resurrection to the emergence of a sprout and the subsequent abundance of fruit.

This metaphor beautifully illustrates the essential sacrifice of Jesus as a means of His glorification, the redemption of the world to God, and the increase and adoration of His future followers. It may also illustrate, as many biblical scholars have proposed, a principle that His followers would likewise experience, either actually or vicariously in their own spiritual lives. (Keep this life-changing principle of *living by dying* in mind as we address spiritual maturity in later chapters.)

Loving by Hating (John 12:25)

The paradoxical statement Jesus made about life and death in John 12:24 is immediately followed with another illogical declaration in which He says, "He who loves his life loses it, and he who hates his life in this world will keep it to life eternal" (John 12:25). Another translation of this verse is, "In the same way, anyone who holds on to life just as it is destroys that life. But if you let it go, reckless in your love, you'll have it forever, real and eternal" (MSG).

In this pronouncement by Jesus, there is a contrast between loving and hating life as relates to losing or retaining life. A man may choose to love his life (or self) and in doing so will lose it. This manner of loving life likely means that he lives as he pleases. He alone prefers and idolizes what the world has to offer in terms of pleasure, security, and the goals he alone establishes as a way of living for himself without regard to living an others-centered and a God-centered life. (See Luke 12:16–21; 18:18–30).

Again John 12:25b states, "He who hates his life in this world shall keep it to life eternal." Here I believe Jesus refers to an individual who does not choose to love his life; he instead elects to hate his life. Some biblical authorities have interpreted the word *hate*, as it is used in Scriptures, to mean to love less. So, to hate his life, or to love his life less, can mean to be so committed to Christ that he has little or no self-centeredness or concern for himself. The hating of life has also been shown to be a prerequisite to being a disciple of Christ (Luke 14:26) and can be easily interpreted simply as the denial of self.

This ironic pronouncement is not unlike the second phrase in Matthew 16:25b: "Whoever loses his life for My sake will find it." Losing a life for the sake of Christ means faithfully carrying on His work that a servant or disciple would be expected to do. It means a work that could involve suffering to the point of death, by choosing to completely deny oneself instead of denying our Lord and Savior. It refers to a person refusing to renounce Christ, even if the punishment were death. It means to sacrifice the lower, natural, and temporal in order to preserve the higher, spiritual, and eternal life. (We will apply this last meaning of losing a life as we consider the topic of spiritual maturity.)

VALUE OF LIFE: A DIVINE WARNING (MATTHEW 16:26)

We need to realize the seriousness of viewing that life lost for the sake of Christ is really an advantage to the person. To thrust this point across, Jesus illustrated the temporal and eternal lives in terms of preserving or losing a person's soul: "For what will it profit a man if he gains the whole world and forfeits his soul? Or what will a man give in exchange for his soul?" (Matthew 16:26). In this verse we see the value and significance of the soul contrasted to the worthlessness of the world.

The principle here is that whatever a person gets at the expense of his being will do him no good in the long run; he cannot keep and enjoy its gains. Our souls are really not our own in one respect (1 Corinthians 6:19), but in another sense a soul is the self, an integral part of us that resides within us while we are on earth. Our souls are worth immensely more than the whole world, are of greater value than all the wealth, honor, and pleasures of this present time.

To show the merit of Jesus' statement, let's consider only one soul or self, or better still, think about your own soul or self. Let's measure your soul's worth compared to total worth as assessed by worldly standards. If placed on a balance scale, the worth of the entire world would be too light to weigh down the value of your soul! We are worth so much to God that He placed the Son of Man on earth to suffer in all the ways of His humanity, as revealed to us in the account of Jesus' Passion. This is how God views the importance of each and every human who lived, is living, or will live.

Note also that a soul can be lost, and there is absolutely nothing that can be paid to make up for it. Verse 26 asks, "Or what will a man give in exchange for his soul?" This question posed by Jesus should be viewed within the context of verse 27, which concerns His prediction of a last judgment of everyone: "For the Son of Man is going to come in the glory of His Father with His angels, and will then repay every man according to his deeds"(Matthew 16:27). At that time, every self will be fully exposed and all the works of each person will be judged, including the motives behind each deed, which within the immediate background of these sayings, would comprise those done "for My sake." Referring back to verse 26b, one commentator has paraphrased Jesus' question in terms of a judicial verdict; there is nothing you can offer to buy back your life at the judgment if you have already forfeited it.

Some view these statements of God's judgments as threats or intimidations made to coerce others to follow Jesus. Those who hold this perspective are likely those who view God as a giant dictator, relying on the propaganda of fear to gain influence over others. Nothing could be further from the truth. Instead, God plainly gives a divine warning in all these paradoxes and sayings. The advice given here by Jesus is what one would expect from a loving, patient, and gracious God who always wants to guide us away from transitory earthly interests toward a higher permanent order of spiritual life.

Closer scrutiny of the seven scriptures that contain key words (see appendix C) discloses more than just counting the number of times a word is used and defining contradictory terms. When examined together as we have just done, they provide insight into Jesus' views on a spiritual life. In these passages, Jesus alluded that His followers should be channeled toward a higher category of spiritual life; the lower life of earthly relationships and activities must be subordinated to the higher and spiritual. The earthly interests may be very desirable and enjoyable in the short run, but those who cling to them and make them supreme are in danger of losing the higher. The spiritual being is infinitely more valuable and should be sought even if other earthly gains are lost.

These contrasting outcomes suggest that believers should consciously obey the commands to deny themselves and carry their crosses daily. For in not doing so, we deliberately risk the vitality of our entire being and endanger our divine security in God. But in obedience to Jesus' directives to deny ourselves and carry our crosses, we will have both the means to reprioritize our lives and the means to detach our self-centered attitudes to God-centeredness.

Last, in anticipation of the last judgment day, the best advantage and preparation for Christians is to deny self, take up the cross, and follow Jesus. These paradoxes all point to the need and importance of salvation and to a life characterized by the high quality or virtuous character of self. In contrast, a self-led life is not the life we should be leading as believers. Instead, we should be championing a life focused and centered on Christ, where He is our one and only gold standard.

Life: Temporal and Eternal Perspectives

I have frequently mentioned eternal life and contrasted it to temporal life. Now I want to insert the topic of perceptions to help better grasp the significant difference of values between temporal and eternal schemes. Table 11.1 summarizes the contrast of these two viewpoints.

TEMPORAL	ETERNAL
Pleasure	Knowing God
Recognition of people	Approval of God
Popularity	Servanthood
Wealth and status	Integrity and character
Power	Humility
↓	↓
Emptiness	Fulfillment
Delusion	Reality
Foolishness	Wisdom

Table 11.1. The Contrast between Temporal and Eternal Perspectives

(Adapted from Boa 2001)

This table shows the sharp contrasts between temporal and eternal value systems. Not only do they describe five differences between temporal and eternal, but also between the seen and unseen, and the natural and spiritual. Perhaps of even greater importance are the great differences of the three projected outcomes between these two perspectives. If one viewpoint is more fully practiced than the other in our day-to-day lives, we should take note as to where these objectives will ultimately end. According to Boa, with a temporal perspective they will terminate in meaninglessness, fantasy, and thoughtlessness. But with an eternal perspective, the results are in accomplishment, authenticity, and understanding. It really becomes a matter of choice whether to focus on the values of one view or the other.

To illustrate the difference between the values of temporal and eternal mind-sets, I offer an example of one person's perspective on these contrasting viewpoints. My wife and I have a very close relative who knew we were professing Christians. On several occasions we talked to her about our faith, hoping to change her earthly perspective. She usually would respond negatively to our words with her favorite comeback: "You two are so heavenly minded that you are no earthly good." Because she was older than us and we respected her, we actually took her advice to heart and became less pious about our Christian faith toward her. In our fallen world, it is easy to side with the attitudes of skeptics and doubters of heavenly values. Many times it is difficult to wean ourselves away from the earthy desires in favor of the divine wishes.

We finally came to the conclusion that she was somehow deceived and had it all backward. It was and still is our opinion that she should have said, "You are earthly good because you are heavenly minded." There is an ever-present tendency to align ourselves with worldly standards of pleasure, popularity, and power. These are not the points of reference for followers of Christ. What we are not to do is specifically spelled out in the incident where Peter chided Jesus not to die on a cross. Jesus told him, "You are not setting your mind on God's interests, but man's" (Matthew 16:23).

Jesus' words to Peter offer a lesson for all Christians as we live out our faith. We can envision a satisfying existence of earthly goodness with a mind-set of keeping and maintaining a self-seeking life. We can also envision a fulfilling life of both earthly and heavenly goodness that is focused on the divine interests of God. Believers must deliberately select one of the two paths—choose to live a self-oriented life or a Christ-centered life. Each of these two pathways is intended to lead to a joyful destination, but the ultimate destiny between the two journeys may be quite different.

BREAKING NEWS AND DEVELOPING STORY

The managers of the television station arranged for the anchor to meet with the two chief investigators who first discovered the S-Factor.

Anchor: "Viewers have been impressed by your research findings, but they want to know more. Is it true there was an incident concerning whose name should be first on publications?"

Dr. Sinton: "Yes, at the time we were hurriedly composing our first manuscript, we both were fatigued and disagreeable with each other."

Dr. Selford: "That's the way it happened. To this day we have not resolved this issue because, in our research community, the one whose name appears first on a publication seems to get most of the credit. Neither of us wants to give up the recognition. It's only part of our human nature to be selfishly motivated and like many others, we just can't help it. Don't worry, though. We'll continue to work amiably together and finish the project."

Chapter 12

... Envision a Fulfilling Life?

Spiritual Maturity

SO FAR, WE have taken a look at the various ways self is understood, the possible obstacles to spiritual growth, the fine distinctions of self-denial, and the multiple meanings of carrying a cross. These realities should provide a solid foundation on which believers can spiritually mature in their pilgrim journeys of faith. Once this groundwork is established, believers require various resources to gain more knowledge and grow deeper in their faith.

With this developing process in mind, the resources in this and following chapters will consist of word pictures and stories. To tell a story and convey a set of ideas, especially of a spiritual nature, it is often difficult to use words alone. Therefore, I wish to present a few simplified graphics along with accompanying narration to help believers better understand Christian maturity.

SPIRITUAL MATURITY: ILLUSTRATED BY STORIES

We will first revisit the hypothetical story of the department store shoppers as related in chapter 1. By analogy, this tale will be one of the resources used to help believers experience the joyfulness of a fulfilling life as they grow in their Christian faith.

Graph 12.1, seen below, visually illustrates the story of the three shoppers and a separate but related story of three individuals who are seeking gratification in Christianity. As you recall, the three shoppers, identified as A, B, and C, individually went to a department store to purchase an advertised item that would dispel their feelings of incompleteness. Lacking knowledge of the location of the desired item, all were lost in the store. Only one willingly followed the clerk, and after finding what he was seeking, considered the item's cost and its utility, and purchased the higher-priced item, which served him well with great satisfaction.

Unfortunately, shopper C became totally uninterested in what he thought would allay his inner needs and left the store. For the remaining two shoppers, there are five points of this imaginary story that we want to emphasize. These issues are associated with (1) the customer's *lostness* in the store, (2) the *guidance* offered by the clerk, (3) the customer's *appraisal* of the item, (4) the choice made to bring about a *resolution* and actions taken to purchase and utilize the item by the customer, and (5) a level of *satisfaction* experienced by each of the buyers.

These five points in the story of the shoppers are also operational and applicable in the lives of believers after they accept Christ as Savior. We use fictional shoppers A and B as equivalents to two hypothetical believers, also A and B, who are examples of new Christians. I purposely use these letter designations interchangeably between the shoppers and believers to enhance the similarity between the two. In graph 12.1 we immediately see the distinct differences between persons A and B regarding their spiritual growth. (It may be helpful for you to mark this place in the book because several references will be made in this chapter and in subsequent chapters to graph 12.1.)

In this graph, the degree of spiritual maturity is plotted on the vertical axis, ranging from low levels to infinity. Values in the graph are incorporated into dashed lines by averaging data, and are shown as a function of time on the horizontal axis. Measured in years, time relates one's life span, which terminates upon physical death. Note that the dashed lines are separated by either a plus sign (+) or a

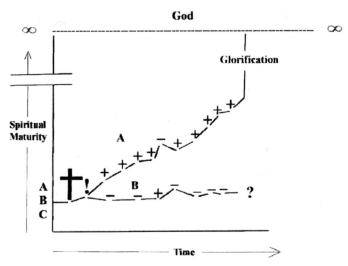

Graph 12.1. A Plot of Spiritual Maturity vs. Time

minus sign (-), each of which corresponds to significant happenings in the lives of individuals A and B.

God is included in the plot and is related to the symbol of infinity (∞) His existence in time, is completely infinite, transcendent, eternal, pure, perfect, and constant; therefore God is immeasurable, having no beginning or end. The infinity of God is used to help us grasp the brevity of our lives and fleeting finiteness when contrasted with eternal existence. As noted in table 11.1, the value or worth attached to a temporal existence is miniscule in comparison to eternity. This distinction of infinity alone should help us gain an everlasting perspective that is decisively different from the common temporal world viewpoint of the finite.

Before the Cross

Of the five points from our fictional story of the three shoppers, only lostness will be used to illustrate what likely occurs in the life of a person before conversion to Christianity. I maintain that a person is in a state of lostness when he or she feels any significant sensations of incompleteness or inconsistencies. In this condition, the individual begins to realize lostness when he thinks his life does not yield lasting and meaningful enjoyment, does not fulfill his earnest desires for peace and contentment, and does not provide any hope that he will experience these three expectations in this short earthly life and beyond. In short, there is something missing.

It is absolutely necessary for one to come to the realization of being lost to satisfy an underlying desire to find something that will overcome this incompleteness. In Christianity, that something is really Someone who will establish a meaningful and satisfying life for a person. Of course the Someone is the Son of God and the Son of Man, Jesus Christ. Without faith in Him and without knowing what He accomplished on the cross of Calvary on humanity's behalf, there is a problem for the lost person and for all humankind. This dilemma can best be resolved in terms of first being found.

Lostness is ultimately related to the dual life forces we have in ourselves; namely, a godly nature and an ungodly nature. Specifically, the extent to which a person is lost is the degree to which one:

- is out of fellowship, out of loving relationship with God and others, and ultimately out of a harmonious relationship within oneself;
- is lacking godly dispositions or characteristics, but possessing those worldly attributes that become embedded as an element in his or her nature and revealed in behavior;
- is retaining the old self, the old unyielding self that manifests the fruit of the flesh; and
- is unwilling to suffer, deny self, and to carry his or her cross.

Conversely, the extent to which a person is found is the level in which one recognizes godly dispositions and has a sincere desire to nourish them. A person who is found accepts herself, receives the free gifts of God, and especially during times of trials and troubles is willing to suffer, deny self, carry her cross and forgive others.

With these definitions in mind we return to the stories of the shoppers and the individuals who seek Christianity by highlighting the five points of lostness, guidance, assessment, resolution, and joyousness.

Out of their particular conditions of being lost came the possibility of being found. What eventually led the three individuals to the department store was admiration of an item that other acquaintances owned, reading an advertisement of that same item, and the motivation to find that item. Lostness was evidenced in all three of the shoppers. Customer A realized this and openly admitted it to the clerk, whereas B and C obstinately denied that they were lost. Note in graph 12.1 that the caliber of spirituality prior to the symbol of the cross is small in all of them. It is my opinion that this low level of spirituality represents a portion of the original image of the Godhead in the creation of humankind (Genesis 1:26–27) that was retained at least in part after the fall (Genesis 3:1–7). This quality and maybe quantity of spirituality may be a segment of God's moral likeness or the capacity to spiritually relate to God, sometimes referred to as one's conscience, which has a limited ability to truly discern right from wrong.

Possessing a conscience without having an awareness of the lostness of one's soul could indicate a lack of repentance and an unwillingness to accept help on the part of customers B and C. This was particularly evident with shopper C. After resisting any help and finding the item he thought might be of some use, he decided it would not be of any value to him. Based upon worth and cost, he refused to purchase it and had no intention of shopping for it again. In terms of salvation, this response by customer C is viewed by most Christians with sadness. Shopper C represents those unsaved who absolutely deny Christ and are to be pitied most of all.

After the Cross

Only small changes in spiritual growth are noted in graph 12.1 for persons A and B at the beginning of their faith walks. Many factors may account for these low levels of spirituality, including a lack of knowledge of sound Christian doctrines or even a lapse back into a state of lostness. Then at a defining moment, perhaps in some crisis experience, something out of the ordinary occurred in the life of A at the time of the exclamation mark shown in the graph. After this point there is an obvious increase in his spiritual maturity that is associated with plus signs. With the exception of one instance without further growth, spiritual maturity consistently ascends until death ends his earthly life.

The explanation for person A's spiritual maturation lies in what occurred during his lifetime. As we shall see, these are step-by-step inward alterations and are completely unlike the extreme cosmetic makeovers of one's appearance. These changes are shown as a preponderance of plus signs, spiritual transformations that are directly associated with certain situations that challenge his firmness of faith. Spiritual transformations are considered by many leading evangelical theologians to be fundamentally necessary to bring about the progressive development of Christlikeness in the believer. These spiritual renovations are further illustrated in figure 12.2 below.

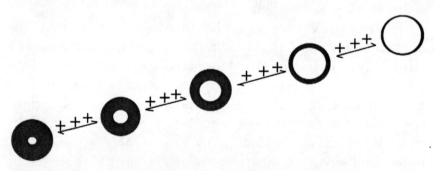

Figure 12.2. A Faultless Progression of Spiritual Maturity

Visualize for a moment several snapshot views of a Christian's self that are taken about every fifteen years. Each self-circle has an inner white area that represents God's image and an element of newly created Christlikeness, which ideally enlarges during the Christian's life on earth. At the same time, the outer area of the circle diminishes. This darkened portion of the self-circle consists of the old tarnished, fleshly self, viewed as the sin nature, which has the capacity and inclination to do those things that in no way bring praise to God.

Overall, this figure shows what transpires between each succeeding circle to bring about these transformations, symbolized by several plus signs. Additional meanings of these signs will be presented later. It should be evident in this illustration of Christian maturity that progression toward the right is associated with a lessening of the fleshly aspect at the expense of the godly life of Christ. It is also important to note that the lines are arrowed at both ends between circles, denoting reversibility. This latter feature indicates that over time spiritual growth can increase, remain unchanged, or, to the detriment of an individual, decrease.

You may wonder how realistic the data of spiritual growth is. Perhaps you're wondering if the dashed lines are really that accurate, or if they have any rational or practical meaning. Maybe you're reflecting on your own experience and noting that it's not quite as even as the lines indicate.

These are perceptive and worthwhile observations. Please realize I am attempting to simplify a major tenet of spirituality that is apparently very complex to many. If we really could quantitatively measure spiritual growth daily in any person, it would surely be very similar to the stock market graphs that show changes in values of stocks, mutual funds, commodities, and so forth. Such financial graphics show fluctuations over time just as the dynamics of spiritual growth data might demonstrate. Variations in spiritual growth do not just happen weekly, monthly or annually, but occur in shorter periods of time, even momentarily.

Regarding only person A after he came to the cross, let's return to the five considerations of our story. It is after the cross until his biological death that we see that miraculous transformations are required to bring about spiritual growth.

1. Lostness

Person A, perhaps in a defining moment, experienced a feeling of being incomplete or unimportant before becoming a believer, and lacked a clear understanding of the phrase "having a relationship with Christ" that he had heard so much about. In this sense, even one who professes a belief in Christ has the capacity to become lost as well as to possess a degree of lostness at any time. Although judicially changed to the level of moral purity by justification, he is still considerably lost because he possesses a sinful, prideful human nature. Deep within himself he realizes that some significant changes must be made in his life. He also realizes that it would be risky and uncomfortable to change.

2. Guidance

Apart from physical requirements, we all have basic spiritual and psychological needs that include the requirements for security, significance, completion, and to be loved and accepted. To meet these needs, many look for guidance from ungodly sources. If we trust that all our needs will be met from one or more sources, we will always look up to, idolize, and adore someone or something.

Person A did not succumb to his self-reliant tendencies to achieve his expectations. He needed someone else to follow; someone to lead him out of lostness to what he thought would serve him best. Any godly person could provide this leadership, but because he learned at least some of the basic doctrines of Christianity he knew he was a child of God, possessing God's Spirit, and his guidance likely came from the indwelling Holy Spirit. "For all who are being led by the Spirit of God, these are sons of God" (Romans 8:14).

3. Appraisal

The Scriptures tell us that a spiritual Christian possesses an enlightened mind that discerns between the natural and supernatural, and understands many of the revealed truths of the Creator. This person is under the influence of the Holy Spirit and examines, scrutinizes, and sees the value of divine things in the past, present, and future. Paul wrote, "He who is spiritual appraises all things" (1 Corinthians 2:15). In this case, person A came to an understanding of the implications involved in Christ's commands to each of His followers to deny self and carry his cross

(Matthew 16:24). Furthermore, he believed the teachings in the New Testament that provided the means of washing the worldly desires out of his polluted human nature.

4. Resolution and a Response

In the department store, person A voluntarily made a calculated, deliberate choice to pay a higher amount for what he earnestly desired and needed. The Christian, acting faithfully on scriptural truths, decided to totally and continually surrender himself to Christ and be obedient to God. He decided to be a faithful follower of Christ and to fully identify with his Savior's life, including the Passion. Knowing these judgments would likely involve a personal cost, he expelled his lingering self-centered cravings.

5. Joyfulness or Satisfaction

Like shopper A who was exceedingly happy about his purchase, the believer experienced a great deal of satisfaction as he progressed in the sanctification aspect of his salvation by serving his Master and others in need. He exhibited increasing manifestations of Christlikeness until his earthly life ended. Notice from graph 12.1 that though his biological life ended, he rose by glorification to a level of spiritual and wonderful completeness, followed by timeless infinity with His God and Savior.

SPIRITUAL MATURITY: ILLUSTRATED BY A PARABLE

Concerning the department store shoppers and their Christian counterparts, we need to further evaluate individuals A, B, and C in order to explain some of their actions and attitudes. To better comprehend the inner selves of these three men, we will look at scriptures that may help us, specifically, the parable of the sower (Matthew 13:1–23; Mark 4:13–20; Luke 8:11–15). In the somewhat cryptic passage, Jesus told multitudes this story about seeds, which represent the Word of God, or as some have suggested, the gospel of Christ or salvation. The seeds were thrown on the footpath, sown in thin soil among rocks, in the midst of thorns, and on good soil. Each of these four conditions was related to the makeup or nature of the soil that in turn represented four types of people and their personal responses. After each heard the message, the specific response reflected the core of that person's human nature.

The parable is explained by Jesus as follows. Sometimes the Word falls on someone whose mind-set within the inner self is as hard as a path made of concrete. That one is like a deaf listener and does not understand the word of the kingdom, and "the evil one comes and snatches away what has been sown in his heart" (Matthew 13:19). The individual who has a rocky core in his or her human nature has superficial spiritual hearing, knowledge, and maturity and "immediately receives it with joy; yet he has no firm root in himself, but is only temporary, and when affliction or persecution arises because of the word, immediately he falls away" (Matthew 13:20–21). Concerning the person who possesses a thorny core, our Lord says, "the worry of the world and the deceitfulness of wealth choke the word, and it becomes unfruitful" (Matthew 13:22). Jesus describes the one who has good soil as the person who "understands it (the Word of God or the gospel); who indeed bears fruit and brings forth, some a hundredfold, some sixty, and some thirty" (Matthew 13:23).

This parable of sowing of seeds in different environments illustrates the responses of the three shoppers and the three people who are challenged with the same good news of Jesus Christ.

In the first category of Jesus' parable, the stony pathway of soil represents those persons who, upon hearing the Word, are faintly impressed, the kind of impression seeds make on hard-packed soil. Because the environment is not conducive for germination of the Word, the seeds are snatched up by Satan. In the stories of the shoppers and would-be believers, person C may well fall into this class, since he was initially impressed with what he first thought might satisfy him. In both scenarios, he denied his lostness, refused help in finding what he sought, and thought that the cost was excessive for what he was seeking. In his case it is no wonder the seeds of the Word were easily and quickly taken away.

The two individuals Jesus described who existed in the rocky or in the thorny soils can be represented by person B in our stories. Referring again to graph 12.1, at a time shortly after the confrontation with the cross, person B had a small increase in the measurement of growth. His immediate reaction to the message of the gospel was joyful. But he probably felt little or no genuine need for salvation. He may never have been totally convinced of his depravity or his lostness, and erroneously thought that a Christian's life should be a state of prolonged happiness; yet he bemoaned any troubles that came his way.

Those with a rocky core are said to hear the Word with initial enthusiasm, but quickly fall away or take offense. Persons in this category likely take offense the moment the life of faith becomes difficult. Mistakenly thinking all troubles will subside and disappear after a church affiliation, they abandon the faith. Not only do rocks become a troubling presence among the seeds of God's Word, but they also provide absolutely no necessary nutrients for spiritual growth. One of the most obvious trends noted in graph 12.1 is the almost constant lack of spiritual growth associated with person B during his remaining time on earth.

Jesus' words about sowing seed on thorny ground may well signify the abiding presence of the corrupted human nature in a once-professing believer. Such would be the case with person B. Worldly worries, a false sense of security brought on by prosperity, and a desire for material things may have plagued him, as do anxieties, uncertainties, and cravings that overwhelm many of us.

Thorns of daily routines and materialistic pursuits often distract believers, strangling God's Word so that it yields no fruit of the Spirit in their lives. Individual B represents those who claim to be led to a saving knowledge in Christ at a time in the past but show little or no evidence of spiritual growth. To whom are we referring? Without becoming explicit, these people are those who often wear overly pious faces in the presence of other churchgoers but fail to display any significant increase in bearing saintly fruit or in any other caliber of spirituality. Like some of these people, person B did not really understand the Word as did individual A. He probably lacked the discipline of Bible study, continued to manifest ungodly traits, and failed to develop Christlikeness.

Many other possible reasons may account for person B's lack of discernable spiritual growth. As previously suggested, he may have continually failed to realize the existence of the thorny sinful nature within him and did not acquire the means to negate its effect on his spiritual growth. It is quite possible that he was satisfied with his life, thought the secular culture was the norm, and felt no need to make his standards otherwise. There is also the possibility that certain idols had a ruling influence in his day-to-day life. One idol worth mentioning here is self, the worship of self, having all the rights and privileges our Western culture places on the individuality of humankind.

Shopper B did not accept guidance from the clerk and manifested a great deal of self-determination in not doing so. Regarding his appraisal, he hurriedly assessed the pros and cons of buying the item; then he primarily based his decision to purchase it on its outward appearance, the personal advantage of having the item, and how much it would cost. The story indicates he did so with little concern about the quality and utility of the article. From these shortcomings, we are led to believe that a determined assessment of what it means to become an active and faithful Christian is the responsibility of every believer.

Regarding the outcome of person B in terms of his spiritual maturity, he may have decided not to obey the command of Christ's admonition of self-denial. As mentioned, every Christian has the choice of either denying self or denying Christ. If this was the case with person B, Jesus was constantly denied, because B was not willing to deny himself. In addition, he undoubtedly thought religion would somehow be a gain for him, yet he likely shunned any idea of carrying a cross. Furthermore, either through ignorance of God's grace or unbelief, or perhaps both, it seems he made no attempt to exchange his worldly nature for a godly nature.

As to any satisfaction with his purchase, shopper B ended up with the cheaper item and showed no evidence of joy. Without following the clerk's help in locating the item or listening to his advice, this customer's item was of little or no worth in the long run. When we relate this unenthusiastic response to the person who was maturing in the Christian faith, we conclude that he too experienced little or no joy, nor any anticipation of future joy.

Customer B continued to possess attitudes of self-dependence rather than those of God-dependence, and of selfish pride instead of humility. Some would call such an individual a nominal or carnal Christian, or possibly even question whether he was a true Christians at all.

The question mark placed at the termination of shopper B's life in graph 12.1 is intentional. It leads one to wonder if his soul will be everlastingly glorified (once saved, always saved) or eternally lost (damned). The debate about this issue still continues among some Christian theologians, but according to my limited research in this writing, most seem to favor the glorification belief.

The man with good soil represents person A. He proved to be a good listener and possessed an understanding of the Word—not necessarily an intellectual knowledge of God's Word, but a spiritual understanding that resulted in bringing forth fruit. Biblically, fruit often means results, manifestations, or expressions. To amplify what Jesus likely meant by bearing fruit in those in whom the Holy Spirit dwells and works, I reference Paul's contrast between the deeds of the flesh and the fruit of the Spirit. Fleshly deeds include jealousy, envy, and so forth, while fruit of the Spirit exhibits love, joy, self-control, and so on. (See Galatians 5:19–23.) Such fruit is vital evidence of a believer who is maturing in his spiritual journey. More specifically, Jesus could have meant that bearing fruit is the quality of virtues that significantly enhances person's spiritual maturity.

BREAKING NEWS AND DEVELOPING STORY

Anchor: "The following report comes from Dr. Barbara Sinton, co-investigator of the study of S-Factor."

Dr. Sinton: "Dr. Selford and I have shown that the total molecular weight (amount) of the S-Factor remains the same in all individuals, but the amount of each of the two subunits was shown to vary between Individuals. As you can see from this chart, these are the results of separate samples taken from subjects 489 and 803. Please note subject 489 has about a quarter of subunit a and the remaining part of the S-Factor is composed of subunit b. Notice that subject 803 has about twice the amount of subunit a as subject 489.

"For reasons we don't yet understand, proportions of the subunits in the S-Factor differ from person to person. However, our research team is considering further studies to clarify this mystery."

Chapter 13

... Envision a Fulfilling Life?

Deliverance from the Power of Sin and Self

IN PREVIOUS CHAPTERS we have claimed that sanctification, an integral part of salvation, is God's way of dealing with the need for liberation from the power of sin and self. Having resolved the issue of being delivered from the penalty and punishment of sin by justification, believers are called to a higher order of spiritual life. My intent in this and succeeding chapters is to help us further understand sanctification in terms of the absolute necessity for deliverance from the power of sin and self as we mature spiritually.

We begin by briefly looking at the recent believer in Christianity who represents the equivalent to shopper A in our story. While person B, also a believer, appeared to maintain a state of lostness and did not eliminate his sinful human nature and its adverse affect on his spiritual growth, person A found what he was looking for and employed the means to eradicate the worldly desires of his human nature, and he grew spiritually. Recall Jesus' parable of the soil and seeds. In a very real sense we see that customer A represents the person whose soil was fertile and in whom the planted seed of the Word took root as he appropriated Christlike features and grew spiritually.

But shouldn't we be very honest with ourselves as we are reminded that there is some degree of lostness in all of us? Is not the ground naturally bad (sinful) in everyone's self, including those in good soil? This is true because we live in an imperfect world with other flawed people, some of whom are dominated by ungodliness. So we need to realize that our soil is not faultless and that we all have ungodly dispositions that hinder us in becoming more like Christ. It would be advantageous for each of us to daily, or even more often, identify the nature of our individual soil. Then and only then can we successfully appropriate the means to eliminate any rocks and thorns that would impede our spiritual growth.

Some may ask, what does it mean to appropriate? Dictionaries define appropriation in terms of taking something for one's own use: the taking of something that belongs to or is associated with someone else. In contrast, a less used term, expropriation, refers to the releasing of something. With these words understood, what exactly do they have to do with obtaining godliness and eliminating that part of our human nature that opposes godliness? Put in another way and specifically, what does the term *appropriation* have to do with the means to deliver one from the power of sin and of self?

To answer the question about appropriation, recall that a vast conflict exists between the two powerful forces within the self of a believing Christian. The conflict is mainly between the flesh and the indwelling Holy Spirit; each wants to govern and be in control. Believers who want to and are willing to follow our Savior to become more Christlike obviously need to put their trust in the power of the Holy Spirit. So our effective goal is to be progressively transformed from a state of self-life and liberated from the power of our sinful natures.

The specifics of how these deliverances occur in lives of Christians now become our center of attention. Although most believers know Jesus suffered, died for us, and was resurrected, few understand what was accomplished on Calvary and how they might appropriate new life.

The magnanimous event of a spiritual transformation, or more accurately a series of events leading to newness of life, constitutes one of the greatest mysteries of all time. In his book titled *The Holy Longing: The Search for a Christian Spirituality*, Ronald Rolheiser connects distinct moments within a succession of events, which he calls a process of transformation or the paschal cycle. He asserts that the cycle has five parts:

1. Good Friday: the loss of life, real death
2. Easter Sunday: the reception of new life
3. The Forty Days: a time for readjustment to the new and for grieving the old
4. Ascension: letting go of the old and letting it bless you, the refusal to cling
5. Pentecost: the reception of new spirit for the new life that one is already living

Rolheiser states that "This cycle is not something that we must undergo just once, at the moment of our deaths, when we lose our earthly lives as we know them. It is rather something we must undergo daily, in every aspect of our lives. We will have many deaths in our lives and within each of these we must receive new life and new spirit. Ultimately our happiness depends upon properly undergoing it. The paschal mystery is the secret to life" (1999, 148).

I share many of this author's views about the process of spiritual transformations. However, I have chosen to highlight only the first two aspects of his proposed paschal cycle. This approach is mainly in accordance with Pauline theology as presented in the New Testament. In my view, transformations will yield new life and virtues by which we can and will be increasingly conformed to the image of Christ. Essentially, these are acts of faith that involve reckoning, considering, and realizing ourselves "to be dead to sin, but alive to God in Christ Jesus" (Romans 6:11). Key aspects of the transformations are illustrated in figure 13.1.

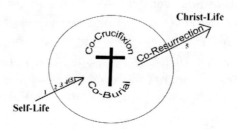

Figure 13.1. Mortification of Self-Life

The word *mortification* used in this figure literally means putting the flesh to death, and it comes from several of Paul's writings. The context of these scriptures shows that the Christian is already spiritually alive and has the indwelling Spirit of God, and therefore must put to death the fleshly nature, which certainly does not belong in the life of a follower of Christ.

John Owen, who was cited in chapter 10, importantly evaluated and amplified Romans 8:13. In this verse, he stressed the importance for believers to mortify the deeds of the flesh. The term *deeds* appears many times in Scripture as an outward focus of actions. In context, deeds are described as good and fruitful. Deeds are also characterized as bad and evil. A lengthy list of these ungodly deeds appears in Galatians 5:19–21, and includes immorality, idolatry, jealousy, and envying. According to Owen, deeds also include the cause of such things, namely the inward fountain of sin—the flesh. In his classic writings on mortification, he concluded that, as Christians, our lives are to be given over to pleasing God by putting to death the deeds of sinful flesh and walking in the newness of the regenerate life.

From Owen's exposition and related scriptural passages, such as Romans 6:21; 8:6, Galatians 6:8, and Colossians 3:5, concerning or alluding to the mortification of self, the following statements are offered:

- The process of mortification directly relates to the one-time sacrificial work of Christ on the cross by the one all-inclusive provision to deal with the deeds of our corrupt nature.

- As believers, we do not put to death anything God has not already crucified with Christ.
- Not only has God dealt with the sin nature in us, that is, the flesh, He has also implanted a new God-like disposition in us through our rebirth into God's family.

Using these analyses and interpretations of God's Holy Word, I view figure 13.1 as a model of the dynamic that energizes the mortification of self-life. It is based primarily upon Romans 6:1–14 and helps to illustrate the transformation of a self-life to a Christlike life. In this model believers see how to evade the bondage of sin, obtain victory through troubles, and bring about conversion of a false self to a true self.

In each of these transformations the underlying rationale hinges on the power of the indwelling Holy Spirit as well as the abiding presence of the Spirit of Christ. The role of the believer is to deny self, take up his cross by faith, and personally associate with the Passion of Christ. This personal recognition and identification of the Passion, which couples us with the historical events of Christ's crucifixion, burial, and resurrection is of supreme importance. Through our unified oneness with Christ in His Passion comes the provision to be transformed to a more Christlike existence.

These statements are admittedly somewhat difficult to comprehend, but should not be overlooked or merely dismissed as hypothetical hype and theological jargon. Hopefully, these assertions will become clearer from the use of the Plot of Spiritual Maturity (fig. 12.1) and the Mortification of Self-Life seen in figure 13.1. As you recall, the graphic of spiritual maturity shows the extent of spiritual growth of two persons who became believers. It is important to note that in this visualization, each plus sign (+) stands for an instance of mortifying the self-life and a minus sign (-) denotes that mortification did not take place.

Figure 13.1 is a model that illustrates the essentials to transform a self-life to a Christlike life. It contains a circle and at its center is a cross. Three crucial aspects of the Passion, His crucifixion, burial, and resurrection are included in the circle. Similar to a cycle, we use the circle purposely to show again that it represents oneself, but as a self-circle without any distinction between godly and ungodly aspects. Keep in mind that these opposing parts of self will be affected as a result, cycling the mortification of self. To become transformed more in the likeness of Christ, we should recognize ourselves in each aspect of the Passion sequences depicted in figure 13.1.

Now let us closely examine the transformation of self by way of looking at the five features person A may have taken in the stories previously told. But before we undertake this discussion, I want to make something abundantly clear. In no way do I want you to understand these points to be a formula or steps to be followed, one through five. That would make this book no different than the self-help presentations that are available in our "wanting to be happy" culture. That style would be mechanistic, like many of the lock-step courses of an academic curriculum. There, you cannot take a second step until you master the first. So if you tried to follow and complete the five steps sequentially, you soon would become discouraged if something didn't work out the way you thought it should.

So, please realize that my intentions are faith oriented and are not to be viewed as methods, stages, or techniques. There is no power in the mechanics of these things. The real power comes from God's grace and love directed toward each believer in every transformation of self we experience.

Now, we go back to our subject. To make this more personal, let's illustrate what might happen if the indwelling Holy Spirit convicted you, a believer in Christ, of possessing an ungodly disposition. Let's choose for our example, the universal attitude of spiritual pride, thinking and acting like you are superior to other believers. In this regard, many people like you have had moments of feeling pious and sensing they were better Christians than other church members. You may even think this feeling of superiority is just natural and you shouldn't worry because surely it cannot be a sin. Have you wondered whether someone was so bold as to describe you to others as self-righteous?

You understand that all of us have a dual nature within ourselves and that there is an active warfare going on between the flesh and the Spirit. You come to realize that this fleshly attitude of spiritual pride is not a godly grace. In fact, suppose that just moments ago you told a friend how much better you looked in comparison to a fellow believer. In response to your recognition that pride is not godly, in prayer you admit or confess that this imposition of the flesh is nothing more than an element of *lostness* in your servanthood relationship with the Master. The indwelling Holy Spirit, who has convicted you that this fleshly nature was never in the personality or character of Jesus Christ, now becomes the *guiding* force conscientiously leading you in a path toward the cross of Calvary.

You remember Jesus' invitation to His would-be disciples to follow Him, as well as the commands to deny self and take up a cross. As a disciple of Christ, you know these sayings are more than printed words in the Bible; they are inspired declarations that are currently expressing Jesus' command for you to face this issue. You also realize that any expropriation of self-life will be painful, particularly something that elicits enjoyable feelings such as spiritual pride.

All of these thoughts and emotions produce distress and you critically begin to *appraise* these various factors, such as the worth of losing a cherished part of your human nature, surrendering your natural feelings of self-adoration, and finding a different kind of life. Once this process of assessing your circumstance is complete, you voluntarily make an unyielding *resolution* to relinquish this prideful trait, pick up your cross, and proceed up the path toward a destiny that most people don't even want to think about, let alone take. And in faith, you prayerfully ask that, with the aid of the Holy Spirit, the attitude of spiritual pride be terminated, destroyed, and mortified.

Suddenly you may realize you are not alone. Someone whom you previously followed from a great distance now waits for you, walks beside you, and quietly whispers, "Don't worry, I know the sacrifice of self hurts, but I've already taken care of this very issue. Don't be bothered, for it is written, 'we know that God causes all things to work together for good to those who love God' (Romans 8:28)."

This Someone continues. "Knowing this truth and your love of our Father God, I want you to consider the cross you are carrying as Mine, the same one on which I chose to be crucified long ago. Then we need to make an exchange. In fact, I have already accomplished My part of the swap by personally taking on all of your problems of self at Calvary. In your particular case, it will be a painful loss of your cherished feeling of spiritual superiority. I am aware that you might miss this part of your disposition, but in its place you will appropriate a part of My nature as a personal gift that will more than make up for your loss. You see, this is what I talked to My disciples about when I told them, 'Whoever wishes to save his life will lose it; but whoever loses his life for My sake will find it.'"

You are now sure it is Christ talking to your inner self. Without your asking, He tells you one more thing. "I know you were once somewhat confused about that word *appropriation*. But that is exactly what mortification of the self-life is about in the process of sanctification. For in your moment of need, in faith you are appropriating My humility. You should know that agape love, patience, joy, or any of My graces are also freely available for you. All of this is accomplished by exchanging your self-life for My life in you."

As previously stated, we use the plus sign [+] to denote the circumstance and actions that brought about the exchange between the believer and Christ. When the plus sign is expanded or magnified we can visualize the transformation in more detail (as shown in fig. 13.2).

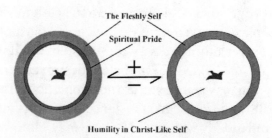

Figure 13.2. An Exchange Christ's Humility for a
Christian's Spiritual Pride

It should be apparent from this figure that the resultant trans-formed self shows a detachment of spiritual pride that existed in the former self. Because of the emergence of Christ's humility in the inner light area, this area of the self-circle is now enlarged with the inclusion of humility at the expense of the detached spiritual pride. From this visualization, we should gain a better understanding of personally expropriating spiritual pride and appropriating one of the character qualities of Jesus Christ's nature.

We are also better able to recognize that the plus sign signifies a spiritual engagement at the battle zone between the flesh and the godly core of self that is inhabited by the Holy Spirit and the Spirit of Christ. The plus sign indicates that the mortification of self has occurred during the co-crucifixion on the cross. With the constant presence of the Holy Spirit and the Spirit of Christ, (symbolized by the dove in the godly core) the battle is won by means of the mortification of self as tracked in figure 13.2. You should also realize that a significant part of the dynamic driving force in this matter is your active faith and the assurance of deliverance that includes an intimate connection with Christ's crucifixion and burial. Without this faith, assurance of deliverance, and identification with His Passion, the transformation may not have occurred or if it did, was reversed, as indicated by the minus sign.

That is not all of your understanding. As a more spiritually mature Christian, you should easily recall some of the scriptures that apply to this supernatural transformation of self. One such passage is the paradoxical rule of death preceding life. (See "Living by Dying" in chapter 11.) Jesus Himself provided this principle when He stated that life was derived from the death of a grain of wheat (John 12:24). Many have concluded that this precept was a reference to Christ's own death and resurrection, and likewise should be taken to mean that death is a mandatory requirement to bring about newness of life in His followers. It should be obvious by now that each of these transformations in Christians do not bring about a bodily death but a death of self.

Jesus spoke of His own death on several occasions, espe-cially near the time of the Passover. On the evening preceding the

183

crucifixion, He told His disciples that His body was to be given for them and bread was to be eaten "in remembrance of Me" (Luke 22:19). Out of this discourse came the practice of Christian sacraments—the Last Supper, Holy Communion, the Eucharist. Clearly, the object for which the Lord's Supper was instituted was to keep Him in remembrance. First Corinthians 11:26 tells us, "For as often as you eat this bread and drink the cup, you proclaim [announce] the Lord's death until He comes." So, regarding the issue of a past and a future event, it seems that a repeated remembrance and participation in Holy Communion becomes an ongoing, declared action on the part of the believer who looks back on Christ's life and death and looks forward to His second coming.

Many consider that Jesus' dialogue with fellow Jews about eating, drinking, and eternal life as recorded in John 6:47–57, helps believers to understand better our identification with Jesus Christ and the reception of His virtues. In the context of contrasting manna, the bread provided by God to the ancient Israelites, Jesus declares to His listeners, "I am the bread of life" (John 6:48). Then Jesus tells them that the living bread is His flesh (body) and relates it to what He is going to give "for the life of the world" (John 6:51). Clearly, this is a reference to His sacrificial death on the cross and the giving of Himself to provide living bread to others.

Jesus then said,

> Truly, truly I say to you, unless you eat the flesh of the Son of Man and drink His blood, you have no life in yourselves. He who eats My flesh and drinks My blood has eternal life, and I will raise him up on the last day. For My flesh is true food, and My blood is true drink. He who eats My flesh and drinks My blood abides in Me, and I in him. As the living Father sent Me, and I live because of the Father, so he who eats Me, he also will live because of Me.
>
> —John 6:53–57

We need to chew on these words and taste their flavor with our spiritual taste buds. What these statements of Jesus mean is that no one will have spiritual life unless the person eats and drinks from Jesus. He wants us to accept, receive, and as hard as it may seem for some people, even digest the essence and the significance of His death in order to receive a resurrected and eternal life.

I contend that believers should intimately and personally identify with Christ's death on the cross by the actions of eating of broken bread and drinking poured-out wine. Jesus may well mean that appropriation of these two essential nutrients in our spiritual diet that are completely necessary to create or promote new and eternal life. Moreover, in these acts of eating and drinking, Jesus says that we abide in Him and He abides (remains) in us (John 6:56). That is, although we are not necessarily consciously aware of it, there is a mutual indwelling of Christ in us. The simultaneous indwelling of two persons in each other is sometimes called a co-inherence or co-inhabitation.

Of all connections and unions, none is as thorough and complete as that which is affected by the digestion of life-giving nutrients. This statement should not be too hard to understand, for even young students are taught in science class that all living things, including plant life, need to take in substances from the environment in order to live. These students learn that what you eat is what you are. Although they are unaware of what is going on inside, these youngsters know that the food they eat is necessary to produce energy and growth; it becomes part of them and helps them to grow.

Jesus, maybe the first biochemist or nutritionist, also knew this fact. When Jesus gives His spirit to the believer for sanctification and spiritual growth, He abides or dwells in the believer. When this happens, His behavioral tendencies of humility and holiness are received and saturate the believer's true self, thereby influencing his whole inward and outward life. Jesus knew this because, spiritually speaking, those who dwell in Him are to remain in the belief of all His teachings.

Thus all believers participate in the benefits of Christ's death and are changed into the very substance of His nature. Christ's substance is His flesh and blood, which refers to His total being, His faultless, unselfish self. This true self lives in His followers, and they in Him; for they are made partakers of His divine nature. (See 2 Peter 1:4.)

185

Jesus knows this sharing of natures is similar to His relationship with the Father. He said He depends upon the living Father for His life and that He lives because of the Father, "so whoever continues to feed on Me [whoever takes Me for his food and is nourished by Me] shall [in his turn] live through and because of Me" (John 6:57 AB). This verse shows that eating blood and flesh is powerful metaphorical language for sharing in the life Jesus bestows on all true believers.

Christians carry out eating broken bread and drinking wine frequently when they commemorate the Lord's Supper and take to heart Jesus' words at the Passover: "Take, eat; this is My body... Drink of it, all of you; for this is My blood of the new covenant" (Matthew 26:26–28). Many Christians believe the ingestion of the elements commemorating the atonement of Christ is necessary to become more Christlike. However, Christians need not limit this to the celebration of the Lord's Supper (or Eucharist); Christians can partake of Jesus daily. In fact, in the Lord's Prayer we petition our Father in heaven to give us our daily bread. Even on a moment-by-moment basis, we need this divine provision as we are delivered from the power of sin and we grow in the likeness of Christ.

Still, that's not the end of the story. As a faithful follower of your Lord, you may have had an undeniable sensation of *joyfulness* in the resurrection aspect of this transformation. All of this would tend to make some people think salvation, particularly sanctification, is only individualistic. That is to say, to experience the joyfulness of a resurrection life is a way of discarding the world to its misery and taking refuge in a private form of eternal salvation. Yet let's not forget that salvation is also communal. It is not just a private matter, but you become an example of a godly person to others.

We should also note that the joyfulness or pleasure did not come from being more spiritual, holy, Christlike, or even more humble compared to someone else. That would be maturing in the wrong direction (signified by a minus sign annotated in graph 12.1 and fig. 13.2), the very thing you possessed and manifested before as a component of self-life. Instead, your joy was based upon a co-resurrection with Christ as well as your obedience to deny self and not your Savior. God was pleased with your acts of self-denial, as well as your readiness to take up a cross and follow His Son.

By following Christ in His Passion in this manner, you became a new person with more of the likeness of Christ than you had before. But did the transformation of becoming a new person lead to an end or purpose in itself? Yes, in part. A better answer is derived from knowing that different purposes are accomplished in transformations. A renovation of character, such as used in this example, should be viewed as an effective goal and is not to be confused with the ultimate destiny God has for you and me. An effective purpose is likely understood where the apostle Peter says, a believer is chosen and is holy, to be part of "a people for God's own possession, so that you may proclaim the excellencies of Him who has called you out of darkness into His marvelous light" (1 Peter 2:9). Thus this outstanding quality of humility is not a onetime proclamation. It is not something you can keep in store for yourself, but really is God's will, a method and purpose of revealing Himself, or, glorifying His virtues through you. These excellencies are perfections of the wisdom, justice, truth, and goodness of God, exhibited in living a holy and useful life, being transformed into the image of God, and walking as Christ Himself walked. Thus we are to conclude that these transformations really glorify the Lord and also achieve a purpose of preparing us for an eternity with the Lord.

BREAKING NEWS AND DEVELOPING STORY

From an audio recording, Dr. Selford narrates his latest analysis using a graph of the measured subunits of the S-Factor. "Even though amounts of subunits in the S-Factor differed in a few samples, we expected that when we calculated percentages of subunits a and b from all of the data obtained from all subjects, they would be nearly equal. But as shown in the graph, this was not the case."

187

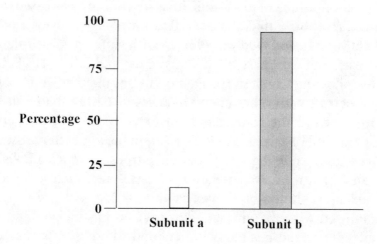

Figure 13.3. Mean Percentages of Subunit Amounts in the S-Factor

"These results show that average amounts of *subunit a* obtained from the entire population of nearly one thousand subjects is 13.5 percent, which is significantly lower than 86.5 percent of *subunit b*. As yet we have not identified the functions of either subunit within the subjects, but we suspect that each of the subunits might be related to some behavioral aspects of the people studied. If it turns out that the behavioral traits are distinctly different from one another, we would anticipate that the number of people having *subunit a* would be significantly less than those having *subunit b*."

Chapter 14

... Envision a Fulfilling Life?

Troubles

GENERALLY SPEAKING, TROUBLES are regarded as conditions of distress or danger primarily caused by worry or anxiety. Responses to troubles vary widely, from people unleashing hatred, bitterness, anger, resentment, and murmuring to less severe reactions from those who merely accept difficulties and try to work their way through these episodes. All troubles are considered to be real, and if troubles are not easily solved they may be more than a person can cope with. Common approaches to solve them include obtaining assistance from friends and family members or from professional sources such as psychotherapy or spiritual guidance.

I readily admit that this short portrayal of troubles and their resolution only begins to touch the surface of these widespread experiences. However, there is a common denominator that we should attach to most troubling situations: suffering. Pain and hurting are usually integral parts of all life's difficulties. Suffering has many faces, whether physical, mental, or emotional. Apart from a purely biological understanding of pain, there is a divine mystery in suffering that has never been universally understood by human reason alone.

Mature Christians, on the other hand, have a divergent understanding of life's painful difficulties. Believers learn that there is a deeper meaning to troubles and the divine intentions they serve. For example, they discover that a major purpose of troubles is to test one's faith and promote endurance (1 Peter 5:1–7; James 1:2–4). These passages and several others portray troubles as an intermingling blend of trials, tribulations, and temptations, all of which have underlying meanings and functions.

Having such an approach, followers of Christ are better prepared to anticipate each troubling situation as a means of maturing spiritually by a transformation of self-life to a Christlike life. They also come to know the enigma of suffering, for a devoted follower of Christ can experience an inward calmness largely because of his or her faithful identification with the Passion of the Son of God.

Below is the model of Mortification of Self-Life introduced in chapter 13.

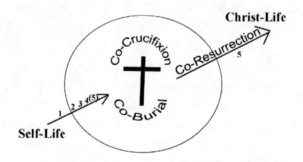

Figure 14.1. The Mortification of Self-Life

I will describe a specific trouble and its resolution as it may have occurred in the imaginary tale of one of the department store customers, person A. Relating his experiences to his equivalent, believer A, includes the same five considerations used previously.

LOSTNESS

If you remember, lostness did not begin in the department store, but in the underlying sensations of each of the would-be shoppers as they sensed something was not right in their lives, having thoughts of incompleteness and a yearning desire somehow to correct their uneasiness, discomfort, and frustration. The combination of these feelings, together with an admiration of an item in the possession of other acquaintances and reading an advertisement of that same item, became the overall motivation that eventually led them to the department store.

Initially, our focus is on the believer, person A. In graph 12.1, we see that he received salvation at the symbol of the cross. He later experienced a keen awareness of his ungodly dispositions as represented by an exclamation mark (!). Thereafter, in conjunction with each cycle of mortification of his self-life (symbolized by a plus sign), there was a significant increase of spiritual maturity during person A's life.

Shopper A's admission of lostness (to the clerk) is of major importance. Regarding believers of the Christian faith, such a declaration could well represent an act of deeper repentance rather than an expression of fear of the consequences of sin before salvation. At this time the declaration was based on the realization of his sinful nature, which is in stark contrast to the infinite holiness of a sovereign and creative God.

To get a better idea of the specific trouble that led shopper A toward the department store and then to the crisis of realizing his lostness, let's hear how believer A might have expressed some of his thoughts concerning his painful frustrations: "Everyone is better than I am and does things better than I do; if I could only look better; if I could only find someone who appreciates me as I am; if I could only cure my hurting and find true happiness." The repeated use of the word, *I* gives us a clue as to the nature of the problem. It is an "I, myself, and me" issue. Following our convention of designating the aspects of self, it is a self problem.

This self disorder is a universal grievance that is unhealthy spiritually, physically, mentally, and emotionally, not only for person A, but for all of us. It is widely known to be a relational disorder in which individuals encounter difficulties with their self-images and with relating to others as well as to God. Before we can be guided toward a resolution of this problem, we must identify the disorder.

Specifically, person A's predicament is *rejection*. To some degree, we all can identify with it from our own personal experiences and honestly admit we are in a potential state of lostness when we sense the spirit of rejection in our lives. As we continue to spotlight believer A, let us discuss the guidance toward overcoming rejection as it particularly relates to all Christians.

GUIDANCE

Christian believers have the privilege of possessing God's manual, the Holy Bible, and the indwelling Spirit of God, both of which are available to grant assistance by leading us toward a clearer understanding of troubling situations and even rejection. On the surface, it may seem easy to understand and manage rejection. But in fact, it may be one of the most difficult tasks, mainly because of our innate stubbornness and our doubts about spiritual therapy that may contrast to the usual reliance on psychotherapy.

Either from a mental illness or a spiritual standpoint, we need to make it clear that rejection or fear of rejection of any severity is not a disorder that is as easily treated as a minor infection. Moreover, rejection is exceedingly complex; there is a wide range of actual and perceived causes, signs, and symptoms. Rejection can be sporadic and short lived, or it can be almost constant and last for many years. The severity of rejection can range from relatively mild patterns to flagrant manifestations of rebellion or aggression, sometimes leading to felonies and suicides. I will address only those less violent or problematical forms of rejection which, according to several biblical authorities, within and outside of our opposing fleshly nature, can and will significantly interfere with developing God-like characteristics.

In his book *Rejection: Biblical Truth Simply Explained*, Steve Hepden identifies two groups of rejection. One group is Self-Rejection, which abides in those who refuse to admit they are renouncing their own being. This pathological form of self-denial creates self-destructive thoughts of a negative image, worthlessness, inferiority, self-accusation, and self-condemnation. The second group is Self-Protection, which is usually the result of painful denunciations from others. Almost always and especially with children, this category creates defensive barriers in relationships. The manifestations of Self-Protection group include self-centeredness, self-justification, self-righteousness, self-pity, and self-deception.

At this point, I pose three questions concerning expressions of rejection:

1. Do you recognize any of these characteristics of rejection in others or yourself?
2. Do you believe some people have fashioned defense mechanisms, although they may be less recognizable at times, as masks that become major obstacles to resolution?
3. Do you think some people who experience rejection wish to continue to wear masks and lead an illusionary life of happiness with little or no substance or meaning?

The honesty of your answers is immensely more important than just a reply of yes or no. So, let us move forward to assess the merits of overcoming this debilitating condition before we consider how rejection can be dealt with in a believer's life.

APPRAISAL

First and foremost, in our appraisal we must discern between seeking God's answer to this life-destroying ailment, maintaining an attitude of indifference, or choosing to seek relief on our own. God's answer will be twofold; first it will provide the spiritual medicine to deliver us from rejection and secondly, it will offer His unconditional divine love to meet our built-in need for recognition. God's solution to this problem of rejection enables us to have peace with God, others, and obviously ourselves.

However, we should not think this first appraisal will be quick and easy. For there is an ongoing battle taking place, and, as in any warfare, there are always risks of harm, pain, and even death. On the battlefield in the core of self are two opposing forces seeking dominance, **self**, the fallen state of the old man and *self*, the godly nature of the new man.

We should be aware of any assessment of life that does not recognize our old man, namely our undisciplined, depraved human nature. Oswald Chambers wrote, "If you refuse to agree with the fact that there is wickedness and selfishness, something downright hateful and wrong in human beings, when it attacks your life, instead of reconciling yourself to it, you will compromise with it and say that it is of no use to battle against it" (1963, meditation for June 24). We should not think the old man is dead. He is very much alive, and his arsenal of weapons includes the planting of deceptive thoughts in our minds.

If we could only record some of these anti-Christ ideas in the old man, they might be saying, "just follow your conscience," "just use common sense," or "just buy and read a self-help book on building self-confidence and self-esteem and everything will work out," or "you can't trust a God who allows His own Son to die." So, armed with the knowledge of deceptiveness in the old man and the awareness of conflicting natures within ourselves, we can then continue to assess this problem of rejection.

For some of us, it is helpful to be reminded about the origin of rejection. The curse of rejection was initiated following the disobedience and denial of God by Adam and Eve. It is clear that this curse from the very first family is hereditary, passing down the affliction through the generations. As we have repeatedly stated, God's plan to lift this curse is wholly and completely centered on the atoning work Jesus Christ. Having experienced and endured a life of rejection from His contemporaries and finally from His Father God, Christ voluntarily took on all of humankind's rejections as well as their consequences.

RESOLUTION

As noted above in figure 14.1, we can visualize how a trouble, such as rejection, can be resolved in the transformation of a self-life to a Christlike life. This overall alteration (signified by a 4 in this figure) is based entirely upon our identification with Jesus' death, burial, and resurrection.

In a more specific manner, we can view this miraculous transformation as one of the plus signs shown in the spiritual growth of person A. (See fig. 12.1.) As you recall, the plus sign represents an instance in one's life in which self is mortified. If this occasion is magnified, it will reveal the resolution of the troubling situation. Graphically, the triumph of rejection is illustrated below in figure 14.2.

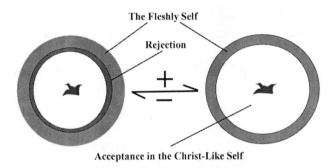

Figure 14.2. The Transformation of Rejection to Acceptance

The figure shows that the rejection in the self-life is replaced with acceptance in the Christlike life. Why did rejection disappear and where did it go? Christ willingly took our rejection, whether actual or perceived, on the cross of Calvary. By faith, on our part of this divine act, we now receive the healing power of loving acceptance.

The redeeming act of Christ can be viewed as a part of the Great Exchange between Him and rejected humankind. Jesus suffered for all our rejection by completely sacrificing His status as God's Son so that we as believers might find and maintain eternal standing as God's sons and daughters. This liberating achievement by Jesus Christ ended the curse on us and allowed our irrevocable adoption into God's family. This should also end any conflict we have within us when we finally decide to follow God's method to resolve the issue of rejection. In a word, God's answer to this barrier between

Him and His children is divine acceptance, a radical acceptance that is sometimes very difficult to understand.

We find this thought more clearly expressed in Paul's letter to the Ephesians, where he wrote, "In love He [God] predestined us to adoption as sons through Jesus Christ to Himself…to the praise of the glory of His of His grace, which He freely bestowed on us in the Beloved [Christ]" (Ephesians 1:4–6). The New King James Version's translation of this passage ends with "by which He [God] has made us *accepted* in the Beloved" (emphasis added). This and many other scriptures relating to acceptance make it abundantly clear that we are not irreversibly rejected, but unconditionally received as loved children into the family of God, with the identical love God has for His only begotten Son.

To help truly value the depths of God's mercy as it relates to bondage from the force of rejection, we are obligated to look even deeper into the meaning of acceptance, the divine cure for rejection. For Christians, acceptance must mean a willingness to take this gift of grace by faith and cheerfully and wholeheartedly believe it is true. Such an agreement calls us to open ourselves to God's freely given love and believe God will never forsake or reject us: "I [God] will never desert you, nor will I ever forsake you" (Hebrews 13:5).

This acceptance becomes a reality as a productive action of love when we encounter anxieties in our lives. In the Sermon on the Mount, Jesus tells us five times not to be anxious (Matthew 6:25–34). Rather, "Seek first His [God's] kingdom and His righteousness, and all these things [all those things about your life that make you unnecessarily anxious] will be added [given] to you" (Matthew 6:33). This verse is not necessarily about gaining things. According to several biblical commentators, the central meaning focuses on the priority of seeking God's righteousness, which is profoundly important in times of troubles for believers.

We must also understand something else about God's acceptance. It is not a one-time authorized gift as justification is. In our sanctification, God's acceptance is an active, recurring principle in our enduring relationship with Jesus Christ. This ceaseless acceptance on God's part allows Him to be intensely involved in our lives for our spiritual growth. Additionally, the Bible tells us to "accept one another, just as Christ also accepted us" (Romans 15:7). From this verse, we readily see God's acceptance of us clearly endorses and promotes our voluntary acceptance of others.

We have come far enough to see that acceptance is a creative action and a process of love. Here we look again at the experience of acceptance that not only persuades us, but empowers us to live by faith. We are empowered to live by faith by the deliverance from the power of the self when we are relieved of the false pride, pretenses, and defensive shells that keep us from living in freedom. Perhaps more importantly, our faith in God's acceptance releases the power to transform self because it gives an assurance of a meaningful life no matter what evil or tragedy we face. The knowledge that we will not be rejected sustains our willingness to forgive others.

As we experience God's forgiveness of our transgressions, we can also experience His acceptance. Where does this profound belief lead? We discover that acceptance, most notably in troubling circumstances such as rejection, plays a vital role in the restoration and re-creation of God's children. So we must also combine our acceptance of God with His forgiveness. Both have empowering features. Forgiveness is the offer to stand by and to love no matter what.

To be forgiven, to experience divine acceptance, is always to venture into a new order of life. The newness of true life begins strangely and wonderfully when we discover God bearing with us in our present life of fear and distrust. It is also of major value to have absolutely no animosity or retaliation toward the one(s) who may have rejected us. For if we cannot truly forgive, which is absolutely essential in the deliverance from rejection, we remain embittered toward anyone who has offended us.

Our acceptance comes from the discovery that God stands by us in spite of our rebellious natures and estrangement from Him. He remains with us in all our needs, at a cost He has already paid on our behalf. This is commonly known as God's grace and is at the heart of New Testament teaching. Surely, this grace is directly related to our experience of acceptance. We know that nothing in our brokenness destroys the possibility of being understood by God and even by others who compassionately care for our well-being.

We now come to the point where rejection approximates all other troubles, those mixtures of trials, temptations, and tribulations that befall all of us, especially followers of Christ. In his letter to the Romans (8:19–23), the apostle Paul was acutely aware of the futility of living in a world of troubles, discord, greed, fear, and distrust. In this ungodly environment he used the words *groaning* or *moaning* to describe the response of all creation to these conditions and the longing for liberation: "We know that the whole creation groans and suffers...even we ourselves groan within ourselves" (Romans 8:22–23).

From Paul's description of this dilemma, we must readily admit that rejection and all troubles in this world produce groaning. I take this statement to mean that inwardly, everyone and everything are intrinsic recipients of troubles. This also implies that all humanity is universally susceptible to and capable of sinning: "For all have sinned and fall short of the glory of God" (Romans 3:23). For the receiver of the troubling situation neither to groan nor to long for its resolution would be irrational and illogical. Anticipating resolution of troubles, however, should be normal and reasonable for a spiritually maturing Christian.

In addition, there is an outward or external component that has the potential of bringing about trouble. It could be a person, a social setting, or any aspect of a natural imperfect world that becomes the stimulus for causing trouble for an individual. Regarding these outward features, the question becomes: How do feelings of rejection relate to and deal with all of these external elements?

Without making any judgments about the external causative agent as to rightness or wrongness, the question can be answered by everyone who is even remotely cognizant of his own inner conflicting human nature and his own sensitivity. It is *how we respond to rejection* as well as to other troubling circumstances in our lives that become a significant indicator of living self- or Christlike lives.

As we react to an offending agent that causes a sense of rejection, the common answer would be "It's only natural that I became bitter, resentful, wanting to retaliate and get even." A good example of this type of self-like life is when we are misunderstood or judged unkindly. Nothing tests the character of Christians more than having something evil said about us. How we respond to this and other trials exposes whether our roots are in the core of our fleshly natures or in the solid depths of our godly *selves*.

Another frequent response to rejection is "My feelings were hurt." That exemplifies the very point; we often respond to the inward pain by retaliating and allowing our fleshly selves to become more dominant, thus manifesting the spirit and deeds of the flesh.

It has been said that hurting people hurt others. If not checked, our instinctive responses could further result in rejection of others. Responses derived from a worldly mind-set will almost always lead to manifestations of hostility, jealousy, anger, disputes, dissentions, and envy, each of which are specifically referred to as "deeds of the flesh." (See Galatians 5:19–20.)

Regarding our part in a developing relationship with Jesus Christ, we should willingly relinquish all of our self-dependent attitudes and totally rely on His help. We are to deny self by denying our rights to ourselves. That is, we must exercise our right to waive our individual rights, and this relinquishment of our old self requires us to perform counterintuitive acts of unselfishness that reflect Jesus' life in us. We will go a long way in resolving rejection by voluntarily waiving any legal and rightful claim to ourselves. Combining self-surrender with the sacrifice of our egotistical and selfish natures by means of the cross will help destroy the very roots of rejection.

Those who are more prone to be led by misguided human nature seem to need to know "Why is this happening to me?" To answer this question from only a worldly viewpoint adds complexity to the difficulties of life. As Christians, we must evaluate troubles biblically. When compared to dealing with the hindering effect of our fallen human natures, as in the case of deliverance from the power of sin and of **self**, people face an increased difficulty with many troubles. Not only are troubles more vexing, but there seems to be a sacrificial aspect for the believer during troubling circumstances, a giving of oneself, not only for the sake of Christ by obeying His commands, but also for the sake of others.

SELF-DENIAL AND CROSS-CARRYING

As we consider the role self-denial may play in troubling situations, we must respond with faith, an overcoming faith that grows and grows as we increasingly mature in the spiritual realm. It is based upon a trust in God, one of total surrender to Him through the denial of self. As we begin to better understand Jesus' directives in Matthew 16:24, we see self-denial is based upon the cross we carry daily in order to direct our minds and attention backward to the reconciling work of Christ. As we shall soon see, obedience to these two commandments of Jesus is based upon the joyous anticipation that for all who love God "all things…work together for good" (Romans 8:28).

As we choose to deal with troubling situations and take into account Christ's many predictions of tribulations for His followers, another perspective becomes vitality important. This is the path Jesus chose to take during His earthly life, and especially the path He took to Calvary. It has been wisely said that Christians live in the shadows of troubles much the same way Jesus Christ lived in the shadow of the cross.

Disturbing as it may seem, *choosing* the path Christ took on our behalf is the prudent and wise choice for Christians to make. His was the straight and narrow way, in which avoidance was not a viable option, and might have prevented His destiny. Christ's decisions demanded complete self-denial and a willingness to take up the cross (Philippians 2:5–8). His path was a path of self-sacrifice, self-giving, and humility.

Any anxiety or worry associated with our feelings of rejection or any other trouble we experience should immediately remind us of the suffering and death of Jesus, who identified Himself with all human problems. That is to say, many troubles may well serve as a jump start to guide us directly into the cross-carrying mode, which may bypass any need to engage points one through three shown at the beginning of this chapter in figure 14.1. More specifically, I believe that, in general, troubles are the major means God uses for us to flashback and associate ourselves with the one-time unselfish act of Jesus on the cross.

In practical terms, trouble is the human expression of God's own sufferings for the believer. It is a revelation of God's will to stand by us. Any unwillingness on our part to accept God's acceptance, love, comfort, and peace in the midst of stormy trials, in concert with an unwillingness to carry our crosses, underscores every hindrance of spiritual growth.

Regarding the issue of undergoing discomfort in troubles, the real question is not *whether* we will suffer, but how we will react to suffering when it comes. We can see it as a miserable experience to be endured, or we can offer it to God for His redemptive purposes. This is the great truth Christians should all know: God will always use that for which we suffer to further His kingdom on earth. Suffering has rightly been called a required course in the school of faith. It is only through difficulties and setbacks that we are brought toward the end of self and forced to trust God alone.

What can be spiritually sacrificed in us is similar to that which was sacrificed in Jesus, and that includes repudiation of self and those human tendencies of survival that cry out and scream, "I do not want to die, I want to live!" These words remind us of what the apostle Paul said about dying and living. In the context of his opposition to legalistic obedience as a means of winning God's acceptance, Paul defended God's plan of salvation, which is available only through the love of God and Christ's death and resurrection.

In Galatians 2:20, the apostle said, "*I have been crucified with Christ; and it is no longer I who live*" (emphasis added). In this somewhat puzzling statement, the two "I's" of Paul could well have been the crucifixion of the self-I, the old self, his natural humanity with all its egotistical inclinations, everything that was contrary to his true self. He faithfully reckoned his old self to be crucified with Christ. That part of his self, the old Adamic nature or the old man, was mortified or separated from the reigning power of the old sinful life. In doing so, he chose to act on his decision to be totally identified with Christ's crucifixion.

Pope Benedict XVI addresses the topics of love and suffering, parenthetic to Paul's usage of the word *I*. He declares, "In the end, even a 'yes' to love is a source of suffering, because love always requires expropriation [the releasing or detachment] of my 'I,' which I allow myself to be pruned and wounded. Love simply cannot exist without this painful renunciation [self-denial] of myself [**self**], for otherwise it becomes pure selfishness and thereby ceases to be love" (2007, 81). I do not know, but perhaps the pope's wording of *expropriation of my 'I'* likewise refers to Paul's I's in the Galatians passage noted above. Nonetheless, these words of the pope clearly underscore his wisdom regarding the fallen aspect of human nature, the importance to deny oneself, and to emphasize suffering in connection with unselfish love.

Again referring to Paul's statement in Galatians 2:20, "I have been crucified with Christ; and it is no longer I who live, *but Christ lives in me*" (emphasis added). The living of Christ in Paul can easily be interpreted to be the true, authentic self of Christ. This being the case, Paul's *self* is then in combination with the true *self* of Jesus Christ! (This spiritual union can be viewed as the white inner portions of self-circles of believers used throughout this book). The true believer can describe his or her intimate relationship with Christ as Paul states in the remaining portion of Galatians 2:20: "...and the life in which I live in the flesh [referring to his human existence or to his body] I live by faith in the Son of God, who loved me, and gave Himself up for me."

Regarding this duality of the two natures in Paul and in ourselves, the self-I and the Christlike *self*, believers also must choose between two paths to walk. One is the wide path to endorse and promote immediate well-being and safety (the path of selfishness), and the other is the narrow path to accept goodness, truth, and justice (the path of love). When we choose the narrow path, the harmonious union between and among the Spirit of Christ, the indwelling Holy Spirit, and the holiness of our spiritual self also permits believers to look beyond the troubling circumstances of life and anticipate living a resurrected eternal life, both in the present and in a future glorified state.

During times of distress and tension, then for Paul and now for us, how important is this anticipation of a resurrected life? Could it be significant, coming on the heels of a flashback, to the historical co-crucifixion and co-burial with Jesus Christ? We'll explore the answer in the following pages.

JOYFULNESS

Any thought of joyfulness in association with troubles would likely be repulsive to those who have only a temporal perspective on life. These individuals naturally link joy with such things as comfort, pleasure, social status, and financial success. Their reality is entrenched in the natural seen world, where characteristics of troubles are anxiety, turmoil, worry, strife, and so forth.

As Christians, however, our reality *also* exists in the supernatural realm since we have an everlasting viewpoint in our loving relationship with God and Jesus Christ. In this spiritual relationship, we need to associate ourselves in every way we possibly can with Christ, including adopting His view of joy during the most troubling time of His earthly life.

The writer of Hebrews states that Christians solidly need to identify with Christ, who possessed staying power on the cross: "let us run...the race that is set before us, fixing our eyes on Jesus,...who for the joy set before Him endured the cross" (Hebrews 12:1–2). In these inspired words of Scripture we find Jesus paradoxically associated joy with suffering.

Many have wondered who and what supported the Son of Man's humanity during the unparalleled sufferings of His Passion that led to a joyous outcome. The Holy Spirit, which we also possess, helped to sustain Jesus during all of His earthly rejections and sufferings. Undoubtedly, the same Holy Spirit will play a major role to help us tolerate sufferings as He did with Jesus.

In addition to the Spirit's assistance, Jesus may have had other things in view that would yield joyfulness—doing God's will and knowing His purpose in making peace between God and humankind, thereby opening the way of salvation to the world. Would any of these viewpoints include the possibility of knowing that death would not be the finality of His life? Could Jesus anticipate life after death as a reward for doing His Father's will? We find answers to these two questions in numerous New Testament scriptures that clearly state Christ's death resulted in His resurrection!

The resurrection of Christ demonstrated that the Father accepted His death for our ransom, sealed His acceptance of us, and guaranteed our resurrection: "He who raised the Lord Jesus will raise us also with Jesus" (2 Corinthians 4:14). Jesus Christ was victorious over death and the grave and thereby gave us assurance of our own resurrection.

We again pose the question mentioned above. How important was Christ's and Paul's anticipation of a resurrection life after death? Along with an expectation of eternal life and joy, and for Paul, the prospect of heavenly rewards, the anticipation of future resurrection was far more than an optimistic outlook, imagination, desire, wish, or inclination. While they patiently persevered through trying circumstances, the enduring faith of a coming resurrection may have been perceived as a present reality for the apostles and early Christians as much as it did for Christ.

To explore this possibility of uniting the future with the present, let us examine some interesting thoughts on anticipation. A clear recall of a past event is described as a flashback, a common experience with many people. Conversely, an expectation of a future act is commonly understood as flash-forward, technically known as prolepsis. This word, derived from a Greek word meaning to take beforehand, is identified as the representation or assumption of a future act or development as if it presently exists or is already accomplished. *The Westminster Dictionary of Theological Terms* says the resurrection of Jesus Christ is proleptic and may be seen as anticipating the consummation and future resurrection of humans.

To add creditability to the expectation of future acts, I cite three biblical passages. Written in the present tense in his letter to the Ephesian Christians, Paul says God "made [them] alive together with Christ...and are raised [them] up with Him, and seated [them] with Him in the heavenly places" (Ephesians 2:5–6). So, in virtue of their close connection with Christ, believers anticipate glory as if they already reside in heaven.

In the gospel of John we read of the troubling situation of Lazarus' death; yet Jesus' thanksgiving for raising him from the dead *preceded* the miracle. "Jesus raised His eyes, and said, 'Father, I thank You that You have heard Me'...When He had said these things, He cried out with a loud voice, 'Lazarus, come forth'" (John 11:41, 43). In an expression of assurance and with anticipation of its certainty, Jesus' gratitude sprang forth *before* the blessing had arrived.

The last reference is again found in the words of Jesus Christ. In the lengthy farewell discourse to His disciples that preceded His trial, crucifixion, burial, and resurrection, Jesus concluded His conversation this way: "These things I have spoken to you, so that in Me you may have peace. In the world you have tribulation, but take courage; I have overcome the world" (John 16:33). The phrase "I have overcome the world" refers to an accomplished task that had not yet totally transpired. Here, we understand that Jesus spoke prophetically about the certainty of life after death. We can follow Christ in the same manner, gaining deliverance in times of tribulation.

This pattern of anticipating the reality of a promised future event is both proleptic and prophetic. So says French theologian and philosopher Jacques Ellul. He notes that a true prophet "already 'lives' the future" (Ringma 2002, meditation for March 18). In living the future, the futurist proclaims in word that which is yet to come. He also demonstrates the newness of future events by the reality of his present actions and deeds.

The thoughts and actions of those who anticipate the reality of Christ's resurrection in the newness of their lives can be of practical value. In the anxiety of troubling times, the future of a resurrection existence is thus made present as a sign of hope and a promise of better things to come. Instead of focusing on the painful trepidations of a current troubling crisis, we are first to direct our attention to the righteousness of Christ and give God praise in anticipation of calming a stressful predicament.

Christians are not thought of as Christ. But we are to fix our eyes on Christ, run the race, and anticipate the joy that is set before us. We are not necessarily prophets, but we can act like those of whom Ellul spoke, and "already live" the future in the present.

Not only do we see a scriptural basis for prolepsis and prophecy, but personal experience plays a role as well. Most of us, at one time or another, while we have experienced distressing or unfavorable circumstances, have projected ourselves to a future place and time when conditions will be greatly improved. To a degree, perhaps due to our faith or spiritual maturity, this form of anticipation becomes a powerful means to endure patiently through troubles small or large. We can view these phenomena as acts of grace that are accessible for the believer both while mortifying his fleshly dispositions and while experiencing troubling situations.

I conclude that the mental attitudes of prolepsis in faithful believers, while unquestionably much different in nature and less in magnitude than Christ's Passion, serve to minimize or allay troubling situations. To emphasize the potential of anticipating resurrection during our troubling situations, I call your attention to the fifth point, which is deliberately placed in front of as well as after the cross in figure 14.1. This feature signifies the joy associated with displacing adverse aspects of the old self-life and taking on elements of a Christlike life. At the same time, we cannot deny that life is lived in the present. Yet, when the alarm is sounded in times of trial, temptation, and trouble, believers can flash back to the events of Christ's Passion (point four) and simultaneously flash forward to an episode of their own joyous resurrection (point five).

Such a concept should not be viewed as a fabricated form of escapism from the present, but as acts of faith on the truth of God's word. For the maturing Christian, this enraptured vision of the reality of Christ's Passion gives credibility to the wise saying, "A flashback pulls the past into the present, and a flash-forward draws the future into the present."

Joyfulness must be one of the greatest aspects of becoming more Christlike and experiencing the resurrection life for the believer as troubles disappear and are eliminated. Yet, we all know that some recur or appear not to end. What can we say about these apparent inconsistencies? Responses vary, but one of the best answers is that we will never know this side of heaven. In our mortality and humanity, we cannot always expect to know answers to questions posed in times of troubles. Rather than questioning, our responses should be those of God-dependence by obeying Christ's commands to deny self, take up our crosses, and follow Him. Based upon God's promises, obeying His commands will lead to life of acceptance, discovery, wonderment, and deliverance. It will be anticipatory, Eucharist-like, winsome, sacrificial, and victorious.

In addition to the joys of this new life, most interpretative biblical scholars maintain that most if not all troubles are divinely ordained in the sense that they are meant to deliver Christians *in* troubles, not *from* them. Expressed in similar ways, God does not give us an overcoming life; instead He gives us eternal life as we overcome troubles. We learn through afflictions and rarely through a series of happy circumstances. Through troubles our Father brings us to a greater awareness of our dependence on Him; therefore, we have the potential to learn more about ourselves and about God through the storms of afflictions.

As a part of this learning and maturing in the spiritual realm, we should look at our trials as opportunities instead of obstacles. If only we could recognize every difficult situation as something in which God proves His love to us, each blockage would then become a place of shelter and rest, and a demonstration to others of His inexpressible power residing in us.

In regard to experiencing the joyfulness of a resurrection-like and Christlike life, we should be clear about understanding three major purposes of troubles. These purposes are found in the Gospel of Mark and in the letter to the Romans. First, there is a definite moral purpose because troubles refine our spirituality in terms of our holiness; second, there is a joyous aspect of our resurrection life; and third, proven character results.

Refinement of Spiritual Maturity

Until times get hard, we do not know whether we are maturing spiritually or if we are fair-weather Christians—the kind Jesus described in the parable of planting seeds in soils in which some "have no firm root in themselves,...when affliction or persecution arises...immediately they fall away" (Mark 4:16–17). But the ones in good soil "bear fruit" (Mark 4:20). We Christians need to examine ourselves and to determine whether during troubling times our roots are in rocky soil, thus causing us to fall away from opportunities to grow spiritually. Conversely, if our roots are in good soil we can envision troubles as opportunities to grow spiritually, and in the process, we exhibit the fruit of the Spirit.

Production of Joy

The second major purpose of troubles is that they result in a joyous response. Paul made this point very clear when he wrote to early Christians in Rome who were experiencing various tribulations: "And not only this, but *we also exult in our tribulations*, knowing that tribulation brings about perseverance" (Romans 5:3, emphasis added). To better understand the joyous aspect of tribulations, we should learn that *to exult* means much more than to experience joy or happiness. We describe a person exulting in high spirits figuratively, as one leaping for joy and exceedingly rejoicing in triumph. It is easy to picture an athlete exulting in a victory over an opponent. Is it too hard to visualize a person who is going through a tribulation in exultation?

Proven Character

Now we need to look at the demonstrated character effect of tribulations: "Perseverance [brings about]...*proven character*; and proven character, hope" (Romans 5:4, emphasis added). Literally, the Greek term for proven character, *dokimen*, means "the experience of being tested and approved." When tribulations come, we persevere in devotion to Christ and do not deny Him; we then come out of that experience with a stronger sense that we are not hypocrites, but we are real and proven. Someone has wisely said that the tree of Christlikeness was bent and it didn't break. Our fidelity and loyalty were put to the test and they passed. Now we have an enhanced, proven character. The gold of our faith was put in the fire and it came out refined, not consumed. This tested and more Christlike character gives us the great anticipation of a joyous resurrection, both in the present and in the future.

BREAKING NEWS AND DEVELOPING STORY

Anchor: "Now, more on the S-Factor. Interest has shifted to the newest researchers to join Drs. Sinton and Selford. My colleague Andrew Jones recently interviewed Drs. Cibalo and Carataker."

Jones: "I had the great pleasure of meeting with these two scientists and hearing their thoughts about the ongoing research of the S-Factor. They told me that first of all, scientists should never introduce any of their own bias into their work. This view is especially important when dealing with less tangible measurements of behavior than with physical properties.

"If and when they begin to conduct their own research, they both plan to use the most modern methodology possible and to statistically analyze the data to find any significance in their results. Therefore, they both resisted making any predeterminations about the study."

Anchor: "Join us tomorrow when we'll bring you more on Andrew's meeting with Drs. Cibalo and Carataker."

Chapter 15

... Envision a Fulfilling Life?

The False Self

IT MUST BE clear by now that one of the major goals of a Christian is to develop Christlikeness. We accomplish this by eradicating or detaching those inner dispositions of ourselves that are counter to the image of God. So far, we have identified these dispositions by many terms that collectively constitute one's ungodly nature. It seems reasonable that the more believers know about this nature that is in conflict with God, the more successful we will be in of replacing this opposing nature with Christlikeness.

While most of Christian orthodoxy chooses the Holy Writ as the ultimate source of all spiritual wisdom, many Christian authorities believe significant knowledge can be derived from those in the behavioral sciences, such as psychology and sociology. For example, one of the more modern theories of human behavior is that individuals function largely by their particular mind-sets, which are fixed mental attitudes or dispositions that predetermine a person's responses to and interpretations of situations. A mind-set also refers to an embedded set of assumptions that is so established that it often resists changes and adaptations held by others.

A leading expert in personality psychology and the author of *The New Psychology of Success*, Carol Dweck, has come to believe that our mind-set is not a minor personality quirk; it creates our whole mental world. She maintains that everyone has one of two basic mind-sets, a fixed or a growth mind-set, ultimately predicting whether one will not or will fulfill his potential.

Not noted for his expertise in psychology, there was another person who also understood mind-sets and clearly contrasted two different types. The apostle Paul wrote, "Those who are according to the flesh set their minds on the things of the flesh, but those who are according to the spirit, the things of the Spirit. For the mind set on the flesh is death, but the mind set on the Spirit is life and peace" (Romans 8:5–6). Paul also may have understood the difference between fixed and growth mind-sets; he certainly could distinguish between the mind-set of a life dominated by the flesh, the sinful inner nature, and one controlled by the Holy Spirit.

I believe Paul's meaning of the "flesh" coincides to a large extent with the "false self." In contrast and in the context of Paul's statement, a person controlled by the Holy Spirit is comparable to the true self of that individual. In this chapter we will dig deeper into the practical meanings of the false self. We shall see that the false self has its own agenda that is largely independent and counter to God's plan for our lives. We will begin by taking a careful look at one's self-image as it relates to the believer's identity, worth, meaning, and purpose.

THE ISSUE OF SELF-IMAGE

A person's self-image is the mental picture that depicts not only physical details, but also subjective features of identity that have been gained from personal experiences or by internalizing the judgments of others.

We learn from sociology and psychology that how we see ourselves is vital, because this sensitivity will affect our behavior, our thinking, and how we relate to others. The manner in which a person envisions him- or herself is one of the most influential facets of a person's worldview. How we look at ourselves, that is, our self-image, is the cornerstone of how we look at everything else. Our personal view of ourselves intercepts our thoughts on everything and helps us determine how we will react to the myriad of life's pleasant times as well as menial and trying circumstances.

Image has to do with perception, which may be a combination of actuality and inaccuracy. Just because we settle on a certain view of ourselves and become comfortable with it does not necessitate its correctness. An inadequate self-image robs us of the energy and powers of attention to relate to others, because many times we are absorbed with our own inadequacies. Throughout our lives, difficult temptations, personal trials, and challenging situations will eventually shake us in our inner selves and leave us feeling uncertain. We never escape the need for a correct self-image, but we may temporarily avoid the issue by becoming content with an insufficient compromise. As we age, we may prefer to ignore the issue, pretending it to be resolved, by simply avoiding changes or challenges that force confrontation with ourselves.

In an attempt to find a superior way to achieve an accurate self-image, let us focus on the hypothesis that self changes over time. We can reasonably assume that one's self-image would also vary over time. In fact, several scientific researchers in the fields of psychology and theology have concluded that people do not possess a static self-image. Instead, self-images are dynamic in nature, some becoming displaced while other emerging self-images gradually evolve and become more perceptible during later stages of a person's life.

THE EMERGENCE OF DIFFERING SELF-IMAGES

There is a version of self that is developmental. Beginning with infancy, each person progresses through three basic periods of maturation: actual, ideal, and true. Each stage is chiefly character-ized by one's self-image. The phases overlap, and often tension exists among the three. Through careful observations of behavioral traits, the initial or actual self develops in a child mainly through the experiences of early life. According to Donald Woods Winnicott, a famed pediatrician and psychoanalyst (1896–1971), these early experiences are crucial to a proper development of personhood.

The person responsible for the infant is largely the mother, and if proper nurturing is not provided, certain deficiencies will manifest themselves later in the child's life. For example, failure to help the child generate a healthy sense of independence during his or her formative years may result in the creation what is known as a false self.

Winnicott asserts that in every person there is a true and false self. The false self is a disguise through which the individual acts, trying to be someone he or she is not. Even in an infant, he states, the primary function of the false self is defensive; in a sense it protects the true self from threat, harm, or even destruction. This is an unconscious process in the very young and as children mature, they commonly mistake the false self for the true self. Generally, the true self feels genuine to the individual, whereas the existence of a false self results in feelings of unreality or a sense of futility.

This actual self, along with its defensive disguises, continues to emerge into young adulthood and beyond. In this initial stage we perceive ourselves to be more independent and different from everyone else, and yet there is a budding inner desire to identify with something or someone else. The actual self simply is what I recognize as being only "me."

Then the ideal self develops in large part out of experience. It is more of a mature nature, a homemade self we began to construct in childhood. It provides a set of attitudes and dispositions that gives us our self-image and guides our lives as we age. Compared to the actual self, the identification of ourselves in the ideal state becomes more directed toward something or someone.

In addition, our ideal self usually is attached to some principle that functions as a personal dogma, a set of standards, rules and judgments, or a belief system we use in our perceptions of others and ourselves. In some cases the beliefs are so unreasonable that the ideal self becomes aggressively judgmental and critical of others who may have opposing persuasions. In these instances, perfection and inflexibility, along with self-deception, are the noteworthy attributes of the ideal self.

Research has shown that we tend to act in harmony with our mental self-portrait or self-image. If we don't like the kind of person we are, we think no one else likes us either, especially those we know or perceive to know who reject us. If we don't like other persons for any reason, our idealist natures are hostile and unforgiving. Such antisocial attitudes influence our communal lives, our task performances, and our relationships with others.

As a result of this unforgiving nature and uneasiness, most of these people in the emerging ideal self experience themselves as flawed or defective, and often as rejected or opposed. Depending on the severity of their sensibilities, some cannot look at themselves without hurting. To cope with this pain, they continue to create differing masks within their psyches.

While most behavioral scientists call this creation a "mask," as Winnicott does, Jungians (devotees of Carl Jung, a Swiss psychiatrist) call this survival mechanism the "persona," while others call it the "adopted child." It is important to see that the false self may be revealed as much in polar opposites such as a super-achieving perfectionist or an abandoned homeless person. By wearing deceptive masks, both are driven to cover up their deep sense of painful self-worthlessness.

How many of us wear masks, try to be something we are not, and consciously attempt to live up to what the "Joneses" are doing, impressing others with our achievements, our fancy belongings, and other attachments to external objects? We wear masks because we are ashamed to expose how unworthy and undeserving of love we think we are. But the mask comes with a heavy price. Whenever we wear it, we continue to fracture ourselves. We divide ourselves into the person we believe we are and the person we pretend to be. We tend to give up our integrity and abandon all hope of being honest as a true self. This lack of truthfulness is really self-destructive and sometimes causes us to experience shame and guilt. The pain of believing we are worthless is bad enough, but now it is compounded by the practice of self-deception.

A. J. Mahari conducted an investigative study of the behavioral illness borderline personality disorder (www.borderlinepersonality.

215

ca/). Each patient diagnosed with this relational disorder gave a history of his or her earlier life, sensing abandonment, yet dependent on safety and security. She identified succeeding layers of masks in these individuals as the disorder became more pronounced. The phony coverings included various forms of denial, unpredictable behavior, and especially blockage of relationships. But behind all masks Mahari claimed these patients were fearful of looking at the unprotected faces of their true identities.

Like Mahari and other specialists who focus on the mental health disorders of their clientele, there are those who claim everybody is shadowed to some degree by an illusionary person—a false self. James Martin, a contemporary of Thomas Merton and other cohorts in the Catholic faith, maintained that all individuals are "clothed" with bandages of the false self. He acknowledges his own possession of a false self and says it is "like the Invisible Man being wrapped, mummy like, in long winding strips of cloth" (2006, 19). After reading this description of a false self, it is tempting for me to believe these coverings could be merely expressions of self-aggrandizement and self-glorification. Such a disguised person would fashion these garments to be perceptible and acceptable to himself and to the world.

These are but a few of the many citations in the literature of mental health that describe the existence of a false self. I only mention these illuminating documents to substantiate the universality of false selves, how potentially debilitating they can be, and to provide an introduction to the last phase of selfhood, that of a true self.

The third category of emerging selves is the true self. This aspect of self is primarily the potential or possibility of oneself. The real self, therefore, is never identical to the actual or ideal self, for it is always more than we are at any moment. That is, the real self is in a state of becoming, transforming, or evolving into a "truer" self.

I will describe the true self more fully in the following chapter, including the means for a Christian to obtain a correct self-image and an authentic self. But first, let's learn more about some of the issues in the middle stage of selfhood, the ideal self. Because of several similarities, morally and spiritually, the ideal self is not identical to but approximates the old self as found in Romans 6:6; Ephesians 4:22; and Colossians 3:9. As we learn more about the emergence of self-images in the ideal phase of maturation, we can also justifiably attach the term *false self* to this duo of the ideal and old self.

THE OLD/IDEAL/FALSE SELF

Although our self-image has great impact upon our behavior, ultimately it may not necessarily reflect the truth. That is the case mainly because this triad of selves—the false, ideal, and old self—is not the true self; instead, this grouping of selves is the pyrite self or fools-gold self. It appears to be real, but has little or no intrinsic worth or purpose compared to real gold. It is like what we see in a plain mirror in contrast to our view in one of those curved mirrors found in most circuses and amusement parks. In this latter case, our features appear exaggerated and distorted and totally unlike a much more pleasant image that is visualized in a common, plain mirror. So we approve of our images in the plain mirror, not realizing that the curved mirror picture is really a more accurate reflection of our inner self, the perverted ideal, old, and false self.

It is in our states of an ideal, old, and false-self, that we identify our self-image, self-worth, and life's meaning, with one or more cherished standards or mind-sets upon which we have come to trust so deeply. To a large part, many in our Western society are dominated by the national and cultural standards that magnify two hyphenated self- terms, *self-confidence* and *self-esteem*. Most psychologists claim that how you see yourself, whether in a positive or negative way, is in accordance to your perceived level of these two hyphenated words. In our culture, these descriptions of self are endorsed by our experiential history, the media, and even by some of our modern religions.

It seems that our secular culture generally idolizes our independent natures (autonomy), and the conventional wisdom of the day measures our standards by the two parameters of self-confidence and self-esteem. In the modern world, these are the major psychoanalytical dimensions to which most people attach supreme importance. From a nonspiritual viewpoint, such individuals are highly dependent on these mind-sets to achieve ultimate happiness in our society. If self-esteem or self-confidence is lower than it should be, every effort is made to bolster the foundation of life to produce a more perfect ideal self.

A person who is squarely in the midst of his ideal self, that is, his old false self, might consciously say this about his own supported standards: "These are the things I can do and with whom I can identify—both to enhance my self-image and self-worth—that give me a feeling of significance and are necessary to bring happiness in my life." If such a concocted statement were uttered by a professing believer who was ingrained in his ideal self, he would likely be repulsed by any standard that espouses self-denial and suffering on a cross. This may be the case if a person's confidence centers on a cross-less gospel, positive thinking, or any of the false worldly standards of enlightenment and success.

With this pretended declaration still in mind, it would behoove each of us to spend some time examining those mind-sets upon which we base our images, value, and purpose. In some cases, these standards could embody deceptiveness and have the potential of enriching a false self; the consequences may produce an incorrect self-image, an improper self-worth, and an unclear purpose of life. If any of the eight standards listed below is so entrenched within our mind-sets that it seems to be right, these principles could hinder or obliterate our true selves. This assertion may be the reason why the ancient sage penned these words of wisdom, "There is a way which seems right to a man, but its end is the way of death" (Proverbs 16:25).

Mind-Sets or Standards of a False Self

Material and Financial Success

The faulty standard of material and monetary success is possibly the easiest to observe in someone else. Almost all of us have witnessed those who are boastful about their material successes.

While many may not exhibit outward tendencies, these false standards can lead us to incredible amounts of stress about our personal worth, fearing loss of our goods, *security, and identity.* To compensate for the loss of identity, one tries to find his identity in performance-based acceptance. The thought process here is chiefly "I am what I do."

Intelligence and Wisdom

Many become accustomed to the praise and glory brought on by this mind-set. Some believe there is power in knowledge. They believe this smartness will protect and preserve them. Often these individuals have an inordinate amount of pride, which feeds their egos. However, if this standard does not meet its expectations, the fall can only bring distress. Overconfidence in our own intellect and understanding can be one of the most dangerous false standards that adversely affects our self. "Do not lean on your own understanding...Do not be wise in your own eyes" (Proverbs 3:5, 7). "Woe to those who are wise in their own eyes and clever in their own sight" (Isaiah 5:21).

Health, Appearance, and Physical Well-Being

Even though these attributes offer some certainty today, they offer no assurance in the long term. When we are younger, these standards may make us feel we are invincible; but as we age, we experience their ill effects and realize more the brevity of life. I suggest reading the colorful yet prophetic words of Solomon in Ecclesiastes 12:1–7 that illustrate the effects of aging. See how he describes older people in terms of a gathering storm, an old house, having weak legs and eyes, few remaining teeth, loss of hearing, and decreased appreciation for music.

Sincerity

This is a subtle way in which we may find ourselves feeling overly confident because we imagine ourselves as having a clean conscience and being earnest in our motives. While we may acknowledge the possibility of error in the way we speak, we often deny its significance because of our sincerity. "Little children, let us not love with word or with tongue, but in deed and truth" (1 John 3:18). "All the ways of a man are clean in his own sight, but the LORD weighs the motives" (Proverbs 16:2).

Skills, Talent, and Ability

These standards tend to provide us with some level of confidence to the point of bragging. However, we must realize that these are gifts from God. "What do you have that you did not receive? But if you did receive it, why do you boast as if you had not received it?" (1 Corinthians 4:7). How can we boast, or be exceedingly self-confident, in something we did not earn but received as a gift?

Admiration and Esteem of Others

A desire for the respect and esteem of others must be the most powerful standard of a false self. No matter how much we mature in our own wisdom, our spirituality, or in worldly understanding, it seems as though we cannot escape the overpowering pressure of needing a positive opinion from others.

Self-Righteousness

This is possibly the most dangerous form of excessive piety. Once we learn to overcome sin, trials, and other troubles, temptations can follow and lead to thoughts and acts of self-righteousness. "And all our righteous deeds are like a filthy garment" (Isaiah 64:6). A significant part of self-righteousness is related to temptations to secure our identities and enhance our value by exploiting distinctions between ourselves and others.

In our illusionary false selves, we often need to label others in ways that give us the advantage. We do this by comparing ourselves with others who—based on appearance, age, education, and so forth—are different than us. Instead of considering others as equals,

220

as God views all humanity, we categorically make distinctions that place us on an elevated level and thereby give us a feeling of superiority. This fixed mind-set is most evident in the religious arena, where we, as individuals or collectively, express our "right way" of believing and doing. In reality and, as Scripture says, such deeds are like dirty clothing.

Self-Will

While this self-defining term seems to be a virtue, in some instances it can be a moral vice. If we have problems we cannot fix, we become frustrated and respond with bad and sometimes immoral choices, and sin is no exception. This was the case with King Ahaz when he became unfaithful to the Lord and sacrificed to other gods. But these sacrifices "became the downfall of him and all of Israel" (2 Chronicles 28:23; see also Titus 1:7; 2 Peter 2:10).

No matter how hard we try through self-will, once we have made ungodly choices we are in a state of lostness and separation from God. On our own we cannot "will" ourselves into anything. Even if sin is not a consideration, further advice about self-will is provided in the book of James. The author, likely the half-brother of Jesus, states that a person who makes plans does not know what tomorrow will bring. Instead, a person should say, "If the Lord wills" (James 4:14–15). Only this godly approach will help neutralize an overly zealous, self-willed Christian.

THOUGHTS ON THE MASKS OF A FALSE SELF

Thus we understand that we, too, can wear masks of being sincere, intelligent, healthy, talented, righteous, and so forth, when indeed these are all tainted with being phony, untruthful, misleading, bogus, and artificial. In addition, when we buy into Satan's damaging lies, we begin to believe him and may believe God is too restrictive and simply intends to take all the fun out of living. We will eventually find ourselves empty, broken, and sidelined in our journeys of spiritual growth.

Although none of the eight so-called standards of a false self listed above should be thought of as sinful in themselves, these worldly life principles are simply not created to bear the weight of our true beings. When we seek to identify our beings in something or someone other than God, we are dealing with an identity theft that is eternally more serious than stealing a Social Security number! We know it was Satan who first stole the original identity, the image of God, from our earliest ancestors. Consequently, the problem is that we inherited either a maligned identity (image) of God or, as some would say, none at all.

These and other false standards such as status, vocation, ethnicity, and certain ideologies can only hinder one's ability in becoming a true self. Why?

- The delusion of being successful, admired by others, and having tangible assets gives way to disillusionment as the possessions and achievements that once nourished our souls fail to satisfy our appetites.
- The feeling of happiness in getting something is a poor substitute for the true joy of contributing something of yourself to others.
- The pursuit of perfection and approval drives us steadily further from peace and contentment with ourselves, others, and God.
- When we focus our attention on our worldly standards and manmade traditions to gain happiness, we only inflate ourselves with boastful pride.

JESUS' VIEWS ABOUT THE DECEPTION AND HYPOCRISY

We all need to come to terms with the chief mind-set that hinders our ability to become a true self. It is that we recognize the falsity of being someone who we are not. In modern terminology, this condition is one of presenting ourselves in disguise, wearing masks. It seems as though Jesus had quite a bit to say about this very issue.

Although the term *mask* does not occur in most translations of the Bible, Jesus came close to accusing a person of wearing a mask when a pretender fasted in the presence of others. He warned, "Do not put on a gloomy face as the hypocrites do, for they neglect their appearance so that they will be noticed by men when they are fasting" (Matthew 6:16). A sour and dreary appearance was intended to impress others, when at the same time the hypocrite was really a fraud, a dishonest charlatan. A hypocrite like this always has a difficult part to act; when he wishes to appear as a penitent, not having godly sorrow nor the genuine principles of inner piety, he is obliged to counterfeit it the best way he can, by a gloomy and austere look. Yet Jesus and others are able to see through this thin veneer of deception.

Jesus witnessed this desire for admiration and esteem in the high-ranking religious leaders, for He taught people to "Beware of the scribes who like to walk around in long robes, and like respectful greetings in the market places" (Mark 12:38; also see Matthew 23:5–7 for additional examples of drawing attention to oneself). Because the scribes needed to be favorably noticed, Jesus accused them of over-concern with appearance and prestige. Jesus' scrutiny of these deceiving individuals who sought public respect and salutations in the marketplace not only marked them as having hypocritical behavior, but also possessing elements of phoniness.

In a confrontational discussion with the Pharisees about who is true and who is not, Jesus told them they had the same desires as the devil, namely, not telling the truth. Referring to Satan, Jesus said, "whenever he speaks a lie, he speaks from his own nature, for he is a liar and the father of lies" (John 8:44). Jesus may be saying here that just as lies come from Satan's nature, the lies of the Pharisees, scribes, and other religious leaders proceed from their evil natures. In turn, we could further say that lies come from the deceptiveness of one's own **self**. (Note that self in bold font follows the convention we use to designate the ungodly aspect of self. When referring only to the godly aspect, self is printed in italics.)

Jesus was adamant about the deception of the religious leaders. It was apparent to Him that the Pharisees had laid aside the commands of God for manmade, religious traditions. Calling them hypocrites, He told them that "what proceeds out of the mouth, this defiles the man" (Matthew 15:11). What comes out of the mouth reflects the corruption of one's inner self. In essence, He said that appearance can deceive people into thinking they are spiritually healthy, when in fact they are spiritually diseased. He said they looked impressive spiritually, but their hearts were contaminated.

According to Jesus, Satan is the master deceiver who casts himself as the one who wants to give us freedom and pleasure, carefully masking his plan to steal from, kill, and destroy us (John 10:10). When we choose to hide our shortcomings, inadequacies, limitations, and ill feelings, are we not wearing masks when we speak a lie about ourselves? Are we not attempting to deceive others, and unwittingly at the same time, ourselves? In doing so, are we not masking a plan like that of Satan to steal integrity, honor, or respect from others? Are we not masking attempts to kill or destroy a potentially caring and lasting relationship with someone else? Honest answers to questions such as these should make us more aware of the seriousness of possessing a controlling false self.

We should not interpret this matter of possessing a dominant false self as a trivial matter. There are dire consequences for retaining the deception of oneself. Self-deception means having misconceptions, false impressions, and false judgments in life. Many of the circumstances in life that bring about the greatest pain and grief are deeply rooted in illusions. Without having the image of God and His true love for and in us, much of the suffering involves inordinately high expectations placed upon someone whom we trust and love. To some degree we want total perfection from that person, who in his or her own imperfect nature cannot be totally faultless; we are innately capable of responding in malicious and vindictive ways. Human history tells us that if the deceptiveness of a false self is not checked and corrected, often sorrowful disharmony will result.

False standards used to achieve at least a modicum of self-acceptance, self-esteem, and self-worth, are connected to a self-referenced being having ever-present pride and selfishness.

The traits of covetousness, possessiveness, and the desire for public recognition, fame, and applause are the very traits we as followers of Christ should seek to uproot from our human natures.

As we have seen from the elaborations of Jesus' counseling and from the consequences of self-deception, the solution to this problem of the false self is observed in God's great plan of redemption. Unable to reclaim the lost identity of our true self on our own, as believers we are provided a way to detach ourselves from a false self and regain a measure of divine uniqueness in our true self.

BREAKING NEWS AND DEVELOPING STORY

Anchor: "This evening journalist Andrew Jones continues his account of his interview with Drs. Carataker and Cibalo."

Jones: "Their immediate task is to reexamine selected subjects who provided samples in the initial study. Using their new data in conjunction with the latest computerized analytical methods, they will determine if there are any correlations between measurements of the subunits of the S-Factor, a and b, and the expressions of altruism and selfishness, along with several other contrasting behavioral characteristics of people who were measured in previous studies.

"Members of our staff have been busily keeping up with this developing story, so stay with us as we present the latest news about the S-Factor."

Chapter 16

... Envision a Fulfilling Life?

The True Self

THE CONCEPT OF humans possessing a true self is known from many sources throughout history. Several ancient and modern customs of philosophy, mysticism, psychology, sociology, and spiritual and religious traditions have advocated the reality of a "true or authentic self." Synonyms of true self include, the pure self, unconditioned self, universal self, no self, essence, pure being, or true nature. In most cases, each is viewed as an internally hidden potency or element within the purest depths of oneself, present in all individuals, and when awakened to a conscious level, true self will lead the person to a genuineness and authenticity of the greatest degree.

These descriptions of a true self have similarities to the beliefs of theosophists—those who hold that all religions are attempts to help humanity evolve to greater perfection. They maintain that each religion, therefore, has a portion of the truth that frees one from the domination of the person, the mask or veil, through which the individual acts. Its reality exists only when one shows forth spiritual or so-called superhuman qualities, all of which are futuristic in this earthly life or hereafter.

BECOMING A TRUE SELF

A myriad of methods has been used to facilitate the achievement of a true self. One such mental discipline practiced for more than five thousand years is meditation, recognized as a component of almost all religions, in which one attempts to move beyond the conditioned, "thinking" mind into a deeper state of relaxation or awareness. Through meditation, a true self is allegedly derived by spiritual practices that are mainly drawn from Yoga, Hinduism, Buddhism, and the New Age Movement.

Orthodox Christianity, generally speaking, utilizes its own unique way to bring about the true self in the followers of Christ. If individual believers are made aware of it after acknowledging fundamental doctrinal beliefs, each sincere Christian is expected to enter a spiritual journey that is designed to develop a true self. In this lifetime expedition, the believer is designated as a set-apart person who aligns him- or herself with God's perfect purpose of redemption. During this heaven-bound journey, spiritual transformations take place in the believer's self. These transformations progress from a predominately "what I do" self to a "who I am" self, and then on to a harmonious balance between the two.

In these transformations, one's understanding of self changes as the false self diminishes. In addition, one's identity, purpose, and worth take on new meanings. At the same time, the person is developing a more intimate loving relationship with God that has practical applications in everyday life. These and many more blessings are viewed as significant parts of a true self.

The question, then, is how does a true self come about? This divine remodeling of oneself is a purposeful result of redemption, God's heavenly plan for our salvation. Fundamentally, it is a progressive spiritual metamorphosis of a Christian who faithfully considers him- or herself united with Christ's finished accomplishments on the cross of Calvary.

As previously described, the transformation of the self-life to a Christlike life is largely derived from the recorded writings of the apostle Paul. In Romans 6, Paul masterfully declares that the design of Christianity is to produce newness of life in us by union with Christ. In this joining together with Christ's life and death, by faith we realize we are "dead to sin, but alive to God in Jesus Christ" (Romans 6:11).

Again, the question is what does it take to be a true self? From the mysterious yet foundational truth of our oneness with Christ, we benefit by becoming partakers of Christ's resurrected life. It is the free provision of God by which a loyal believer becomes progressively transformed into a true self. In these two statements, the use of the words *becoming* and *becomes* is highly significant. For the Christian, the importance of becoming a participant of Christ's resurrected life and a truer self is evidenced by experiencing transformations that are associated with spiritual maturity. This phenomenon is not a onetime event, but should be viewed as a series of active, dynamic alterations of the inner self.

We can be a true self if we are released from the distortion of our own false judgments, our self-deceptions, our preoccupation with always getting, and from blocking our power to grow morally and spiritually. So it is obvious that these obstacles are to be separated and done away with in order to develop our true selves. The means by which these transformations are accomplished may be better understood using a simplified description in the translation of a self-life to a Christlike life.

We have seen this model to be useful for illustrating the deliverance of Christians from the bondage of sin and through the anxiety of troubles. In both of these conditions, believers must possess an earnest desire and willingness to deny self, take up the cross, and personally identify with the Passion of Christ.

As noted in figure 16.1 below, the model of a transformation of the false self to a true self focuses solidly upon the inner mortification of self in the mystical revelation of Christ's crucifixion. The term *mortification*, also translated "putting the flesh to death" or "death to self," is referred to in the New Testament as the lethality of oneself that is in opposition to the nature of God.

229

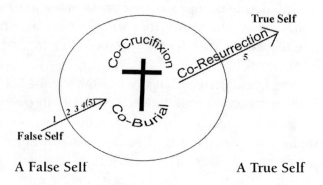

A False Self　　　　　　　　　　　　**A True Self**

Figure 16.1. The Mortification of a False Self

In this model, the reconstruction of a false self to a true self uses the five considerations referenced in the make-believe tales of a shopper in a department store and a not-so-make-believe story of a maturing Christian, both labeled person A.

1. Lostness

Customer A said, "Yes, I'm really lost," after the clerk asked him if he needed help. Now we all need to ask, "Am I lost?" To respond to this query, we are reminded that lostness is the biblical concept of a person's disharmony in his relationship with his Creator. For the one who is unsaved, the discord is total. For the saved, it is the degree to which one possesses a predominance of ungodly dispositions that are embedded in his or her inward human nature (being) and outer behavior (doing).

Following our convention of bolding the letters of self when it denotes the fleshly nature of self (an individual controlled by sin and directed to selfish pursuits rather than service of God), we can define lostness as the level of **self**, the old unyielding false person (being) that is manifesting the fruit of the flesh (deeds, conduct, or actions). Such a person is described by Paul as one who sets his mind on the things of the flesh, and "The mind set on the flesh is death…because the mind set on the flesh is hostile toward God; for it does not subject itself to the law of God, for it is not even able to do so, and those who are in the flesh cannot please God" (Romans 8:6–8).

To use a common analogy employed by most biblical writers, lostness equates with darkness. Contrastingly, being found (discovered, ascertained, discerned, revealed, and exposed) is associated with light. Even a cursory reading of the Gospels tells us the repeated reference to light is Jesus Christ. He is "the Light of the world" (John 8:12). Believers are told not to participate in the unfruitful deeds of darkness. "When they are exposed by the light...everything that becomes visible is light." Paul emphatically tells these believers to awaken and rise from the dead and "Christ will shine on you" (Ephesians 5:11, 13–14).

From this spiritual understanding of deadness and sleepiness in connection with Paul's admonishment for believers to come around to the reality of their darkness, we see the great need for those among us who are frustrated, restless, and discouraged to wake up regarding our sense of incompleteness. We are to wake up to the truth of our lostness and the presence of an antagonistic, counterfeit false self within our beings. If we cannot arise out of this state of slumber, we cannot begin to let Christ shine in us in order to become a *self*. With these meanings of self understood, what might be your answer to the question, "Am I lost?"

2. Guidance

Guidance in the context of spirituality centers on the indwelling of the Holy Spirit in the believer. The third person of the Holy Trinity is certainly involved in directing the maturing Christian out of a counterfeit self-life. This unlit path of darkness must be enlightened by God's Spirit to reveal its phoniness and to light up the passageway to a *self*, an illuminated true self.

The Holy Spirit guides us in many ways. He could initiate enlightenment through a preacher, relative, or friend; by reading the Bible, Christian literature, or a newspaper article; by viewing or listening to a Christian television program, radio program, or podcast. To be sure, these and many other helping measures can be exquisitely orchestrated by God, who mysteriously yet with purpose guides the growing Christian toward a greater desire to become authentic, a *self* who is pleasing to God.

However, for young children and grandchildren whose knowledge of God's creation and plan of salvation is relatively small, the Bible makes it abundantly clear that parents and grandparents are to be the guiding forces. It is their responsibility to instruct children in the ways of the Lord and their obligation to share with them what their "eyes have seen" in their walks of faith, and to "make them [God's ways and commands] known to your sons and your grandsons" (Deuteronomy 4:9). As trustworthy followers of Christ, we are accountable to convey this knowledge to our progeny.

3. Appraisal

At this juncture, we need to evaluate the use of various standards in discovering the true self. We have already claimed that many people have been deceived or have deceived themselves by applying worldly standards, which largely yield an ideal but false self. If we are wise enough to acknowledge the incorrectness of these standards, we might further assess appropriate norms by turning to and relying upon institutions, such as governmental and private organizations, or certain scientific disciplines that include promises of fostering a betterment of humanity. Such groups, including some religious institutions, often fall short in directing their followers toward a goal of developing a true self.

If we recognize the shortcomings of these institutions to provide true selfhood, we may then turn to certain friends or acquaintances with whom we can identify and whom we trust in some way, hoping for self authenticity. Should these individuals lack experience and education, we might conclude they are recommending a substandard means of attaining a more perfect true self.

If and when these valuations of self prove to be flawed, we are seemingly left with only ourselves. As it was with acknowledging the reality of our lostness, are we capable of accurately judging ourselves? It has been said, "Self-revelation precedes divine revelation." An honest examination of one's lostness and one's spirituality may not seem important, but a sincere self-appraisal might be the springboard that reveals wrongful attitudes and gives us insight into the destructive aspects of a false self. Spiritual searching often includes asking probing questions to be truthfully answered, such as "Have I refused to forgive someone even as I prayed, 'forgive our debts, as we also have forgiven our debtors' (Matthew 6:12)?" An honest answer to questions of this sort helps to expose our false selves.

You may recall from chapter 10 that the Bible does not overlook the assessment of oneself; self-examination can help determine whether godly characteristics of a true self are really present in the hearts of Christians. "Beloved, if our heart does not condemn us, we have confidence before God" (1 John 3:21). The psalmist prays, "Search me, O God, and know my heart [inner being];...see if there be any hurtful way in me, and lead me in the everlasting way" (Psalm 139:23–24). The apostle Paul exhorts believers to look within their inner selves, saying, "Test yourselves to see if you are in the faith; examine yourselves!" (2 Corinthians 13:5). In this same verse, he further states that this assessment of self reveals whether Jesus Christ is present in their inner beings.

Similar to the use of quality control most businesses practice, sustained appraisal of personal faithfulness is extremely helpful in the process of the transformation of the false self to a true self. Remember, you are unique, and, apart from the fact that only God Himself knows you completely in every regard, you are the best and only person who can appraise your spiritual nature.

Related to self-examination, another possible means of appraisal is to compare yourself in your present state with the past. Assuming you can correctly remember, it's time for you to reflect back over your life and estimate your own levels of Christlikeness and spiritual growth up to this point.

Ask yourself two questions: Do I see myself progressing in Christlike qualities such as forgiveness, patience, hope, and love? Referring to graph 12.1 in chapter 12, do you mimic to some degree the spiritual growth of person A, person B, or somewhere in between? Realize, of course, that because all of us retain a certain measure of spiritual immaturity and its corollary, our tainted human nature, our spiritual acuity is likely less than accurate.

For Christians, it is essential to have a right standard to effectively discriminate between truthfulness and deceitfulness. Why? The lack of a true criterion can lead us further on the wide dark road to degeneration and lostness rather than regeneration; the narrow pathway leads to that *something*, which most true believers come to believe is joyous and wholesome fellowship with our heavenly Father.

This leaves us with only one authority on the subject of our developing a true self. And that is the Triune Godhead. As regenerating Christians, we should see that Jesus Christ is our standard, or better yet, our gold standard. As noted in chapter 7, He is our supreme example. He is the model of worth, significance, identity, and purpose that is derived from our increasing knowledge of Him and our growing personal relationships with Him. The apostle Peter clearly tells the early converts that Christ is " an example for you to follow in His steps" (1 Peter 2:21). Scripture also tells us, "He [Jesus]... is a man of truth; there is nothing false about him" (John 7:18 NIV). Only those who want to follow in His footsteps can recognize Jesus for who He is—God's Son who is totally true in every respect.

To follow Christ and to hold Him as our gold standard means that we obey God's two greatest commandments, to love Him and others (Matthew 22:36–39), as well as Jesus' commands to deny ourselves and daily take up our crosses (Matthew 16:24; Luke 9:23). We believe these two sets of divine commandments constitute the essence of sanctification and deserve daily responses.

Rather than acting on suggestions, recommendations, or guidelines, we act on commands, either positively or negatively. Endowed with the freedom of choice by our Creator, self-denial and taking up our crosses are two separate, yet related, determinations we repeatedly are to make during our spiritual journeys with Christ. We make these choices as we continually seek to be delivered from the false self while simultaneously gaining the status of a true self.

The New Testament tells us we become obedient servants to whomever we choose to follow; if we follow in obedience to God, sanctification will result. Paul clearly states this in his letter to the church at Rome. Using the metaphoric language of slaves and masters, he tells them we are either obedient to and are "slaves of sin [or]...slaves of righteousness, [and having been emancipated from sin by becoming willing servants of God, we are to commit ourselves as] slaves to righteousness, resulting in sanctification [holiness]" (Romans 6:17–19). Could this passage indicate that spiritually maturing believers who are committed to God and faithfully follow Christ are involved in the sanctification aspect of their salvation?

In the Old Testament, Joshua, the conquering captain of the Lord's army, tells the people in the tribes of Israel, "Choose for yourselves today whom you will serve...but as for me and my house, we will serve the Lord" (Joshua 24:15). At this point, we should have all the evidence we need to make a decision between which we will follow—the true Lord or the ungodly desires of our false self.

4. Resolution

We have decided to get rid of the false self, the ruined part of our selves, or, following our pre-stated terminology, the **self**. All deliberations and assessments are over; it is time for action. The Bible says the one who hears the Word should act upon it. If he only "looks at his natural face in a mirror" and carelessly leaves and forgets "what kind of person he was" instead of looking at the truth, he deludes himself (James 1:22–24). In other words, to see what needs to be done and not to do it is to deceive oneself.

In a nutshell, if we say yes to Jesus, we are required to be renewed in the spirit of mind by laying aside **self** and putting on *self*. "In reference to your former manner of life, you lay aside the old self [old nature], which is being corrupted in accordance with the lusts of deceit, and that you be renewed in the spirit of your mind, and put on *self* [the new nature], which in the likeness of God has been created in righteousness and holiness of the truth" (Ephesians 4:22–24; see also Colossians 3:8–11). In both of these

235

passages and elsewhere in the New Testament, Paul tells us to put off the old Adamic nature, the false self, and put on the new Christlike nature, the original factual self. First we will address the laying aside the old self and ask ourselves, "How do we put off the old self?"

Author M. Robert Mulholland Jr. says that putting off the old nature is "a proactive acknowledgment of losing our self for Christ's sake, of denying our self, of taking up our cross, of being crucified with Christ: a radical abandonment of our entire self-referenced structure of being" (2006, 110). He goes on to describe the abandoning of our false self as the relinquishment of the deep inner desires of our fleshly self, an acknowledgment of the deadness of the old nature, and, in a single word that has been a central spiritual discipline throughout the centuries, a *detachment*. This term can be defined in many ways. From a biblical perspective, detachment is an orientation of the inner self *away from* narcissistic enslavement to earthly desires, possessions, and motivations and *toward* an other-centered pursuit of God.

Concerning the oneness of ourselves with Christ, scripturally referred to as "Christ in us" and "us in Christ," how can we specifically detach and put to death the false self? The realization of our unity with Christ should make it obvious that we cannot do it ourselves. As our representative, Jesus in oneness with His heavenly Father has already put our false self to death on the cross of Calvary: "one died for all, therefore all died" (2 Corinthians 5:14).

The apostle Paul emphasized this death of the false self when he wrote, "Even so consider yourselves to be dead to sin, but alive to God in Christ Jesus" (Romans 6:11). Through our co-crucifixion with Christ, as illustrated by feature number four in The Mortification of a False Self (fig. 16.1), God has already accomplished the detachment of false self.

Author Kenneth Boa maintains that followers of Christ are engaged a spiritual warfare with the flesh, which is the capacity for sin within us. He says that as we await the fullness of our redemption, the old appetites, attitudes, memories, and habits can surface at any time and wage war against the life of Christ in us. The warfare with the flesh...will continue throughout the time of our stay on earth. The flesh can never be reformed or improved; it can only be put to death....Because of our union with Christ in his death and resurrection, we can approach the spiritual warfare from a position of victory. It is true that the flesh or power of sin is still with us, but it need no longer have dominion over our lives. To overcome the force of the flesh we need to reckon or consider ourselves to be dead to sin but alive to God. We must believe what God has said is true of us, regardless of how we feel. (Boa 2001, 330–332)

Application of this victory over our fleshly nature can be visualized above in figure 16.1, when we vicariously lose our lives with Jesus on the cross.

If a believer is living in unity with Christ and by the indwelling resurrecting power of the Holy Spirit, he is "putting to death" those fleshly, ungodly aspects of himself (Romans 8:13). Incomprehensible love for His Father and for each of us was Christ's motivation to accept willingly any and all of our liabilities, such as a false self, that separates us from our God. Similarly, our incentive centers on our love toward Jesus Christ. He tells His disciples, "If you love Me, you will keep My commandments" (John 14:15).

We should be quick to emphasize that this detachment of the inner false self through our identification with Christ's crucifixion in His Passion should not be a simple intellectual agreement to a theological fact; nor is it an adherence to a prescribed dogma. Furthermore, detachment is not a onetime reckoning of faith, nor totally accomplished while one is alone in a meditative mood. In our everyday world of work or play, detachment is experienced and accomplished in every relationship and situation on a moment-by-moment basis.

Some have described the necessity of repeating the means of detachment as on the job training, OJT. Perhaps this is why Paul used the word *renewing* in his exhortation, "do not be conformed to this world, but be transformed by the renewing of your mind" (Romans 12:2). Continual repetition and renewing of this spiritual undertaking in the mind is necessary to detach the false life from our selves.

Regarding the solution to problems arising from the false self, some may ask what is the importance of obeying Jesus' directive to deny one's self, carry his cross and follow Him? We can interpret the verse that immediately follows these commands as an explanation. Jesus says, "For whoever wishes to save his life will lose it, but whoever loses his life for My sake will find it" (Matthew 16:25).

We have already acknowledged that Jesus may be referring to the likelihood of the physical death of the disciples. However, I believe Jesus' statement in this verse goes much further than mere facts of losing a physical life because of the disciple's faithfulness to his Master. So I am taking the liberty to separate verse 25 of Matthew 16 into two parts: a false self and a true self. An amplification of the first part of this verse is offered in the following manner:

A False Self: A Non-Follower of Christ

The first part of Matthew 16:25 reads, "For whoever wishes to save his life shall lose it."

For—a word used as a link between what was previously said (including Jesus' retort to Peter's rebuke by revealing him as having a mind-set not in tune with God's interests in verse 23 and Jesus' commands to deny self and carry a cross in verse 24) and what is next said; a word used as a function to indicate purpose, an intended goal, or the recipient of an activity.

whoever—anyone who does not voluntarily choose to deny self, carry his cross, and follow Jesus Christ, as exemplified by persons B and C.

wishes—has the desire, the aspiration, the craving, the fixed mind-set to use worldly standards as a means to achieve happiness, security, and worth.

to save his life—to spare himself, his false self, his fleshly life, his old nature (old being) with its practices (doing); his life of deception and his life of self-reliance; retaining all the natural tendencies or dispositions of his human nature, hoarding or accumulating tangible assets that seemingly protect against the loss of his temporal life.

will lose—a firm declaration of something that is non-recoverable and wasted.

it—life and all the aspects of his false self and also in jeopardy is his true self.

Throughout the centuries, many have adamantly wished not to relinquish their false selves and their protective masks. Sadly, these would-be followers of Christ, and even some nominal believers, willfully chose to maintain or retreat to the state of existing independently. Regarding the so-called believers, there they stayed as non-followers of Christ, like customer B did. Seeds planted in the rocky and thorny soils of these individuals (Matthew 13:1–23) yielded no firm roots, and because of afflictions, worries of the world, and the deceitfulness of riches, they fell away and became unfruitful.

Even more sorrowfully, they could be like shopper C, who had serious misgivings about purchasing the desired item, and person C, who was seeking satisfaction in the Christian faith. In these stories, both saw what they thought might serve themselves, however believed what they found was overpriced and would be of no use to them. Maybe they were like those who ask, "What's in it for me?" and answer, "Nothing. I am the captain of my ship and I don't want anyone to tell me what to buy, when to buy it, and how to live my life!" In both stories, they abruptly left with no intention to return. Such a person is totally unwilling to participate in God's plan of redemption and seeks to correct his lostness by other means.

Jesus knew that a certain portion of humankind would be like persons B and C and would refuse to deny themselves and to carry their crosses, thereby rejecting God's perfect plan of redemption. For them, Jesus says in Matthew 16:26–27, "For what will it profit a man if he gains the whole world and forfeits his soul? Or what will a man give in exchange for his soul?" Those who seek only their own rights, assets, self-fulfillment, and sufficiency will find they have lost the most valuable possessions of all—their souls.

Each of us should ask, "What will I personally lose if I do not make a total obligation to follow Christ by denying myself and carrying my cross?" To drive the question home for us, consider this: Jesus, in essence, asks us to imagine a balance scale. On the left side He places our old false selves and adds the whole world with all of its glamour and allurements. On the right side Jesus places just one thing—that part of our total being that is not false, namely *self*, the true self. Then, watching the scales tilt to the right, He essentially asks each of us, "What good will it be if you gain the whole world and be deprived of the true self you could become?"

The only answer we can give centers on the fact that God was willing to offer the life of His Son, and did so while we were still alienated from Him (Romans 5:6–8). There is no one in this world who is not worth this high price that was paid in our behalf. According to the Word of God, we must conclude that our worth is the same value placed on His Son's sacrifice for us, and each of us is infinitely valuable regardless of gender, nationality, race, church affiliation, and so on.

After Jesus asks what one will give in exchange for his soul in Matthew 16:26, He shifts the focus of our gaze to history's end in verse 27. The Son of Man is going to come in His Father's glory and will compensate all for their good deeds. Not only does becoming the person God wants us to be outweigh this world, but in choosing to deny ourselves, take up our cross, and follow Jesus we receive eternal rewards as well. To contrast the person who is dominated by a false self, I will now amplify Matthew 16:25b in the same way and describe in this verse an individual who has a predominant true self and who follows Christ.

A True Self: A Follower of Christ

The second half of Matthew 16:25 reads, "but whoever loses his life for My sake will find it."

but—however, on the other hand, in contrast to one who does not voluntarily choose to deny self, carry his cross, and follow Jesus Christ.

whoever—anyone who has already voluntarily chosen to comply with Jesus' commands to deny self by not sparing himself, carry his cross, follow Him and *acts* on this judgment by the inner mortification of the self-life, that is, unification with the Passion of

Christ as illustrated by consideration number four in figure 16.1. In our stories, this individual is represented by person A. He is the one whose seed is sown in good soil and produces valuable fruit. A true follower is one who lays aside the old self, his old nature, as described in the death of a self-life. We continue to look at him as one who puts on the new self; he puts on Christ.

loses—detaches, denies, abandons, releases, expropriates.

his life—his false self, his **self**, his fleshly temporal life; those selfish and prideful natural tendencies or dispositions of his human nature that hinder and obstruct an ongoing and perpetual relationship with God and Jesus Christ; his deeply entrenched inner core of a self-referenced and a self-absorbed being that holds back from a relationship with God and his Christ-referenced mode of being, and his "me first" attitude of the mind.

for My sake—for the truth of who Jesus is, the Son of God, and for the truth of the gospel.

will find—a promise to discover, detect, become aware of, uncover, disclose, receive.

it—eternal life. *It* is appropriating the virtuous character of Jesus Christ. *It* is *self*, the real, authentic self, in a loving relationship with God; the radical supernatural life with all the worth, purpose, meaning, identity, and joy God intended it to be from eternity past. *It* is the condition of wellness; the peace we have with God, others, and ourselves. *It* is the developing mind-set derived from the Holy Spirit that is directed toward God's interests. *It* is the experience of the power of resurrection in his life. *It* is to put on new clothing with a new orientation toward Christ. These six "its" that describe eternal life are not merely substitutes, nor are they behavioral modifications, but are some of the promised replacements for those things that are willingly and purposely denied, relinquished, and lost.

5. Joy of Putting on Christ

Where has this journey of faith toward Christlikeness taken us so far? The answer is from the radical nature of our deadness of the false self to experiencing the joyful resurrection and eternal life of a true self. This response is illustrated by the number five in figure 16.1 and more precisely in figure 16.2 below. We have now reached that point in our stories where the emphasis shifts from putting off a mask of the old false self to putting on Christ.

Those of us who elected to enter into the sanctification aspect of our salvation soon realized that the journey toward the reality of a true self is at times uncomfortable. With a sense of incompleteness and restlessness, we admitted we needed help. Through a variety of means, divine prompting led us out of lostness toward assessment, in which we could more fully evaluate the pros and cons of continuing toward the Suffering One on the cross. We had to consider whether the painful loss of the mask that had protected our false selves for so long would be worth choosing to obey Christ's commands to follow Him.

From the clear teaching of Holy Scriptures, we then faithfully acknowledged our mystical role in Christ's Passion. It was there on His cross, the cross that rightfully should have been ours, that Christ took our cherished mask from us in trade for His maskless true self. Out of and through the co-crucifixion with Christ and the co-burial of our old phoniness came the acquisition of a true self. This miraculous change is depicted in figure 16.2.

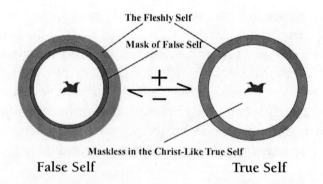

False Self   **True Self**

Figure 16.2. The Transformation of a False Self to a True Self

We should not despair or let our hearts be troubled, for at this juncture we can joyfully begin to discover what Paul refers to as putting on the new self (Ephesians 4:22–24; Colossians 3:11). What does it mean to put on the new self? As depicted in figure 16.2 above, a part of putting on a new self means that the masquerade is over; the divine switch is consummated by putting off the fake image of the old self while concurrently putting on the excellencies of Christ. As previously explained in our deliverances from the power of sin and through troubles, the believer becomes aware of his virtuous characteristics that flow into his new Christlike self. Maybe this awareness and the anticipation of its reality gives credence for placing the number five (representing the experience of joyousness that is associated with resurrection part of Christ's Passion and Christlikeness) before or in conjunction with the co-crucifixion (fig. 16.1).

This discovery of passing on the old life and experiencing a newness of life may have been part of what the apostle John was thinking when he wrote, "that whoever believes in Him [Jesus Christ] should not perish, but have eternal life." Using these well-known words of John 3:16 as a springboard, let us delve even deeper into our understanding of a true self by taking a closer look at putting on a new self. In practical terms, it consists of our identity, worth, purpose, and meaning.

IDENTITY

Identity is the believer's characteristics that come from putting on a new self. The major point of becoming an authentic self through sanctification is to progressively develop the image of God. The redeemed person is said to be in the image of God the Creator. These are the spiritual likenesses or nature of God that were best portrayed in the innocence of the pre-fall Adam. The redeemed person is "renewed to a true knowledge according to the image of the One who created him" (Colossians 3:10).

Similarly, Christians are gradually changed into the image of the Son of God as they appropriate the glorious characteristics of Christ, such as His traits of love, patience, self-giving, and obedience. Our progressive metamorphosis involves not only moral and spiritual likeness to Christ, but ultimately the Christian's future glory, including glorified bodies.

In our spiritual journey, we are constantly being transformed into the brilliance of our new images. Second Corinthians 3:18 tells us that we all are beholding as in a mirror the glory of the Lord, and "are being transformed into the same image from glory to glory, just as from the Lord, the Spirit." This means that the shining features of Christ's character are to be revealed from one degree of glory to another in our new true selves by the Spirit of God. The result of these transformations provides an ongoing emergence of Christ's image and gives us a new identity during our spiritual maturation. This sanctifying action is illustrated in figures P.2, 9.4, and 12.2. In these visualizations of self-circles, the white concentric circles can be viewed as ever increasing splendors of glory. As we are conformed more into the likenesses of Christ, it will then be His illuminating image that we will portray, and less of our darkened and unrepentant false selves.

So, within the scope of putting on a new self, identity takes on a heightened significance for the follower of Christ. He begins to joyously realize that by His grace, God is desirous to change the believer's self-image and thereby he can live for something vastly bigger than himself. This all fits into God's plan of redemption and further allows him to have worth and purpose in life.

Worth

Worth is the moral goodness, usefulness, and availability of a true follower of Christ. These are descriptions of value and are associated with putting on Christ. We may wonder if Jesus Christ was ever concerned with His self-worth. If so, His worth came only from His Father God. As God's children, is it possible for us to find our worth in God alone? If we are concerned with self-worth, upon what should our self-worth be based? We should be repeatedly reminded that our self-worth is based upon how God sees us, for He and He alone knows our true worth.

As Christians, can we define our self-worth? Yes, but not in the way our culture defines us. Rather our self-worth comes from the way God sees us in our justification. Justification provides us with an excellent idea of our true worth. Our conversion from unsaved to saved is a judicial provision that established our standing of holiness with God. After receiving this unearned divine gift, we are invited to live up to this holiness. We are then invited to be set-apart Christians to begin an intimate, ongoing, and personal relationship with God. It is through this Lordship relationship with Christ and putting on Christ that we find many scriptural affirmations of both our true identity and worth. (To state a few in the first person, see appendix F, What Christians May Know about Themselves.)

PURPOSE AND MEANING

Purpose is the reason for which someone exists, and the meaning or significance of that existence is the consequence of putting on Christ. To grasp the truth of these claims better, we can cite a philosophical analysis of life's purpose and meaning. Aristotle explained life in teleological terms by proposing a detailed progression of all life through intermediate provisional stages toward an end or goal. In our modern way of thinking, the end or goal is thought of in terms of the effect or result. But he called the terminal phase of this process the "final cause." For example, the essence or nature of coal is the final cause of plant life (vegetation) that began with the absorption of power from sunshine thousands of years ago. The essence or nature of an oak tree is the final cause of maturity that began with an acorn. The essence or nature of the human being is the final cause of the development that began in the impregnated female.

The words of the following song, "Hymn of Promise," capture elements of a Christian's purpose and meaning in life as he or she progresses toward his or her final cause.

In the bulb there is a flower; in the seed, an apple tree;
In cocoons, a hidden promise; butterflies will soon be free!
In the cold and snow of winter there's a spring that waits to be,
Unrevealed until its season, something God alone can see.

There's a song in every silence, seeking word and melody;
There's a dawn in every darkness, bringing hope to you and me.
From the past will come the future; what it holds, a mystery,
Unrevealed until its season, something God alone can see.

In our end is our beginning; in our time, infinity.
In our doubt, there is believing; in our life, eternity.
In our death, a resurrection; at the last a victory,
unrevealed until its season, something God alone can see.

Applying Aristotle's final cause to a Christian's sanctification, author Richard Neuhaus states that the direction of our lives is not determined by what we want to do, a wish to be someone, or a choice to be decided. Instead he says that our final cause, intention, or goal of life here on earth is to find who we really are, a truth that is in the making, or purpose to be discovered. Personally speaking, Neuhaus states, "What I want and what I choose may be in conflict with who I am, with who I *really* am" (2000, 128). Apparently, Neuhaus discerned that there are two natures residing in one's self, for he uses the word self twice in his statement, "The question is whether the self is an objective truth to be discovered or a subjective choice determined by the self" (129).

It is of great interest that these descriptions of a final cause quoted from Aristotle and Neuhaus's statement are in direct contrast to the direction sought by many worldly belief systems. These culturally based systems are known as naturalism, relativism, materialism, and secularism; they promote the physical realm and social idealism. Their general viewpoint engenders little or no substance in spiritual matters and usually measures a fulfilled life in terms of pleasure, security, and comfort.

We also interpret Neuhaus's view of a final cause to be God's will in our lives, as an ultimate destiny in our earthly lives, which is best described in terms of one's nature and authenticity. If indeed these assertions are correct, we should be able to justifiably couple them with the concept of becoming a true self. However, in the physical biological world, when we start by looking at the grand scheme of life in terms of alpha to omega, from green vegetation to black coal, from a seed to a mature tree, from a germinated ovum to a grown person at his life's end, sometimes it is difficult to grasp the details what occurs during the growth process of becoming a true self.

One should recognize the possibility that the final cause of human life may be assessed in terms of daily or shorter occurrences and not in one's entire life span. If this is a logical and acceptable option, we can readily claim that the means of becoming a true self within the framework of a Christian advancement of Christlikeness is accomplished every day, even by the momentary transformations of a false self to a true self.

During these spiritual and moral metamorphoses the final cause is revealed, namely our true natures and who we are at each point in time. Whether they are labeled provisional or final causes does not matter. Just as a seed finds its fulfillment in a flower, the believer finds degrees of completeness in becoming spiritually mature. If our responses to every situation or episode truly reflect the character and nature of Christ, we should also experience the joys of a resurrection life at these various times.

Some might challenge such statements by saying that all of this heavenly peacefulness is only subjective, not real and objective. While I readily admit that the unseen world of spirituality is less tangible than the visible creation, our faith and trust in the promises of a holy, loving God become a reality as we plainly manifest the virtues of God and Jesus Christ.

This is no imaginary realization, but one that can be joyfully anticipated and experienced as a result of following Christ obediently by denying ourselves and carrying our crosses. Conversely, having little or no conscious degree of cheerfulness, peace, and contentment may indicate that the false self still has dominance in our lives, holding us in bondage of selfishness and worldly pride.

We should be quick to remind ourselves again that these joys are not something in which we can exult or retain for ourselves. Instead, the attitudes of our minds should be like that of the psalmist who said, "I delight to do Your will, O my God" (Psalm 40:8). We should be like our gold standard, Jesus Christ, whose joy was His absolute self-abandonment to His Father and the readiness

247

to obey His Father's will, "who for the joy set before Him endured the cross" (Hebrews 12:2).

In like manner, we find the purpose for which we exist and which gives life meaning, significance, and completeness. But there is an unrelenting quandary that arises from doubters and skeptics. They question whether the problem of finding purpose is one of low-esteem, low- confidence, or an assortment of self-centered thoughts, rather than biblically God-centered thoughts about who we are and how we become the genuineness of a true self. Is the issue one of exalting ourselves, or one of praising God, His plan, and His revelation concerning who we are?

Significantly, our value and providence can be readily available to others who witness our faithful responses, especially in times of challenges and distress. For example, all of our counter-culture Christlike responses to our troubles appear to be radically different from the common-sense reactions of many individuals. But this may be the very way you are unwittingly serving God's purpose of being "a people for God's own possession, that you may proclaim the excellencies of Him who has called you out of darkness into His marvelous light" (1 Peter 2:9).

You may recall in our story of the department store shoppers that other people observed the great satisfaction of customer A's purchase and sought to buy one for themselves. Substituting yourself for person A in the saga of Christian maturity, might another person's observations of you be the very key that opens that individual's heart to the gospel of Jesus Christ?

If we recognize virtuous attitudes in a follower of Christ as public advertisements of God's nature, we can understand that our Christlike virtues were not meant to be adornments for ourselves. It is through the everyday manifesting of these qualities that from our inner selves "will flow rivers of living water" (John 7:38). The Bible tells us that our chief duty is to glorify, reflect, and show forth Christ in all we do. Furthermore, we are told, "Let your light shine before men in such a way that they may see your good works, and glorify your Father who is in heaven" (Matthew 5:16). This is the chief aim of putting on the new created self.

In regard to experiencing the joyfulness of the resurrection life, the Bible tells us where to direct any pride or boasting: "let not a... man boast of his wisdom,...might...[and]...riches; but let him who boasts boast of this, that he understands and knows Me, that I am the LORD who exercises lovingkindness, justice and righteousness on earth; for I delight in these things" (Jeremiah 9:23–24). Here the prophet Jeremiah is telling the people of Judah that God knows that all are prone to boast, but the real issue concerns the source from which boasting results. Many boast of false standards as the basis for attaining completeness and happiness. For those of this mind-set, God warns that such values will not create contentment or serve an eternal purpose. Instead, knowledge of Him will produce the fruit of love, fairness, and virtue, on which He places His stamp of approval.

Knowing that all good comes from God—"Every good thing given and every perfect gift is from above, coming down from the Father of lights" (James 1:17)—we must acknowledge that we are poor and powerless, unable to attain the joys of a true self on our own, and we have nothing but what we have received as we put on Christ. It is then and only then that we can boast in God alone, for we look beyond the gifts we receive to the Giver and beyond the blessings to the Source of life.

BREAKING NEWS AND DEVELOPING STORY

Anchor: "After nearly six months of silence, we're pleased to bring you an update on the latest discoveries regarding the S-Factor. In a moment we'll show you video footage of lecture recently given by Drs. Selford, Sinton, Carataker, and Cibalo.

Sinton: "The data of the two indices, Selfish Index and Altruism Index, obtained from each of the individuals in the study are seen on the dark line. On the horizontal axis are increasing measurements of the Selfish Index (SI). On the vertical axis are increasing values of the Altruism Index (AI)."

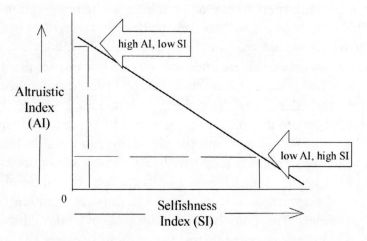

Figure 16.3. Plot of Altruistic Index vs. Selfish Index

Selford: "The result of tracking these two indices is called a negative correlation. A positive correlation would show the line low at the left and rising to the right. The finding of a negative correlation is similar to results shown in previous studies using these same parameters of SI and AI, or when evaluating opposing traits such as humility and pride. However, the most exciting result of our S-Factor study was derived from the analysis of the paired data of levels of subunit a or subunit b with the measurements of SI or AI. Not shown graphically, the other major result is summarized as follows."

Carataker: "There were significant correlations between the amounts of the S-Factor's two subunits and the two traits of altruism and selfishness. Increasing amounts of subunit a of the S-Factor is associated with the trait of altruism, an attitude or a behavior marked by unselfish concern for the welfare of others. On the other hand, increasing amounts of subunit b in the S-Factor is coupled with selfishness, a prideful attitude of possessiveness marked by means of benefiting oneself at the expense of others."

Anchor: "This appears to be the first time a biological substance like the S-Factor has been shown to be associated with a behavioral trait in humans.

"Now, to simplify the doctors' language just a bit, let's suppose you were randomly chosen as a subject in this study, and the battery of physiological evaluations revealed that you possessed a high level of altruism. According to the data of the scientists, in your case, the amount of subunit a would predictability be high. Indeed, when a measurement was made of your S-Factor, the results showed an elevated amount of subunit a compared to a low subunit b. In another person, a high level of subunit b would expectably be linked with selfish characteristics.

"That's it for tonight. We will keep you informed regarding any further developments in this highly unusual story."

Chapter 17

... Envision a Fulfilling Life?

Marks of Spiritual Maturity

IN ESSENCE, THE characteristic marks of biblical maturity in a Christian are the products of true spirituality. In fact, biblical spirituality can be described by the term *maturity*, since Christian maturity is the result of growth. So with this association between spirituality and spiritual maturation in mind, the defining questions are threefold: (1) Who causes spiritual growth and by what means is it produced? (2) What are the marks of spirituality? and (3) How do the marks of spiritual maturity fit into God's plan of redemption in a practical way? These are the three major considerations in this chapter as I invite each of you to envision a fulfilling life for followers of Christ.

THE CAUSE AND MEANS OF SPIRITUAL GROWTH

The Bible says it is "God who causes the growth" (1 Corinthians 3:7). This is the claim of the apostle Paul, given to early church members concerning their spiritual maturity. Undoubtedly, God in His sovereignty has a myriad of ways to providentially bring about spiritual maturity.

I will mention only one method that is often overlooked by many Christians: daily circumstances. These events are asserted by many theologians to be ordained by God, who in His providence brings believers into situations that cannot be totally explained in terms of purpose and meaning. God shepherds the believer to places, among people, or into conditions to accomplish His definitive purposes. The implications of God's intervention in our lives in this manner are numerous. Spiritually speaking, one suggestion is simply that God's involvement produces a measure of spiritual maturity. There is vagueness as to whomever and whatever else may play a role in the life of a believer. But one thing is certain: it is the sovereign God, our heavenly Father, who ultimately causes the Christian to grow spiritually.

I have proposed throughout this book that the specific means by which Christlikeness develops in an individual is centered on the finished work of Jesus Christ on the cross of Calvary. With the power of the indwelling presence of the Holy Spirit in a believer, inner transformations of self-sacrifice (or self-mortification) take place that result in maturing spiritually. Thus, in the context of spiritual maturity, we have an opportunity to briefly and concisely glance into the mystery of the Holy Trinity. Acting in unity and in perfect harmony, the three eternal persons of the Godhead—the Father, Son, and Holy Spirit—have functions in the spiritual growth of each child in God's family.

THE MARKS OF SPIRITUAL MATURITY

The elements or distinctive marks of a Christian are selected personality attributes of God, the likeness of which are communicable as supremely evidenced in the life and character of Jesus Christ. This is to say that the incarnate Jesus Christ reflects and portrays the essence of His Father's personality. Many believe these qualities similarly constitute the inherited image of God as recorded in Genesis 1:26–27. Thus, greater and greater levels of these distinguishing marks are key indices of spiritual growth, and are basic for believers to be concerned about in their own lives. From my research, I believe these marks are not imagined, but in many cases are objective and can be sensed or experienced.

Is it possible to know which of the many attributes of a holy and sovereign God are revealed in a spiritually maturing Christian? The simple answer is that these attributes are Godlike and Christlike qualities imparted in and manifested by the believer. To more fully answer this question, we must know what Christ looked like. This still begs the answer to the question what is there about Jesus and His character that will reveal what a true Christian looks like?

We approach this question by taking a close look at the apostle Paul's words to the Ephesians. He states that maturing Christians should continue, "until we all attain to...a mature man, to the measure of the stature which belongs to the fullness of Christ... [and] grow up in all aspects into Him" (Ephesians 4:13, 15).

Before we focus on "stature" as it might represent a mark or set of marks of spiritual maturity, let us delve into the meaning of a mature man as used in verse 13. The Greek word used here for "mature man" is *teleios*, meaning, "having attained the end, purpose, complete, perfect." In the common language of the day this word described a full-grown, mature adult. In a spiritual sense, a mature man also describes one who is fully developed and perfected, having achieved a degree of his complete purpose in harmony with the desirable spiritual qualities found throughout the New Testament.

A derivative of the term *teleios* is also used in Greek literature to denote a final cause, intention, or destiny of an individual's life. You may recall that this same word was used in the previous chapter as we discussed a human's purpose in life. In this regard, it is interesting to note that one's maturity is analogous to one's final cause. The implication here is that when we have attained a level of spiritual maturity, we have completed a particular purpose in our lives. If this is so in the progressive development of sanctification, spiritual maturity corresponds well with the level of Christlikeness derived from transformations of the self-life.

Returning to Ephesians 4, the gospel standard of Jesus Christ is used to measure the stature of each member of a local church. Most likely, the term *stature* can be understood as an individual's level of goodness, achievement, or any of the human qualities attributed to spirituality. Whatever the measure of stature to which Paul refers, it must be a virtuous or moral feature that qualifies a believer for the ranks of true followers of Christ and makes him or her worthy for heaven.

In this passage of linking the stature of Christ to the maturity of believers, it should be stressed that the church members are to attain full maturity in every way and in all things of Christ's fullness. We also see in these verses that there is fullness or completeness in Christ and a richness to be derived from Him. It could be that a measure of that stature is assigned in the sovereign counsel of God to every believer. This measure of stature can also be interpreted as the final cause or life's purpose. Furthermore, it is possible that such obligations differ in quality and quantity for each believer, much like the different spiritual gifts given to believers in the early church (1 Corinthians 12:28–30; Ephesians 4:11).

We are not given a definitive measurement of this stature in the Bible; nonetheless, many theologians believe we never come to its full measure while we live in an imperfect world. Based upon the eternal position provided in the justification aspect of salvation, it must be gratifying for all believers that even without coming to a full amount of the stature of Christ, we still retain God's unconditional acceptance and have an acceptable height of Christ's fullness in heaven.

It is reasonable to think that the specific characteristics that constitute the stature of Christ would have the same labels used in the plot of spirituality versus time as noted in graph 12.1. These qualities would also be the same selected features of God ascribed in the life and character of Jesus Christ. They would not be those that only God possesses absolutely, such as all-knowingness or unchangeableness, but instead would include traits universally associated with humankind, such as truth and love.

In a broad sense, the term stature as it is used in Ephesians 4:13 may be understood as an individual's level of a true self. When we are referring to Jesus Christ, we can boldly state that He is not only our standard for the wholesomeness of His human virtues, but also for purity. Christ's completely sinless nature did not allow fabrication of any masks; therefore we can justifiably say the truest self of all is Jesus Christ. "Christ is all, and in all" (Colossians 3:11).

Jesus experienced a life of trials and temptations, and at least to a common-sense way of thinking, surely there were moments when a mask would seem to have benefited Him. Take for example those two major temptations of Jesus, first in the desert and then at the time of His crucifixion. In each situation, the temptations focused on His humanity. A mask may have tempted Jesus to be someone other than who He really was, such as the following:

- someone who fit in,
- someone who never posed a threat to the status quo,
- someone who craved only respect and self-esteem, or
- someone who was in tune with his contemporary Jewish religious leaders.

Nevertheless, together with His attitude of self-denial, the aid of the indwelling Holy Spirit, and His total submission to His Father's will, Christ's true self remained perfectly intact. He did not need to make any pretensions as to who He was and what purpose He was to fulfill on the cross of Calvary. So we conclude that these temptations were thwarted by means of self-denial as He rejected all attempts to be a false self. Instead, He embraced His true self, the Son of God and the Son of Man, and therefore was true to the Father God, to Himself, and to all humanity.

If you want to know how real you are, that is, how much you reveal your self in your Christian faith, test yourself by these words of Jesus: "Follow Me." In every dimension in which you are not real, your self will argue or evade the issue altogether rather than follow Him. Most of us will go through any number of twists and turns to avoid denying ourselves and to stay away from carrying our crosses daily, actions Jesus plainly said were necessary to follow Him faithfully.

Oswald Chambers (in *My Utmost for His Highest*) and several commentators evaluated various responses to Christ's invitation to "Follow Me." Generally, these scholars seem to be in agreement on one point. They think that as long as we have even the least bit of spiritual disrespect for the clearly spoken words of God's Son, it will always reveal itself in the fact that we are seeking an alternative route to God and expecting God to provide blessings of deliverance and joyousness. Yet, in biblical words and in a spiritual sense, all the time Jesus is telling each of us:

"Come to Me" (Matthew 11:28).
"Follow Me" (Matthew 16:24).
"I am the true vine" (John 15:1).
"I am the way, and the truth, and the life; no one comes to the Father but through Me" (John 14:6).

This is not a "winner takes all" quiz, but did you pass the test?

Time and time again we use the standard or measure of the stature of our Lord Jesus Christ to help explain what a Christian looks like. However, rather than the usual approach, which is to consider His righteous and virtuous qualities, we can identify what He is *not*. In addition to avoiding becoming a false self, some notable examples include the absence of retaliation, hatred, and at least twenty hyphenated self- terms that are so common in our secular world, and shamefully, also in our Christian community. (Refer to appendix A, Hyphenated Self-Terms)

There is yet another way to test our self in order to determine whether our *self* has dominion over any remnants of the old self. We have asserted that the true self in all people is always in a state of becoming. Morally speaking, this condition is dynamic; it can go from vice to virtue or virtue to vice in both non-Christians and believers. The test is then is one of trends. Over time, what and who are we becoming?

Regarding spiritual maturity, there are at least two major differences between a non-Christian and a follower of Christ. One difference centers on what and who the nonbeliever and the believer are becoming. The nonbeliever likely exhibits a trend that is focused on some self-adoring feature, a set of worldly standards, or some figure other than Jesus Christ. For the believer, he has a trend to become more like Christ; this is his one and only goal. Second, unlike the nonbeliever who is internally pointed toward moral betterment only by the guiding influence of his conscience, the Christian's sense of right and wrong is supplemented by *self*, the inner core of his true self which is united with and directed by the Holy Spirit and the Spirit of Christ. I maintain that the motivation to become Christlike combined with the cohabitation of spirits in the believer is the energizing force that fosters greater levels of spiritual maturity. This trend is most noticeable in person A as noted in figure 12.1.

If we accept the thesis that a Christian has the potential to develop the virtuous characteristics of Christ in his or her true self, there are startling implications to consider. Immediately, we realize we are automatically at one with the Spirit and we are at one with Christ, the companionship of the truest self of all.

To help illustrate becoming part of a self spirituality, let's return to the disciple Peter. Based upon several Scripture passages, his self was evident because he possessed oscillating patterns of brashness and self-assertiveness, and vacillated in his allegiance to Christ. If Jesus used worldly wisdom to judge Peter's potential usefulness to advance God's kingdom, Peter would have been summarily rejected without delay. But even when Peter vehemently denied Him three times, Jesus demonstrated His loving true self and God's divine grace by not discarding him. Somehow, He recognized early on that Peter had potential to become a truer self as a faithful leader in the early church.

For the true believer in modern times, this unconditional recognition of our potential illustrates not only the detection of our budding worth but also of God's unchanging love and acceptance of His children. However, we mortals are unable to visualize completely the potential of others, let alone ourselves. Likewise, neither can we accurately understand anything about our exact purpose, because God is using us for *His* purpose. Only God has these sovereign insights. So in our fallen humanity we often live by common sense that arises out of fallen, fleshly human nature, even though we are continually exhorted to "Trust in the LORD with all your heart, and do not lean on your own understanding" (Proverbs 3:5).

So what are some of the implications here? If and when we can shed our masks, the false identities that hinder the actualization of our true selves, we can better live in a manner that pleases God. For when we please Him, our wills coincide with His will, and we make decisions based upon the Christlike natures that exist in our reconstituted true selves. As always, all of these choices involve ourselves, others, and ultimately God.

We need to come to the point when we affirm God's love for us but at the same time realize we are unable to know absolutely our ways. Then we are in much better positions to improve our relationships with others. How? We should consider others in this same light, knowing that they, too, are loved by God, made in His image, and are in a state of becoming. If all people really were to think and view everyone else in this manner, it would upset the entire world. If this scenario is limited to interactions among our brothers and sisters in Christ, I believe it would revolutionize the church as we know it!

What, then, are the some of the inferences we can make from these understandings? First, because we know we should not judge others and because we do not know with any accuracy their levels of selves and what kinds of masks they are wearing (or what kind of identities they are portraying), we can only interact with them and see them as they are in their own beings and in their own becoming.

Here are some specific implications. It has been estimated that the number of abortions in the United States is 1.4 million per year. The records also show that 93 percent of all abortions occur for social reasons, because the child is unwanted or is an inconvenience. In each of these murders a decision was made to end the life of a growing fetus whose self was already initiated. The perpetrator of this action was totally ignorant of the child's potential. If a decision was made not to abort, the would-be mother might eventually discover what that infant would become; perhaps he would be an average person like most of us. But she will never know. One of the take-home messages here is that before we act or speak on behalf of or in opposition to a person, whether or not he or she is vulnerable like the unborn, we need to give some thought to the possible consequences of our actions or speech.

In regard to a maturing Christian who is attaining the characteristics of the stature of Christ, keep in mind that these qualities would also be the same selected features of God that are ascribed to the true self of Jesus Christ. I have categorized these attributes into nine areas: wellness, fruit of the Spirit, outer garments, spiritual acuity or discrimination index, holiness, humility, persecution, loving and serving others.

SPECIFIC MARKS OF SPIRITUAL MATURITY

Wellness

Wellness is defined as a condition of healthiness, most often associated with physical or mental health. Wellness is also understood simply as a condition of happiness. While specific definitions vary, I believe wellness is explainable when viewed as an umbrella term. In this manner, it refers to a state of being that takes into account subjects such as contentment, fulfillment, security, worthiness, peace, and joyfulness. Exceptions may exist, but every person, whether Christian or not, conscientiously desires personal satisfaction in one or more of these conditions.

As a mark of Christian maturity, the wellness of the believer can be defined as a condition of well-being that is both experiential and prophetic, for it corresponds to what is promised, predicted, or foreshadowed. Jesus may have understood and applied wellness in terms of peace when He told His disciples, "My peace I give to you; not as the world gives do I give to you" (John 14:27); and also when He gave a universal call to come to Him and "I will give you rest" (Matthew 11:28). Referring to keeping His commandments and abiding in His love, Jesus said, "These things I have spoken to you so that My joy may be in you, and that your joy may be made full" (John 15:11). When Jesus caused the blind beggar to see, He said, "Your faith has made you well" (Mark 10:52). In other biblical texts, this last reference about the miraculous healing of the beggar states that his faith has made him complete and whole.

We then can conclude that the wellness of a believer is a faith-based condition of well-being that is satisfactorily established and secure with no need for the believer to wander or look for something or someone else to improve his or her well-being. (As a side thought, this definition ties in with our stories, particularly of person A, who, before finding what he was seeking, perceived himself to be unsatisfied, incomplete, and lost.)

Dallas Willard, noted author of several books that deal with the spiritual life of Christians who are becoming more Christlike, equates inner self-denial with death of self and links this process of mortification of self to wellness. In his book *Renovation of the Heart*, Willard writes that being dead to self is the settled condition that:

> represents…a fundamental, indispensable element in the renovation of the heart, soul, and life. Being dead to self is the condition where the mere fact that I do not get what I want does not surprise or offend me and has no control over me….[Those who are] dead to self will certainly not even notice some things that others would—for example, things such as social slights, verbal put-downs and innuendos, or physical discomforts. They appropriately look after things that concern them, but they do not worry about outcomes that merely affect adversely their own desires and feelings. Those who are dead to self are not controlled in thought, feeling, or action by self-exaltation or by the will to have their own way, but are easily controlled by love of God and neighbor. (2002, 71–72)

The settled condition of one who is becoming Christlike, which Willard describes above, can be viewed as a mark of spiritual maturity. Certainly, such a person who denies himself, carries his cross, and detaches those unsettling thoughts and dispositions that are counter to Christlikeness will progressively move toward states of contentment, fulfillment, security, worthiness, peace, and joyfulness.

The Fruit of the Spirit

"The fruit of the Spirit is love, joy, peace, patience, kindness, goodness, faithfulness, gentleness, self-control" (Galatians 5:22–23). Any of these virtuous characteristics can be marks of a maturing Christian. Believers whose lives are adorned by these virtues cannot be condemned by anyone or by the law, for the whole purpose and design of the moral law of God is fulfilled in those who have the Spirit of God producing these fruits in their true selves.

At this point, I want to single out the second fruit of the Spirit, joy, and connect it to point five in our model used to represent transformations of a self-life to a Christlike life and a false life to a true life. Some might think joy is just another synonym for happiness and that this state of contentment would be the cure for all our anxieties. Rarely does happiness come from those who fabricate or seek it directly. No, here I am speaking of true pleasure that is true joy. Joy comes only from a life of integrity, because this fruit is not sought, but is a by-product we experience when we live in faithfulness and obedience to God and Jesus Christ.

Outer Garments

I believe the apostle Paul uses allegorical expressions such as "put on" or "to be clothed with" to signify the appealing qualities of the wearer. Perhaps, in another sense, Paul wants the early Christians in the church at Colossae to replicate certain mercies fashioned by the greatest designer of all time, Jesus Christ. This outer attire can become the medium of contact between the wearers and those nearby. For the wearers, Paul wants them to feel the slightest touch of another's misery so the believers' sharpened sensitivity of mercy would always be within reach of the depressed. For those in close proximity to the wearer, they can touch the Christians' clothing and sometimes feel the "texture" of the believers' moral fiber.

Several of these garments coincide with fruit of the Spirit, but also include others, such as compassion, humility, forbearance, and thankfulness. (See Colossians 3:12–16.) Note that in the context of this passage these garments are characteristics of Christ's followers and are to be worn every day. It is also important to note that the overall purpose of wearing this metaphorical clothing is not for overly glorifying the person, but its function is one of attractiveness. The clothing is to display the aesthetic appearance of the outer garments that modestly reflects the inward beauty of the wearer. Someone might summarize this mark of Christian maturity by the statement, "You are what you wear."

Spiritual Acuity (SA) or Discrimination Index (DI)

SA and DI are two terms I've created that seem appropriate to describe a mark of spiritual growth. There is scriptural evidence that links the maturity of a Christian to discernment of what is good and evil. The major theme in the book of Hebrews is the superior goodness of Christ, which is further described with words such as *better*, *perfect*, and *heavenly*. The author of this letter contrasts the immature person as an "infant" who feeds only on milk to the "mature" individual who eats solid food. This wholesome diet is ingested by adults who are "mature, who because of practice have their senses trained to discern good and evil" (Hebrews 5:13–14).

In this verse, the word *mature*, translated from the Greek *teleios*, is identical to a spiritual adult who attains a measure of Christ's stature. (See Ephesians 4:13.) Solid food is the nourishment used by complete believers whose "senses and mental faculties are trained by practice to discriminate and distinguish between what is morally good and noble and what is evil and contrary either to divine or human law" (Hebrews 5:13–14 AB). I concluded that SA or DI was an essential element of Jesus' self and should be a virtuous characteristic of a spiritually maturing Christian. This inner sense is viewed as another one of God's graces that is available for a believer who is able to recognize good from evil, right from wrong, factual from misleading teachings, and even discern in him- or herself or others a true self from a false self.

264

Holiness

"Be holy yourselves also in all your behavior; because it is written, You shall be holy, for I am holy" (1 Peter 1:15–16). This passage clearly states the basis and purpose of holiness in the lives of believers. In addition, three related statements can be derived from this passage: (1) the reception of having the holiness of Christ in us is the grand object of a genuine Christian's pursuit of spiritual maturity; (2) Christians progressively perfect holiness by receiving the nature of Christ; and (3) the means of accomplishing this authenticity of holiness is to resist and avoid sin, and with persistence, continually detach any form of ungodliness from our self. God is holy, and He calls upon those who believe in Him to express His holiness in our character and behavior every day of our lives.

Humility

You may recall figure P.1, An Inverse Relationship between Humility and Pride. This graphic illustrates that an increase of humility is accompanied by a decrease of human pride. With this thought in mind, it is appropriate to designate the virtue of humility as a mark of Christian maturity. Author Andrew Murray says a believer's life must bear this stamp of deliverance from sin. He further states, "Humility is the only soil in which the graces root; the lack of humility is sufficient explanation of every defect and failure. In the life of earnest Christians, of those who pursue and profess holiness, humility ought to be the chief mark of their uprightness" (2004, 3–4).

Persecution

There are ample warnings throughout the Bible that those who claim an affiliation with God and Christ are subject to trials and tribulation. We are quite aware of this hostility through accounts of opposition to the people of God, the prophets, Jesus Christ, and the apostles, in addition to historical facts surrounding human atrocities committed against Christians. Jesus said, "If the world hates you, you know that it has hated Me before it hated you....If they persecuted Me, they will also persecute you" (John 15:18, 20).

If the naiveté of many Christians was replaced by simple awareness, they would know of this intolerance. So to ascertain that persecution is a real mark of spiritual maturity in our lives, can we say without any doubt that we have been discriminated against or maltreated because of our Christian beliefs?

Love

Many people hesitate to even touch on this subject of love because it has been discussed at such great length in both secular and religious realms. I suspect that expanded definitions and stories of love would fill volumes. Nevertheless, let us place love in the context of spirituality and God's plan of redemption by focusing now on 1 John 4 and 1 Corinthians 13.

By way of introduction, I pose two questions: Why must we love others? Why is loving God a prerequisite for loving and caring for others?

The answer to both questions is easy, for they are both answered in one verse of Scripture: "If God loved so us, we also ought to love one another" (1 John 4:11). It doesn't get simpler than this. The second question is related to the first but says nothing about the necessity of responding to His love before caring for other people. Maybe we'll gain more understanding by taking a closer look at the encounter Peter had with the risen Lord. In John 21:15–17, just before His ascension into heaven, Jesus charged Peter with the task of caring for the Shepherd's sheep. Notice that Jesus' commands to Peter were predicated on only one thing—his answer to a piercing question Jesus asked three times: "Do you love Me?"

Three times Peter must have experienced increasing inner pain because of his bold defiance only a few days before when he declared, "Even if I have to die with You, I will not deny You" (Matthew 26:35). But now, everything was quite different; Jesus had defeated death and was asking about Peter's love toward Him.

An interpretation of this encounter is that Peter's affirmative answer to Jesus was the realization (or the beginning of recognition) of Jesus' unconditional love toward him, even in light of Peter's three steadfast denials at His trial, and of his growing true love and devotion to Jesus. Obedience to do what is commanded by one's merciful master demands utmost devotion, loyalty, and especially the denial of self that is shown by the submissive one. Instead of following his natural tendencies of self-preservation and denying his Master, Peter humbly obeyed Jesus and thereafter, even in the face of persecution and death, willingly cared for others by shepherding Christ's followers.

In regard to loving God, it seems that we have gone full circle. In chapter 3, we concluded that a person's self is to truly love the Lord God with all of his heart, soul, mind, and strength (Matthew 22:37; Luke 10:27). In other words, the love comes from the totality and purity of one's being—not from a false or a fleshly self, but from a person's true self.

I especially admire C. S. Lewis's response to the issue of loving God. In his book *Mere Christianity*, he says many often are worried and cannot find feeling in themselves to love God. His recommendation is not to sit on manufactured feelings but to act as if we did. He says to ask ourselves, "If I were sure that I loved God, what would I do? When you have found the answer, go and do it" (132).

Regarding the second greatest commandment, found in Matthew 22 and Luke 10—"You shall love your neighbor as yourself"—Lewis suggests the same approach:

Do not waste time bothering whether you 'love' your neighbor; act as if you did. When you are behaving as if you loved someone, you will presently come to love him....Whenever we do good to another self, just because it is a self, made (like us) by God, and desiring its own happiness as we desire ours, we shall have learned to love it a little more or, at least, to dislike it less (131).

Whether one agrees with Lewis's approach to loving God and others, the commands to love are not negotiable. These mandates remain intact, and our part as followers of Jesus Christ is to obey them from and in our entire beings.

Loving Others

If this heading of loving others was put in the form of a question, it might be phrased: What about loving others relates to spiritual maturity? My firm opinion is that when followers of Christ obey God's second greatest commandment, they are growing spiritually and are directly involved in the center of God's plan of redemption. Too often, Christians have come to believe that redemption centers only on themselves. The Bible tells us otherwise. For when we are released from the bondage of our fleshly self, we then can deliberate on our true selves, let God transform us into Christlikeness, and become sources of love and new life for others. (See fig. 17.1.)

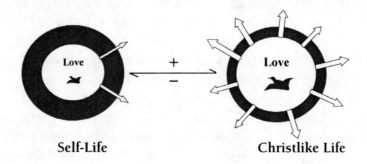

Self-Life   **Christlike Life**

Figure 17.1. The Transformation of Self-Life Results in Love to Others

This visual illustrates that the very nature of God and Christ is manifested in the life of the believer. The transformation of the self-life to the Christlike life is visualized by the changes that occur in the two self-circles. Even though both circles depict Christ's love in the core of a person's true self, only small avenues of love are burrowed through the outer carnal nature of the self-circle on the left. As previously described in the graphic Spiritual Maturity vs. Time (fig. 12.1), the plus sign signifies an inseparable identification of a believer with Christ's Passion and the resultant transformation of self such as this.

The Christlike *self*-circle on the right shows an enlarged inner core that is primarily comprised of the love of Christ, which is not purposefully retained but is more abundantly released through the outer tough cortex of self. If at any time, this corrupt aspect of self is not denied and is allowed to become a dominant force, the transformation is reversed as indicated by the minus sign. In the past, the term *backsliding* was used to describe the occurrences of continued reversals. Regardless of which label is used to describe this reversal, the likelihood of manifesting the love of Christlikeness is diminished in the life of a Christian.

This figure also helps us to understand that those having the supernatural nature of divine love also possess Christ in them. In addition, the graphic illustrates the presence of Christ's *self* in them as overcomers, "because greater is He who is in you than he who is in the world" (1 John 4:4). The "he" in this verse is Satan, the same one who is external and whose defiant spirit yet remains to some degree in one's inner self.

To more fully understand the full dimension of the two greatest commandments, we first must see what the Bible says about love. Most who have even a minimal knowledge of the New Testament will likely recall the great love chapter in the Bible, 1 Corinthians 13.

In this letter to the Corinthians, chapter 13 ends with the often-quoted verse 13: "But now faith, hope, love, abide these three; but the greatest of these is love." These three virtues are Paul's standard for all believers. Judged by this rule, love is greater than either faith or hope.

Why does Paul conclude that love is the greatest? According to most Bible commentaries, in a comparative sense, love is the more important virtue. Faith saves us and, along with hope, concerns individuals. Love also pertains to persons, but additionally is relevant to society and benefits others. Love exerts a wider influence and overcomes more evils. It is the great principle that binds the universe in harmony, unites God to His creatures and His creatures to Himself, and connects and allies all holy beings with each other.

The expression "greatest is love" designates love to be of true religion. True religion, or love to others, will prompt one to seek others' welfare and promote their happiness and salvation, even at great personal sacrifice and self-denial. If attaining happiness instead of abiding love is a person's main goal, it proves he or she is supremely selfish; selfishness is not, and never will be, a mark of spiritual growth.

In the preceding verses Paul tells us what love is and what it is not. One of those things love is not is found in verse 5 of 1 Corinthians 13: "it does not seek its own." There is, perhaps, not a more striking or important expression in the New Testament than this that more beautifully sets forth the nature and power of the love produced in a disciplined follower of Christ. This love is not of our fleshly natures but from our *self*, that is, our authentic self. Its evident meaning is that love does not seek its own happiness exclusively or its own happiness at the expense of injury to others. The manner in which love does not seek its own is illustrated above in figure 17.1. The implantation of God's love in the believer can only increase as the features of a self-life, such as self-love, decrease.

Serving Others

In this understanding of love we can return to Scripture to seek guidance on finding another characteristic that is closely related to love. In our quest to identify solidly the marks of mature spirituality, we must not bypass the quality that so completely characterized the life of Jesus Christ, the quality of an unselfish servant to others.

Jesus said, "For even the Son of Man did not come to be served, but to serve, and to give His life a ransom for many" (Mark 10:45). The apostle Paul added to this focus when he wrote, "Do not merely look out for your own personal interests, but also for the interests of others" (Philippians 2:4). But then pointing to the Savior as our great example, he promptly added, "Have this attitude in yourselves which was also in Christ Jesus" (Philippians 2:5). Paul followed this exhortation with a strong reminder of the humiliation of Christ (Philippians 2:6–11) who, though being the Son of God, emptied Himself by taking the form of a servant.

There is no question that if we are going to grow and mature into Christlike character, we must progress in giving ourselves to and for others. Servant living opposes the primary concerns and focus of our culture, personal happiness and comfort.

Further, a servant is, first of all, one who willingly yields or surrenders to somebody. For Christians, this means deference to God first and then submission to one another. To put it another way, a servant waives personal rights and meets the needs of others rather than those of self. It means to give oneself willingly to minister for and to others and to do whatever it takes to accomplish what is best for another. That doesn't sound like selfishness, does it?

Christ's plan of redemption that produces maximum blessing to the world and the church includes believers becoming servants to others. As representatives of the Lord Jesus, our failure to live as servants throws up huge barriers for effectively providing for others and for becoming active participants in God's plan of redemption. There are three questions about marks of Christian spiritual maturity that we might consider at this time.

1. What are some of the hindrances to developing an attitude of serving others?

As you consider the following, think about your own life and natural tendencies. The most direct, to-the-point answer is that these barriers are the remnants of the old man, the false self, the fleshly self, with all of its selfish and prideful tendencies. More specifically, they include a desire for status or to feel important, human strategies to meet one's own felt needs, and self-centered living or seeking happiness from the world rather than in the Savior.

2. Which of the nine marks of Christian maturity would be most practical?

This is probably the hardest question of the three to answer. As previously stated, there is little or no difference between serving and loving others. Therefore, perhaps the best answer is both of them together. This question is similar to the one posed at the beginning of this chapter: How do the marks of spiritual maturity fit into God's plan of redemption in a practical way? Most of them are sensed or experienced, but the most practical is this combination of loving and serving others.

3. How does Jesus' command to deny self and carry a cross fit into these marks of spiritual maturity?

The answer is derived from almost everything we have already said about these two commands. To illustrate this view, we can expand the matrix of Jesus' commands to deny oneself and carry a cross in order to be identified as a follower (see table 8.1). In doing so, another "yes" must be included under the column "Serve and Love Others." (See table 17.2.) According to this graphic, if one fails to obey either or both of Jesus' commands, not only is he or she considered a non-follower of Christ but this person has a decreased desire or capacity to truly love and serve others.

Jesus's Commands Matthew 16:24 Luke 9:23 Mark 8:34		Follow Christ	Serve and Love Others
Deny Self	Carry Cross		
Yes	Yes	Yes	Yes
Yes	No	No	No
No	Yes	No	No
No	No	No	No

**The Responses to Jesus's Commands
Determines Following Christ and Serving and Loving Others**

Table 17.2. An Expanded Matrix of One's Responses to Jesus' Commands

Serving and loving others is to deny self to the point of sacrificing oneself for the sake of others. Coming anywhere near to tangibly accomplishing this charge requires the surrendering of oneself to the Creator and the detachment of any natural affinities that are counter to serving others. The means of detaching our selfish fleshly self is by faith unifying both our crosses to Christ's cross and ourselves to the One who already mortified our old fleshly natures.

Throughout history, Christians who made sacrificial efforts to follow Christ and to joyfully serve others endured discomfort, but rarely to the extent that our Savior bore on the cross. In Hebrews 12:3–4, the writer tells believers not to "grow weary and to lose heart. You have not yet resisted to the point of shedding blood." Christians can know that when they surrender themselves for the sake of others they can anticipate the experience of holy joy, which has always been linked to the blessedness of Christ's resurrection.

Those of us who are willing to endure as faithful followers of Christ with attitudes of servants can be God's representatives, knowing that when we feed the poor, visit those in prison, and clothe the naked, we actually do it to Jesus Christ Himself (Matthew 25:31–46).

The Real Breaking News and Developing Story

Unlike the Breaking News and Developing Story sections inserted in this book, I need to tell you about a quite different narrative. It is not about the fictional biological scientists who attempt to determine the biochemical function of make-believe genetic material. Although an attempt was made to show some analogy to a story of Christian maturity, it is not about three people who had inner longings for completeness and sought resolution in a department store. The developing story about which I now speak is a continuation of the breaking news narrative recorded in the top-selling book in the Western world, the Holy Bible.

The real breaking news story had its beginnings from the foundations of the world and was partially revealed by prophets hundreds of centuries ago. Not until shepherds were led by a bright shining star to a manger in Bethlehem did the breaking news story begin to unfold. This historical account took place about thirty years before reaching its pinnacle on a small hill outside Jerusalem called Calvary. There, on a crudely constructed wooden framework, innocence became guilt, sinlessness became sin, and righteousness became unrighteousness; the purpose provided deliverance to all humankind. Theologically, this divine intention supplied the means of redemption for all people.

273

More accurately, the breaking news story is not followed by only one developing story; it concerns a huge number of developing stories, namely the story of every professing follower of Jesus Christ. In contrast to any fairy tale, each of these stories chronicles a real life. Each story line is distinctive in that it provides an account of how every believer throughout the ages has dealt with troubles, trials, temptations, and interpersonal relationships. It deals with detaching a false self and becoming a true self, and how well one has been available to unselfishly help others in their times of need, thereby representing Christ as His ambassadors. These are but a few of the very inward and outward features that frame the picture of a Christian's true self-image, worth, and purpose in life.

The Bible speaks of a "book of life." Paul mentions individuals by name and includes other unidentified fellow workers "whose names are in the book of life" (Philippians 4:2–3). The apostle John speaks of the book of life in connection with a New Jerusalem, a heavenly city, the place Christ is preparing for His people, saying, "no one who practices abomination and lying, shall ever come into it, but only those whose names are written in the Lamb's book of life" (Revelation 21:27). We find in Luke's gospel an account in which the disciples came to Jesus and told Him of their joyous successes over demons. Jesus responded to their story, saying, "do not rejoice in this,…but rejoice that your names are recorded in heaven" (Luke 10:20).

Whether taken literally or metaphorically, these references to the Book of Life seem to speak of the roster of righteous believers who are to inherit eternal life. Perhaps each person recorded in the book of life who is saved and whose name is not blotted out will have checkmark next to his or her name, indicating justification, the perfect righteousness of Christ. This simply means that the free gift of salvation has been imputed to the person's account; he or she is fully justified, lovingly accepted by God, and worthy of living eternally in heaven.

The point in considering such a book is twofold. First, Christians are assured that their names will not be blotted out of the book of life. Second, up to this very moment, a portion of the developing story is complete for each believer; there is no changing it for any of us. Perhaps, the Chief Accountant in heaven has tracked all the marks of maturity for each of us and prepared a plot of Christian maturity similar to the one seen in graph 12.1. To be sure, as we have already pointed out, in our humanity of possessing opposing natures, it will show the ups and downs much like a stock market graphic.

We should realize that the Chief Accountant possesses an attribute of omniscience (knowing all actual and possible things). So, in addition to tracking our marks of spiritual growth, entries in the book may include moments or periods of time we have not denied self, carried our crosses, and followed Christ. Let's assume each of these actions was simply entered in the Master Ledger as a yes or no that represents our responses to the commands of Jesus' noted in the matrix above (fig. 17.2). Similarly, a plus or minus sign is also entered to signify each of our successful or unsuccessful transformations of self-likeness to Christlikeness, respectively.

Most assuredly, you will ask what the usefulness of this data is. I really don't know. But one thing we must know is that at the end of the day, for every Christian every no and every minus sign will be blotted out from the book of life. All true followers of Christ understand this happens only because of the overflowing love and grace of God.

In our humanity, none of us is able to perfectly detail our own past spiritual growth, but with some form of accuracy we should reasonably be able to provide a spiritual autobiography. In addition to some trivial matters, we may remember feelings of being lost and longing for calmness and freedom. Most people can recall seeking resolutions to those feelings and inner tensions. Then, our choices and actions would indicate whether peace, contentment, and true joy resulted. This is all history, and we cannot change any of it.

But we know we have the capability to create our own story lines by disciplining ourselves to deny ourselves, carry our crosses and allowing God to transform us now and in the future. What will our personal graphs of spiritual maturity look like in the upcoming minutes, hours, days, weeks, months, and beyond? Over an extended period, some trends of our spiritual growth may be revealed. Will our graphs demonstrate an elevation, remain relatively level or maybe even exhibit a decline?

Remember that the book of life is one in which some names will appear, while others will not. The Bible does not tell us anything more about this book, but it might also include information concerning the believer's rewards and conduct. In 1 Corinthians 3:13–14, the apostle Paul advises believers that there will be a time at which the quality of our deeds or conduct will reveal whether we will obtain a reward. In His wisdom, God has not revealed much in the way of what these rewards will be; however, we can be assured that because God is good, the rewards will also be good.

Paul says the rewards will really depend on the foundation or standard used to obtain them (1 Corinthians 3:10—4:5). He counsels us to be careful to build on the only foundation needed by a Christian—Jesus Christ.

Regarding the importance of foundations, remember Jesus' parable of the seeds and soil. The seed sown in soil among rocks produced temporary growth because it had no firm root; the seed sown among thorns produced growth but no fruit, because of worldly concerns; the seed sown in good soil produced fruit because of the high quality of the soil (Matthew 13:20–23). In each case, the result was directly dependent on the nature of the soil, which is analogous to the foundation used to produce the Christlike qualities of life. Here, the message for believers who envision a fulfilling life of peace and contentment is that we must choose the right foundation or standard to achieve our desires.

We know there are many worldly standards people use to elevate themselves. In regard to defining a self, these standards have been described as material and financial success, intelligence and wisdom, and so forth, and they seem to be based on self-confidence and self-esteem. Again, there is only one foundation on which to build, Jesus Christ. With these thoughts in mind about who and what else might be in the book of life, it would be prudent for each of us to evaluate ourselves in terms of lostness. Let us then seek guidance, assess our options, make a decision to deny ourselves, carry our crosses, faithfully share in the Great Exchange that took place on Christ's cross, and finally, anticipate rewarding resurrection lives.

BREAKING NEWS AND DEVELOPING STORY

Anchor: "The following is a taped discussion held by the four chief investigators of the S-Factor."

Sinton: "The discovery of the S-Factor has turned out to be the most exciting episode of my life."

Selford: "We were very fortunate to attract two colleagues who masterfully helped us to determine that each of the two components of the S-Factor is linked to one of the two opposing behavior characteristics, namely selfishness and altruism."

Carataker: "I view our part in the overall study as a blessing. Maybe it was providentially planned."

Cibalo: "I agree with everything you've all said. It seems to me that the correlations we found between the subunits of the S-Factor and the virtue of altruism and the vice of selfishness are truly amazing. It is also remarkable that in the total population we evaluated, we identified about seven times more subjects as being selfish than those who manifested altruistic characteristics. But we need to ask what are the practicality and other implications of these findings."

Sinton: "You are correct. Our results indicate that all the individuals we studied have predispositions of behavior that are somehow based upon their individual genetic makeup. But, remember, our results were static, obtained only at a point in time. We really do not know if genetics, over time, can modify psychological aspects or, alternatively, if character traits such as altruism and selfishness can alter their genes."

Selford: "I agree. Never before has anyone even thought of such things. So to understand the correlations found between parts of the S-Factor and two diametrically opposed human dispositions better, we need to design and conduct another study. It would be made up of people in whom we periodically and simultaneously measure both the two subunits of the S-Factor and the traits of altruism and selfishness over a period of time."

Carataker: "You know there are groups of religious people who believe that, over time, they can fundamentally change their conduct and behavior patterns. If these changes really happen and were shown to be related to their genetic makeup, we might win the Nobel Prize!"

Cibalo: "Of the many religious views held in our society, Christianity is one of those groups that have within its body of believers those who profess to have the capacity to change from ungodly to godly people. If such alterations really occur, they would be a likely group to exhibit transformations of selfishness to altruism in conjunction with changes in the quantities of S-Factor subunits."

Selford: "That's an interesting theory, and testing it will require much more funding. So, if anyone wishes to contribute, please contact us at our web site, www.sfactorresearch.org.

"By the way, Dr. Sinton, I am willing to have your name appear before mine on all of our future research publications."

Sinton: "Thank you, Sir. That's mighty altruistic of you!"

Chapter 18

...Envision a Fulfilling Life?

The Illuminated Self 1

IN THESE FINAL chapters, I wish to interject two very important questions. First, "What about Christianity is attractive to unregenerated, unconverted, unsaved individuals?" Second, "What about Christianity is appealing to those who have professed this faith but have not yet embarked on the journey of becoming a true follower of Christ?"

To help answer these two separate but related questions, we will explore the topic of Jesus' assertion that He is the light of the world and His declaration that those who wish to become His disciples are also to be lights: "I am the Light of the world; he who follows Me will not walk in the darkness, but will have the Light of life" (John 8:12). When He spoke of spiritual matters, Jesus frequently used certain features of the physical world metaphorically. In doing so, He engaged our senses, such as seeing and hearing, to help us understand divine revelations. In concert with these physical senses, we also use our spiritual eyes and ears to see and hear these truths from Scripture. With that in mind let us examine a few of the properties of physical light, and, by analogy, relate them to the biblical use of the word *light*.

Light in the Natural Realm

We will begin with a brief scientific assessment of selected properties of light. We learn from the discipline of physics that there is a narrow band of wavelengths called visible light within the total electromagnetic spectrum. Typically, when we use the term *light* we are referring to all wavelengths that stimulate the retina of our eyes, which in turn result in the sensation of sight. Regarding the transfer of light from the sun, commonly known as white light, there are three properties of light or three things that can happen to a light wave. Depending upon the nature of the object the light wave hits, it can be reflected, absorbed, or transmitted and dispersed.

Reflection

Solid substances, for the most part, will reflect light. Light, as it is produced from a luminous object such as the sun, can illuminate certain matter, such as the moon, that is capable of reflecting that light. It is only by reflection that we see most solid objects in the physical world. This is most evident when we look ourselves at ourselves in a mirror. We see a reflection or image of ourselves; it is what we look like at that given moment.

Another example of reflection would be our perception of color. The object is colored because a specific wavelength within the light spectrum is reflected. If the object is a red apple, the fruit appears red to the observer because it reflects red light.

Absorption

If the object is totally black, all the wavelengths of light hitting that object are absorbed and no light is reflected. Moreover, no color can be perceived because all visible frequencies (light waves) of color are absorbed. If the object is not entirely black, and depending on the nature of the item, both absorption and reflection may result. A common example of light absorption is when a dark-colored vehicle is exposed to white light. This light is largely absorbed and most of its energy is converted to heat.

Transmission and Dispersion

Another feature of natural light is that its wavelengths can be transmitted. In this case, for light to enter a target object it must be clear, like a glass, quartz, or water. When all the wavelengths of the natural visible light spectrum strike one's eye at the same time, white is perceived. But in reality white light from the sun contains all possible color variations or hues, numbering in the hundreds or more. Classically, the major colors sensed by receptors in the eye are red, orange, yellow, green, blue, and violet. Each of these six colors and the multitude of other hues are characteristic of distinct wavelengths within the visible light spectrum, and during transmission in a transparent medium they can be dispersed.

This dispersion of light in a transparent object leads to a separation of the various colors. In the natural realm the best example of light dispersion is the appearance of a rainbow following rainfall. The remaining transparent droplets of atmospheric water transmit the incoming white sunlight and thereby separate the sunlight into its component colors.

We can also witness the phenomena of light dispersion with the use of a crystalline transparent prism. When white light is directed into one side of the prism, there is separation of colors which correspond to the many wavelengths of the source light. Dispersion can be viewed as a scattering of light from a fixed source. Thus, the original colorless light is divided or partitioned into its component colors.

LIGHT IN THE SPIRITUAL REALM

We see light initially introduced in the first book of the Bible, in which the created earth was formless and in darkness. The next ingenious act was uttered by God, who said, "'Let there be light'; and there was light. God saw that the light was good; and God separated the light from the darkness" (Genesis 1:3–4). So, from the very beginning, continuing to Revelation, God's Word makes an interplaying contrast between darkness and light as a recurring theme.

Borrowed from the natural world, light is inherently suited to portray spiritual realities. For the most part, however, light and life go together. We see this concept illustrated in the sun, the fountain of light, the source and sustainer of life on our planet. By its life-giving properties, all things exist; neither animal nor vegetative life could survive were it not for the sun.

The word *light* is divinely rich in its comprehensiveness and meaning. Its splendor is used throughout Scripture as a symbol and synonym for all that is luminous and radiant in the mental, moral, and spiritual realms of humankind. Of these three, light, figuratively used, has to do preeminently with spiritual life, including also an illumination of the mind that floods all the faculties of the soul: intellect, conscience, reason, and will. As we shall see in these final chapters, there is an enlightenment of these faculties in the moral and theological domains. The purposes of these illuminations include individual spiritual growth and a display of the marks of spiritual maturity.

SOURCES OF LIGHT

Any light we may reflect, absorb, or disperse will depend on the source of that light. Therefore, we must first identify the sources of light. There are many sources of light, which we will classify under three categories: true light, false light, and hybrid lights.

The True Light

True light is godly light, emanating primarily from God the Father and Jesus Christ. Some may consider that Christ Himself is the luminous object and capable of generating His light. After all, He said, "I am the Light of the world" (John 8:12). Others may say that Christ is illuminated and capable of emitting light obtained from a source other than Himself, namely from God. This interpretation is possible, for the Bible tells us that all good comes from God, who is identified as "the Father of lights" (James 1:17).

The apostle Paul helps us understand light in regard to God when he wrote to Timothy of the "King of kings and Lord of lords, who alone possesses immortality and dwells in unapproachable light, whom no man has seen or can see. To Him be honor and eternal dominion!" (1 Timothy 6:15–16). Due to our moral and spiritual incompleteness, this impasse is merely a temporary reality, for in our glorification we will see Him face to face (1 Corinthians 13:12; 1 John 3:2).

Even Moses, the leader of the Hebrew nation, could only see the symbol (a burning bush) of the God's divine presence (Exodus 3:1–6); but no man could ever see the face of God. Because He is infinite and eternal, God is incomprehensible; if He is incomprehensible to the mind, consequently He is invisible to the eye.

In the Bible, light often symbolizes the deity of God (Psalms 27:1; 36:9; 1 John 1:5) and the divine being of God's only begotten Son, who became comprehensible and visible to the eye.

Thus, we will consider Him as the luminous object and capable of generating His light to the world. Jesus is not merely a light or another light, He is *the* one and only true Light. As the light, Jesus illumines the truth, gives God's elect spiritual understanding, and reveals to us God Himself and what He has done for us. Christ calls Himself the light and asserts what He is in Himself; He possesses the essential attribute of divine nature and moral perfection but has absolutely no darkness of immorality.

In reference to the metaphor of light signifying holiness and godliness, Christ's assertion that He possesses absolute moral perfection, truth, and the freedom from moral evil can be illustrated in figure 18.1. The completely white circle of Christ's self in this drawing represents His holiness and purity. In His inner being there is absolutely no darkness at all, no ignorance, no imperfection, and no sinfulness to barricade His holiness from the dark world around Him. By virtue of not possessing any darkness, the only light emitted by Christ is true light that originates from a true self.

Radiating directly out from the core of holiness are four emissions of light, which appear cross-like in the backdrop of an obviously darkened world. This figure is intended to illustrate that

Figure 18.1. The Illumination of Christ's Self

Christ is the fountain of light. He is the true light that, because of His finished work on the cross, brings life. Those who walk in His light live in the life of Christ and the life of Christ is in them. This is the light that brings about and supports the supernatural life of Christ's followers.

Because physical light is also diffusive, it spreads out or is transmitted. It can be seen by people in the vicinity of its source. Light also illuminates, reveals, and clarifies. Although light is analogous to holiness in many ways, spiritually speaking, light might also symbolize all other distinguishing attributes of Jesus Christ. As illustrated in this figure, most notably on the cross, these traits would include both the divine and human natures of Jesus that radiate out of His being into the darkness of the world.

The False Light

The Bible provides Christians with enough information to identify the ultimate origin of false light—the archenemy of God, namely, Satan. The apostle Paul said there are "false apostles, deceitful workers," who disguise themselves as apostles of Christ. He says this is "no wonder, for even Satan disguises himself as an angel of light" (2 Corinthians 11:13–14). This fallen angel is sometimes described as Lucifer (Isaiah 14:3–20); in Latin Lucifer means Light Bringer. Lucifer is also likened to the day or morning star, both of which refer to Venus, the brightest object in the sky besides the sun and the moon. Perhaps the perpetual presence of this shining star acts as a reminder for all humanity that, although defeated during the events of Christ's Passion, the angel of light is a master of deception and still maintains a powerful force throughout the world.

There is plenty of evidence of Satan's influence on Christians. Satan:

- tempts them to lie (Acts 5:3).
- snatches the Word from their hearts so they may not believe and be saved (Luke 8:12).
- accuses and slanders them (Revelation 12:10).
- employs demons to attempt to defeat them (Ephesians 6:11–12).
- hinders or prevents their plan to advance God's kingdom (1 Thessalonians 2:18).
- tempts them to immorality because of humankind's lack of self-control (1 Corinthians 7:5).

In relation to unbelievers, as in some susceptible believers, Satan's supervising power is evident in his ability to seize the Word from their hearts so they may not believe and be saved (Luke 8:12); and he blinds their minds so they may not see the light of the gospel (2 Corinthians 4:4).

The Hybrid Lights

Throughout the ages many philosophers and religionists have tended to look at the world only in white and black. This is entirely appropriate when we contrast the true, pure, white light of God with the false light of Satan. Thus, differentiation can easily be made between absolute values of good and bad, right or wrong, just and unjust, and so on. But when we view the state of a fallen world, including humankind, it is neither wise nor true to divide the world into a simplistic schema of opposites.

Throughout this book we have consistently viewed a self living in a fallen world, having the dual natures of godliness and ungodliness. In this latter state of corruptness and defilement, it is impossible for anyone to produce pure, true light or a totally corrupt false light. Moreover, it is also impossible to be recipients of these two types of light from others, because they, too, possess divided selves.

In addition, we are flooded with a variety of hybrid lights, each of which is a combination of true and false lights. But before we take a closer look at the significance and consequences of receiving and emitting hybrid lights, we need to return to our discussion of physical light and its relation to the spiritual realm. In this regard, we can view the interactions of the true light, the false light and hybrid lights with the prisms of the mind.

LIGHT'S RELATION TO PRISMS OF THE MIND

In the technical and scientific world, many filtering devices are used in optics and sound. They function to selectively separate various electromagnetic wavelengths for a desired purpose. One such item is generically known as an optical prism. It is usually a triangular shaped transparent or semitransparent glass with flat surfaces.

By analogy, the human mind can function to some extent similarly to its physical counterpart, the optical prism. Before we begin to probe more deeply into this proposed similarity, let's look briefly at the function of the human mind.

In general, the mind is a philosophical and biological term for the center of all mental activity. It refers to the aspects of intellect and consciousness, manifested as combinations of perception, memory, emotion, will, and imagination. Also, the human mind often refers especially to the thought processes of reason. Thus, the mind is a strategic and integral part of self that can operate in a manner dissimilar to and in contrast with other aspects of the body.

HERITAGE LINKS TO THE PRISM OF THE MIND

Consider that every human being has a unique mind, which at least in part acts as an optical prism. This prism functions as a filter in the complex array of nerve and brain tissue, filtering every conceivable experience, happening, or situation into an integral portion of the mind's prism, sometimes identified as a person's heritage. This legacy was received genetically or environmentally as light from one's family, acquaintances, culture, and so forth, and thereby became the person's exclusive philosophy or mind-set, way of thinking, belief system, and particularly one's value system.

As suggested in an earlier chapter, we change chronologically from an actual, to an ideal, to a becoming self, and our prisms of mind are altered throughout these stages of development. Each prism provides a rather small but almost indelible set of values and the underlying perception of virtues derived from our genetics and environment. As stated above, lights can be viewed as experiences or those happenings that that engage the prisms of our minds. They are filtered, and if retained as having value, function as major mechanisms of the mind from which to view the world, people, and events. All of this constitutes our heritage.

In this context, it is important to note that values make up the core from which we operate or react to various situations. The direction an individual takes in his or her life is influenced and controlled by his or her personal mind-set. For example, among the many types of polar opposites in the world it seems that there are two kinds of people: those who have a predominately eternal viewpoint and those who are preoccupied with the present. One

287

group is absorbed with seeking treasures in heaven; the other accumulates assets in the here and now. They are different and often opposing perspectives.

Spiritually speaking, for the unconverted and for some nominal Christians, the incoming hybrid lights have been filtered through the prisms of their minds and they likely retained the absorbed, darkened false lights instead of the true light. Such people may be limited in understanding due to lack of experience and education, or they may have succumbed to the seductive influence of the particular culture in which they lived. These individuals may have assimilated a heritage that readily and mindlessly accepts only what has been passed on to them through the prisms of their minds, disregarding any thoughts or ideas that are counter to their particular mind-sets. Such a biography almost always results in a heritage that is dominated by the old self. These individuals lack a critical perception or mind-set.

At times, some of these people may question their heritage because of dissatisfaction with the narrow foundation of standards on which they seek success and happiness. In this state, they undoubtedly struggle with the idea of changing their long-held worldviews. If, for example, such a person was inordinately influenced by secular humanism, he would have to come to a point when he must make a choice whether or not to comply with modern cultural norms. Put another way in more general terms, he would have to make a decision to maintain his self-oriented heritage or, alternatively, to seek a new lifestyle and heritage that is based upon a different foundation of values.

THE ADVERSE AFFECT OF FALSE LIGHTS ON THE PRISM OF THE MIND

Holy Scriptures provide us with further insight into those persons who rigidly oppose many of the traditional Christian beliefs. Paul plainly says that the good news of Jesus Christ "is veiled to those who are perishing, in whose case the god of this world has blinded the minds of the unbelieving so that they might not see the light of the gospel of the glory of Christ, who is the image of God" (2 Corinthians 4:3–4).

It is not difficult to view these people as being blinded by false lights (notice the plural) from a variety of sources—such as people, experiences, and institutions of learning—all of which contain elements of belief systems other than the Judeo-Christian tradition. Paul identified these ideologies as the "tradition of men, according to the elementary principles of the world" (Colossians 2:8). Now we would label these ideologies materialism, secularism, individualism, and pragmatism.

God told Paul He was sending him to the Jewish people and the Gentiles to "open their eyes so that they may turn from the darkness to light and from the dominion of Satan to God" (Acts 26:18). Here, Paul's preaching was the vehicle to enable people to open their eyes to an understanding of the things of God and to turn from heathenism and superstition to the knowledge of God. Thus, they were brought from under the power and authority of Satan to be under the power and authority of God.

False lights can be indistinguishable from the true light. The tragic effect of these false lights is that they illuminate the old self, further harden its dense core, and thereby hinder the entrance of the one and only accurate light. Like the hard shell completely encloses a hickory nut or a hazel nut, the dominance of **self** encapsulates the inner core of a true self, and it is a hard nut to crack (pun intended).

Overall, false lights serve to edify and glorify the false old man. Not only are these illuminations absorbed in the ungodly nature of humankind like natural light is absorbed in darkened objects, but they adversely affect one's ability to recognize the true brilliance of Christ's lights. In other words, these individuals are spiritually blind or are visually compromised. So it is with those living in darkness and under the dominance of a false self, who have been deceived; they highlight their personal core philosophies and ways of thinking, rather than illuminate the kingdom values of God.

The apostle Peter said believers are "partakers of the divine nature" and should possess a number of virtuous qualities (2 Peter 1:4). If we demonstrate such virtues as "self-control,...brotherly kindness,...[and] love," we are "neither useless nor unfruitful in the true knowledge of our Lord Jesus Christ." But those who lack them are "blind or short-sighted" (2 Peter 1:6–9). Such conditions would indicate that they were also stunted in their spiritual growth in the Lord and not fully exhibiting the distinguishing marks of Christian maturity.

Another apostle also focused on the issue of blindness in terms of light and darkness, and stated, "The one who hates his brother is in the darkness and walks in the darkness, and does not know where he is going because the darkness has blinded his eyes" (1 John 2:11). Such a bitter person may still be in an unconverted existence; he ambles throughout his life in the absence of light and his grudge-bearing behavior is ample proof that he is basically a nonbeliever. In this verse, John essentially says that a person who intensely dislikes another is lost and has no eternal purpose, all of which can be attributed to blindness and a darkened and false mind-set.

THE PROPERTIES OF LIGHT THAT AFFECT THE PRISMS OF THE MIND

Light Reflection

The scientific world tells us that natural light can be reflected, so it is not difficult to suspect that spiritual light is also mirrored. Images of our inner selves, our lifestyles and conduct, values, deeds, and so forth are manifested in our everyday lives and can be observed by others. Most of these character traits and actions are outwardly visible and, if virtuous, are generally prized in most cultures. In addition to being in accord with godliness, these behaviors have the capacity to commend Christianity to the world. When the reflections are Christlike, there is evidence of human goodness. These are manifestations of acting as Jesus would and talking to others as if He somehow were speaking through us.

In the current state of ungodliness in our world, even non-Christians still honor such righteousness (goodness), which helps demonstrate the new life and the new heredity the gospel brings.

If, on the other hand, one's actions and words reflect and replicate badness, having an image of evil, wickedness, immorality, lacking mercy, being cruel, and unforgiving, then one would conclude that one's image was anything other than that of Christ.

Light Absorption

Likewise, knowing that natural light can be absorbed into objects, spiritual light also can be absorbed into the prisms of our minds. In both the natural and supernatural spheres, absorption can be defined as a preoccupation; a state of whole attention being occupied, assimilation; passage of something into another place, or ability of the object to absorb energy. When these meanings are collectively applied only to spiritual light entering the human mind, one gets the idea that absorption of light—whether true, false, or a blend of the two—has the propensity to *infiltrate* or to be incorporated into a prism of the mind, and in doing so to modify its very nature. Again, like the reflection of light, results in this alteration depend on the source of the light. If the provider of the light is false, the lights are readily impregnated in the mind's prism of the recipient in the ego or false self.

Light Refraction and Dispersion

Depending upon the particular nature of a nonspiritual prism, light is refracted and dispersed, as previously discussed. This phenomenon is used to separate a beam of white light into its constituent spectrum of colors that are visible to the human eye and is illustrated in the following figure.

While in the natural world we can readily distinguish the stark difference between the presence of light and that of darkness, we cannot see any of the separate wavelengths that really constitute white light. This is because the wavelengths of white light are invisible to the naked eye. In like manner, we cannot see God, for He is a spirit in both the natural and supernatural worlds. However, we, as born-again believers, can see symbolically and thereby understand by faith what God has miraculously accomplished in

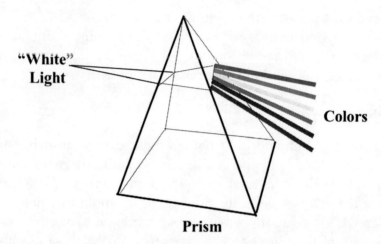

"White" Light

Colors

Prism

Figure 18.2. Dispersion of Natural Light into a Spectrum of Visible Colors

the atonement of Jesus Christ; namely, that Jesus' death brought triumph over evil, and His subsequent resurrection from the dead wondrously substantiated this victory.

So, besides seeing by faith and knowing God in connection with the victory of life over death in the historical Passion of Christ, can we see God in a real and tangible way? If the answer is yes, how do we approach such a mysterious subject? We can choose to answer this by relating virtues, one or more of God's attributes or Christ's characteristics, in a manner that is perceptible to the natural human mind. These attributes of God and the character features of Jesus become visible when we consider them as appropriated gifts that we joyfully receive through the prisms of our minds.

As we present this concept of actually visualizing these gifts within our minds and through our biological eyes, we should have a workable definition of virtues as they can be expressed in the lives of believers by means of receiving the true light.

TRUE LIGHT: AS VIRTUES

Virtues can be correctly placed into and under a broader context of values. Individual virtues (listed in appendix G) can be clustered into several categories of values. Simply stated, a single virtue is a character trait or quality that is valued as being good. Personal virtues are characteristics that are valued as promoting individual and collective well-being, and thus they are good by definition. The opposite of virtues is vices.

It is also necessary at this point to understand that I do not intend to suggest that only Christians do good acts or understand the value of possessing virtues. Everyone, including young children, understands goodness, for it is the conscience that provides the basic knowledge of right and wrong, good and bad. This understanding is a part of what Christian theology calls common grace—the recognition that God's good things can be tasted by all; they are not entirely reserved for those who believe in Him. Common grace refers to the countless, undeserved gifts of God that make our lives more comfortable, or even possible. God gives sunshine and rain to all, whether we are grateful or not.

However, these mercies of God that we depend on are meant to help lead us to a more personal category of grace (Romans 2:4). This second expression of kindness by God is given on the condition of faith and is commonly known as saving grace. It refers to all that God is ready to do for those who faithfully trust in His free offer of salvation in Christ, becoming righteous and good in His sight. This value of goodness and having virtuous behavior is at the core of Christianity and Judaism. Any goodness believers can attain always centers on the biblical belief of God's love.

With that said, we will focus now on selected virtues within only two categories of values: theological and aesthetic values. It should be emphasized that within all groups of values, whether good or perceived to be so, virtues have as their final scope to dispose us to attitudes and acts conducive to our happiness and joy.

Theological values and virtues center on monotheism, the belief that there is only one God; Judaism, Christianity, and Islam are all monotheistic. Any pleasure we derive from these theological values is twofold: (1) natural, which is attainable by our natural powers; and (2) supernatural, which exceeds the capacity of unaided fallen human nature. Since merely natural principles of human action are inadequate to a supernatural end, it is necessary that we be endowed with supernatural powers to enable us to attain our final destiny. These supernatural principles are theological virtues. In Christianity, virtues are called theological because they have God and Jesus Christ as their immediate sources and because, in sanctification, they are divinely transmitted progressively through the presence and power of the Holy Spirit.

AESTHETIC VALUES AND VIRTUES ARE FOUND...

In Nature

From both secular and spiritual perspectives, the artistry of and in nature has captured the thrill and imagination of humankind throughout history. There is splendor in viewing nature in all of its modes, whether in reality or through art, that conveys an illustration of beauty. Regarding just natural color, every drop of water in the ocean has in it the possibility of rainbow colors. In fact, all matter has color, of which the rainbow is only a specimen.

In Scripture

It is evident that the Bible is an ethical book. Righteousness in all relationships of humankind as moral beings is the key to its inspiration and the guiding light to its correct understanding. But all of Scripture inspired and penned is in an atmosphere of aesthetics. Beauty of form and color were integrated into the revelation of God's Word, and the suitability of that association has been seen and felt through the ages. We see evidence of this attractiveness in the writing of poetry and in the use of allegory, illustration, and metaphor that would charm and hold the reader's attention. The parables of Jesus are notable examples of this method. They use the imagery from familiar natural surroundings to reveal supernatural spiritual truths of God and His kingdom.

In Harmony

Harmony can be defined as a pleasing arrangement of parts, whether it be music, poetry, or even color. In visual experiences, harmony is something that is pleasing to the eye. It engages the viewer and creates an inner sense of order and balance. When something is not harmonious, it's either boring or chaotic. The human mind tends to reject what it cannot organize, or what it cannot understand. To achieve acceptable harmony requires a presentation structure that has dynamic equilibrium.

In the context of Christian spirituality, harmony becomes increasingly apparent in the relationship established between the believer and God. Harmony in the life of the follower of Christ extends beyond into the lives of others and, as evidenced by the settled condition of his or her well-being, yields a personal life characterized by orderliness, calmness, and peace of mind.

In God and Jesus Christ

Author R. C. Sproul states,

Beauty is around us everywhere, seen in the handiwork of God in nature, in the holy words of scripture, and in the harmonious works of the artists whom He has gifted in His common grace. But while all of these things are beautiful, they pale in comparison to the loveliness of the Creator Himself [and His Son]. All the travails of his life and the sacrifices that we make to serve the Lord will be more than worth it when on that day we gaze upon His beauty. (August 2009, 55)

In True Followers of Christ

People generally appreciate artistic values, even as evidenced in others, but principally in Christians. There is beauty in personal virtue, for virtue can be attractive, good-looking, striking, appealing, alluring, pleasing, pleasant, lovely, charismatic, and desirable. On the other hand, vices can be repellant, ugly, disgusting, revolting, hideous, and repulsive.

For Christians who are maturing in the grace and knowledge of Christ, there is a multitude of beautiful experiences and expressions of their life that include the following:

- Finding their true selves as they become more Christlike.
- Losing their old selves.
- Witnessing spiritual maturity in other Christians.
- Experiencing shalom, the peace of mind.
- Having the joy of a growing, harmonious, and intimate relationship with Jesus.
- Realizing fulfillment and contentment by the faithful obedience to God's commands to love Him, others, and self.
- Experiencing the reality of seeking and finding Christ.
- Knowing they are in Christ and He is in them.
- Knowing that faithfulness toward God in the daily journey is pleasing to Him.
- Seeing in themselves the creativity of Christlikeness by the renewing of the mind.
- Anticipating goodness and joy that result from faithfully following Jesus.
- Receiving and sharing the love of God and Jesus Christ with others.
- Realizing that others who are observing their attitudinal transformations may come to a saving knowledge of their own.
- Helping to motivate others—by the attractiveness of their own virtues and other marks of Christian spiritual maturity that resonate in the minds of these individuals—to become followers of Christ.

Beauty is contained in all of these observations, and especially the last three points. Paul may have had in mind these considerations when he told early believers to *put on* or *be clothed with* new garments, a distinguishing mark of Christian maturity. In fact, these aesthetic features in true believers should help answer the two questions posed at the beginning of this chapter: "What about

Christianity is attractive to unconverted individuals?" and "What is appealing to those who have accepted the gift of salvation by faith but have not become true followers of Christ?"

The answer must be that there is a good type of covetousness that is created in the minds of these individuals. With their natural senses, they can see, hear, and feel some of the magnetism that makes them desire something believers have but they do not. These individuals may not accurately define that something in Christians, but in many cases it is a combination of the caring, trustworthy, peaceful, humble, helpful, and joyful nature of believers.

Basically, we are talking about goodness. Most people instinctively know there is something worthy about goodness. Goodness functions as a potent attractant that has a unique true beauty of its own. More specifically, goodness is the attitudes and the character traits outwardly manifested in the daily lives of believers, which if really known, are the same ones that Jesus displayed during His life here on earth.

Chapter 19

... Envision a Fulfilling Life?

The Illuminated Self 2

TRUE LIGHT: ITS TRANSFORMATIONAL POWER

LET'S RETURN TO the model of transformation established in preceding chapters. This is a model of spiritual transformation that includes Christian doctrinal features one through five, which we will further discuss in this chapter. Essentially, this renovation solidly plants our minds on a particular matter in a contemplative mode (1–3) then propels our minds backward (a flashback) to Jesus' Passion (4) and forward in time (a flash forward) to joyousness (5). In essence, the concern here is a change of a person's perspective. Even more specifically, in the parlance of Christian theology, the issue is one of sincere repentance leading to a transformed life. This model is graphically summarized in figure 19.1 below and relabeled the Transformation of a Mind from Old Self to a New Self.

1. Lostness

Someone has said, "The proof of spiritual maturity is not how pure you are but your awareness of your impurity." This awareness awakens the conscience of a person and captures the essence of lostness. Because the issue at hand concerns the illumination of ourselves, it should be obvious that there are impurities of both

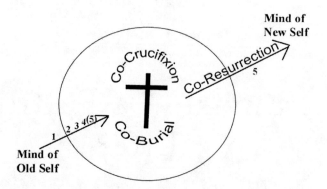

Figure 19.1. The Transformation of a Mind from an Old Self to a New Self

darkness and blindness in our depraved and defiled minds that need to be dealt with. At this stage, it's not a matter of determining when, where, and how these pollutants originated, but one of realizing that their internal existence hinders the flow of true light and the progress of growing spiritually.

2. Guidance

Many times the Bible tells us that the conviction of lostness opens the door for the Holy Spirit to escort us to a place where answers to perplexing issues of life are found. Surely, routes taken to maneuver us toward such a place vary widely, but the one we are most familiar with is the truth found in God's Word. By hearing and reading to internalize the Word, we are directed to the source of true light, and we find the remedy to cure the blindness in our minds.

3. Assessment

We refer to biblically based appraisal as self-reflection, self-evaluation, or self-criticism. It has been said that no one is as blind as the person who is incapable of self-reflection. This kind of reflection is not to be a guilt-driven pursuit, but rather an accurate sign of our dual natures of purity and uncleanness. Where do we get this inner reflection? The answer is that it mainly comes from the piercing Word of God and also possibly from a trusted brother or sister in Christ.

If we fail to reflect on ourselves in this manner, we will stifle personal growth and development. Just like we do spring cleaning to get rid of clutter and to organize our lives, the Scriptures encourage us to examine ourselves frequently within, taking an honest inventory of the motives and desires from which we act, so that we may find ourselves glorifying God and not anyone or anything else.

4. Decision and Action

Unlike the transparent crystal prism into which natural light is immediately dispersed and observed as colors with our natural eyes, to some extent the spiritual prisms of the mind are fogged. This cloudiness is due to a depraved mind that obstructs the transmission of true light. In the New Testament we find that the depraved mind is linked to argumentative behavioral traits and impurities of thought and conscience.

Paul talks about unceasing quarrels between individuals and tells Timothy there is "constant friction between men of depraved mind and deprived of the truth" (1 Timothy 6:5). The arguments cannot be settled, not only because some individuals will not listen to the truth (a hearing problem) but because their minds are corrupt.

On a different occasion, in his letter to Titus Paul states that "to those who are defiled and unbelieving, nothing is pure, but both their mind and their conscience are defiled" (Titus 1:15). Paul is saying that in their consciences and minds, both to offered and received grace, nothing is pure and these people have no part in Christ. Their minds are contaminated with impure and unholy images and ideas, and their consciences are defiled, possibly with the guilt of their sins. At least in part, we take this indictment to mean that the believer's ability to emit true light is decreased because too much false light is lodged in his mind and is actively being radiated outward from his self-oriented nature.

As we previously discussed a resolution of our old, false self life in chapters 12,13,14 and 16, and now labeled Decision and Action, we need to find a way to both reverse this hindering effect of blindness and to correct our vision. The only way to detach the cobwebs from the prisms of our minds and to alter the perceptions of our old heritage is by an unyielding identification with Jesus' Passion, as indicated by consideration of number 4 shown in figure 19.1 above.

I also have come to believe that the way to achieve these actions is through renewing the mind! Within the context of believers offering themselves as living sacrifices, Paul urges each us to "not be conformed to this world, but be transformed by the renewing of your mind" (Romans 12:1–2). From the commentaries and other resources I have read, the meaning of these two verses is that we should not cherish a spirit that is devoted to the world, following its vain fashions and pleasures, but cultivate a spirit that is attached to God, His kingdom, and His cause. This is a transformational experience Christians are exhorted to practice, not to bring about a mere external change, but to bring about an inner change that results from the continual replacement of the old shaded mind, to an entire alteration of the state of the mind, a new heritage.

On another occasion, Paul spoke to the need to look at eternal instead of temporal things. As we do so, we are likely to experience affliction, but at the same time, we are to realize that our "inner man is being renewed day by day" (2 Corinthians 4:16–18). This renewal of self is one that is constantly renovating, strengthening and invigorating. The powers of the mind are expanded and we gain clearer views of the light of truth and an enhanced faith in God.

Both of these passages bring together the thoughts of recurring troubling situations for believers who are accompanied by the continual need to renew our minds. For our immediate instruction, to renew something, such as our mind, means to regain or revive, to be metamorphosed or renovated, or to appear as a new creation with a clearer view of true knowledge.

In fact, we find a link between true knowledge and the likeness of God. Paul tells the believers to lay "aside the old self with its evil practices and…put on the new self who is being renewed to a true knowledge according to the image of the One who created him" (Colossians 3:9–10). *The Message* renders these verses in a very contemporary and descriptive way: "You're done with that old life. It's like a filthy set of ill-fitting clothes you've stripped off and put in the fire. Now you're dressed in a new wardrobe. Every item of your new way of life is custom-made by the Creator, with his label on it." From this novel wording of Scripture we get the idea that renewal of the mind also results in regaining the reflection or image of the divine nature that was originally placed in humankind (Genesis 1:26). Is this not a wonderful way to understand God's intention of changing one's perception and transforming self?

The word *renewed* cited above in Colossians refers to a transformational nature and can be partially illustrated in computer terminology. The system tools section of most personal computers includes two valuable software utilities that are commonly known as a cleaner and defragmenter of a hard drive disk. Respectively, use of these programs allows a person to delete temporary or invalid files and to reduce file fragmentation by physically reorganizing and restoring the contents of the disk. The computer operator can periodically choose to run these utilities to minimize computer crashes and errors, thereby increasing the overall performance of the computer.

In a sense, the use of these beneficial operations allows a computer's hard drive to be revived or renovated, and thereby can be likened to mind renewal. A renewed mind of a believer can be viewed as cleaned and defragmented; it is cleansed of cloudy impurities and better organized with true knowledge. Marvelously, this resemblance between the cleaning of a computer's hard drive and renewal was predated by a psalmist living sometime in the tenth century B.C. He associated cleanliness with renewal of self when he wrote, "Create in me a clean heart, O God, and renew a steadfast spirit with me" (Psalm 51:10). Amazing.

Is it also possible that the renewing of the mind is simply analogous to the transformation to Christlikeness by mortification of the false self? Is it feasible that this scriptural truth of mind-renewal is the divine means to change one's old self-seeking heredity to a new heredity in the family of God? Without the true light of God and Jesus Christ penetrating and exposing our false perspectives, could we by ourselves ever do away with our old false, corrupted philosophies and ungodly attitudes and dispositions? These synonyms of old perspectives are the very derivatives of the false self that must be stripped off and done away with by the Spirit so that the true light of Jesus Christ can manifest itself in our lives.

Over the years, I have had the opportunity to engage in conversations with others, whether Christian or not, about their religious beliefs. Almost invariably, if they were forthcoming, some would staunchly focus on a few pet peeves or irritations about particular religious matters. Without becoming specific or judging them as right or wrong on these issues, I was constantly struck by the tenacity with which these individuals held onto their ideas. You might say, "Well, that's the way it is; some people think one way and others think another." That's entirely correct. But that is the very point I am making. We each have our own particular mind-set, value system, or philosophy. We have identified these things as the core of perspectives, firmly lodged as the heritage that resides in the prisms of our minds. For the Christian, this heritage is to be expected as normal and is acceptable if it is not cluttered with excessive worldly values that conflict with kingdom values.

If you are evangelical in your Christian doctrine and believe the thesis of dualism as shown in Romans 7, you must realize how difficult it can be to convert a mind that is clouded by the input of excessive false lights. But that is the challenge for us who support and work for individual and cultural transformations.

However, in this regard, all followers of Christ have a common starting point. We simply have to claim the new heritage God has so graciously provided. The Bible tells us our heritage has been changed because when we received salvation we obtained "the adoption as sons" (Galatians 4:5), and "if a son, then an heir through God" (Galatians 4:7). Paul also tells us, "For all who are being led by the Spirit of God, these are sons of God" (Romans 8:14), and further, "The Spirit Himself testifies with our spirit that we are children of God, and if children, heirs also, heirs of God and fellow heirs with Christ" (Romans 8:16–17). This can only be viewed as one of the great added blessings we have as followers of Christ.

So it is obvious that, by the grace of God, Christians experience a positional change of heritage when we receive the spirit of adoption as sons and daughters of God. Our part in this gift of grace is to claim and reclaim by the daily renewing of our minds—our glorious heritage—and by the responsible growing into greater spiritual maturity. Referring to figure 19.1, this is accomplished by transformations from a mind-set according to the flesh and the impulses of the old nature (in the old man) to a new mind-set (in the new man).

Through the Great Exchange on the cross of Calvary, Christ has provided the means to appropriate a new mind-set and utilize the light of His mind in the minds of believers. We, as followers of Christ, have the great privilege to convert our minds to the likeness of Christ's mind as it is revealed to us by His Spirit. In fact, this claim is supported by Scripture. We are told that believers have a matching mind that was in Jesus Christ! "We have the mind of Christ" (1 Corinthians 2:16). By the high merit of His Spirit dwelling in us and since we possess the light of Jesus' mind, we can reflect, absorb, and disperse His true light. These spiritual properties are best carried out in the mind's eye that is healthy and not clouded with darkness.

Someone said that "Sin and our fallen nature is an eye and mind disorder that is diagnosed and cured by the Great Physician." In the context of placing one's desires on earthly or heavenly things, Jesus Christ contrasts the value of things within these two domains in terms of one's good or bad eyesight, and of the presence or absence of light: "If your eye is clear [good and healthy], your whole body will be full of light. But if your eye is bad, your whole body will be full of darkness. If then the light that is in you is darkness, how great is the darkness!" (Matthew 6:22–23).

Some biblical authorities interpret this passage to mean that good eyes receive and fill the body with God's light so that the light would serve God, self, and others. If the clarity and purity of good light are clouded by worldly standards, the light which is within becomes darkened. If this condition is not successfully treated, loss of sight and union with God could result. This state of being may be precisely what Jesus meant when He said, "How great is the darkness."

Regarding the treatment and cure of this eye problem, I think being spiritually blind and having a mind dominated by falsity is like having ocular cataracts. In this visually compromised condition, especially in older people, objects appear blurred, the sense of brilliance is lowered, and colors lose their natural beauty. The treatment for this decreased vision is surgical removal of the old corrupt lens, accompanied by a replacement with a totally new, transparent intraocular lens. In the spiritual realm, this miraculous feat of exchanging our defective human natures for the purity of Christ's character can only be accomplished by the divine Ophthalmologist. In this case, not only is Christ the Chief Diagnostician and Surgeon, He is also the willing Donor of Himself to replace the loss of our imperfect eyesight.

Because true followers of Christ believe this doctrine of sanctification, we do not play a passive or unconscious part in this spiritual operation. In a partnering manner in obedience to Jesus Christ, we deliberately deny ourselves, take up our cross, and submissively come to the Lord, asking in faith for emancipation from this debilitating illness. Knowing we have the mind of Christ (2 Corinthians 6:16), our minds are united with Christ's and directed to the time and place when Jesus took upon Himself our depravity for all times with all of its ungodly forms.

In that historic event, Christ's pure white self-circle became the blackest self-circle ever, even to the point of God's face turning aside. Part of that intense blackness in Christ was our own darkened depravity; therefore, as a flashback experience, we should not make any mistake about our role in the co-crucifixion with Jesus on the cross. The necessary price has already been paid on our behalf, to deliver us from the darkness and blindness of our minds.

5. Joy

If there is any joy associated with the transformation from an old to a new self, it necessarily will be joy in which hope and the assurance of resurrection come into play. The author of Hebrews made this plain as he summarized many of the lives of saints in ancient times, saying that all of them, "having gained approval through their faith, did not receive what was promised, because God had provided something better" (Hebrews 11:39–40). He goes on to say that even Jesus, "the author and perfecter of faith," had "joy set before Him" and endured the cross (Hebrews 12:2). It would seem that we will not fully receive the promised glorious light while we continue our daily activities on earth, but we must await that heavenly call.

This same idea is conveyed by Paul, who, in the first chapter of Ephesians told the believers at Ephesus how blessed they were because of their association with God and Jesus Christ, and that he prayed for each one that "the eyes of your heart may be enlightened, so that you will know what is the hope of His calling, what are the riches of the glory of His inheritance" (Ephesians 1:18).

On the other hand, although we have not been fully glorified and cannot see God, in brief moments of glimmering illumination we may experience elements of joy associated with His love that is all around and in us. The love that is in us may be better understood by the Hebrew word *hesed*, translated loving-kindness, which is used to describe the Lord more than 250 times in the Old Testament. It is a loyal, steadfast, and faithful love that stresses the idea that those involved in the love relationship belong together. It is this type of love that is imparted to us during our transformations to ever-increasing Christlikeness. Expressions of loving-kindness become visible when followers of Christ manifest His virtues, not any we conjure up on our own. If the prism of our minds is transparent and relatively free of thoughts that impede the transmission of true light, our minds can disperse Christ's unseen radiation into a visible array of colors as illustrated in figure 19.2.

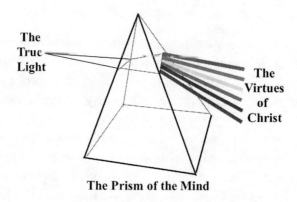

The True Light

The Virtues of Christ

The Prism of the Mind

Figure 19.2. Transmission of True Light Disperses the Virtues of Christ

You may ask, what do light dispersion and colors have to do with Christianity? We will continue to use prisms to answer this question, as appropriate metaphors to show the result of incoming true light as it is transmitted and dispersed in the minds of believers. I trust that this well-confirmed property of light will illustrate the spiritual means to understand a biblical worldview. To accomplish such an undertaking also should help ultimately to illuminate our minds as to our identity and purpose(s). (Again, refer to appendix F, What Christians May Know about Themselves.)

The variety of colors seen in figure 19.2 is derived from the true light from Christ and the true lights of fellow Christians. We need to be reminded that as the entire spectrum of colors can be dispersed from white light in a natural prism, so can a multitude of colored virtues be seen in our spiritual counterparts, the prisms of our minds. In this latter case, each of the hundreds of hues can be equated to one of Christ's numerous virtues. (You are encouraged to view the list of virtues in appendix G or make your own list of desirable virtues.)

The Importance of Right Thinking

One of the main functions of the mind is that of thinking, which encompasses our beliefs, reasoning, and outlook on life. Thinking, whether morally good or bad, positive or negative, creative or destructive, constitutes the very essence of every human being. In the book of Proverbs, the author tells us about a man's thoughts: "as he thinks within himself, so he is" (Proverbs 23:7). The verb *thinks* probably means as he is in himself, so he is in action. If he thinks selfishly, he is selfish. If his thoughts focus on kindnesses, he is kind. If this is an accurate interpretation, then it is imperative that a follower of Christ rightly thinks righteous thoughts through the clear prism of his or her mind.

We are told to think and dwell on excellencies or virtues: "whatever is true, whatever is honorable, whatever is right, whatever is pure, whatever is lovely, whatever is of good repute" (Philippians 4:8); and when such thoughts are practiced, "the God of peace will be with you" (Philippians 4:9). Many have sought the peace of God in their lives by meditating on such virtues, but have been unsuccessful because practicing the excellencies was lacking.

The Importance of Rightly Appropriating Virtues

One of the major reasons for this shortage of success is that believers have not faithfully or actually appropriated the means to acquire these unmerited blessings and virtues. While prayer and other Christian disciplines are necessary for daily living, God has lovingly endowed us with One who says "let him deny himself, and take up his cross and follow Me....Whoever loses his life for my sake will find it" (Matthew 16:24–25). In these words of Jesus, as mentioned, the *it* means life, and moreover, is equivalent to the true light of Jesus in the world. Jesus tells the listener who follows Him, " shall have the light of life (John 8:12). As suggested above, the light of life in His followers includes the visible manifestations of the beautifully colored virtues of Christ.

In the Sermon on the Mount, Jesus used the metaphor of darkness and light as He pictured one who lives in God's kingdom as a light. Jesus told His disciples, "You are the light of the world" (Matthew 5:14). The graphic seen in figure 19.3 might represent what Jesus meant when He said His followers would be lights of the world. It portrays a believer's self embedded in what seems to be a cross made up of four light emissions. The radiance of the cross's true light originates within the center of self and filters through the darkened shell of self into an even darker world.

Figure 19.3. The Illumination of a Believer's Self

As you recall, the justified self of a believer (see fig. 9.1) who has faithfully established his citizenship and heritage in heaven, is identified as a totally white self-circle. Throughout this book, depictions of a believer's self-circle during sanctification salvation show both the whiteness of purity and the darkness of uncleanness. We now use this same self-circle of a true follower of Christ as he is slowly but surely becoming transformed from living a self-oriented life to a life of Christlikeness.

You will notice a great similarity between figure 19.3 and figure 18.1, which illustrates Jesus Christ as the Light of the world. Both figures show the brilliance of light in contrast to the blackened backgrounds. This similarity provides the context in which the true light's power is best realized in the darkened nature of humankind and in the world. The only difference between the figures is that Christ's self is entirely white, whereas the self-circle of a believer contains the persistent, darkened outer portion, which signifies the residual fleshly nature. By having a self-absorbing part of his inner self, the believer retains the innate capacity to radiate his or her selfish nature into the world. In this figure, these particular rays of self are not shown because these bogus radiations are unworthy and essentially no different than the falsity of worldly illuminations. Only Christ-inclined radiation is produced.

The Purpose of an Illuminated Self

We reminded of Paul's words, that "we are His [God's] workmanship, created in Christ Jesus for good works, which God prepared beforehand so that we would walk in them" (Ephesians 2:10). Rather than selfishly acquiring any of Christ's virtues for ourselves alone, we are to display the character of Christ in practical ways through our good works. In other words, we are not to be transformed, renewed and re-created to Christlikeness just for ourselves, but to exhibit the magnificent hues of Jesus Christ's light to a watching world.

After Jesus instructed His brethren to be the light of the world, He directed each one, "Let your light shine before men in such a way that they may see your good works, and glorify your Father who is in heaven" (Matthew 5:16). This verse unmistakably discloses the purpose for the righteous followers to shine their lights. It has nothing to do with their personal achievements or earthly rewards, but everything to do with good deeds that are to be observed (and experienced) by others and thereby demonstrate the glory of their heavenly Father. This is the type of radiation that exalts God and not self. It is the radiation that God looks at and finds favor in us. It is these "what I do" actions that constitute our good works and pay tribute to our heavenly Father.

My intention here is to equate the true light of mature believers with the observable virtues or marks of Christian maturity. Viewing spiritual growth in this manner should indicate that the greater one's maturity, the greater the potential for generating greater intensities of true light.

Conversely, those who have little growth because of sizeable amounts of self-interest will be encumbered. The author of Hebrews may have had these obstacles in view when he wrote, "lay aside every encumbrance and the sin which so easily entangles us " (Hebrews 12:1). It is noteworthy that the word *encumbrance* in this verse can mean whatever weighs us down or whatever gets in our way that effectively hinders us. Also, in this same verse, the phrase "entanglement of sin" has been illustrated as an inner barrier or hindrance of corruption that surrounds and binds us.

In fact, this entanglement has been aptly described in *Adam Clarke's Commentary on the New Testament* as a prisoner enslaved in a strong fortress, being bound by it and "often hemmed in on every side; it is a circular, well-fortified wall over which we must leap or must break out." Note that the commentator's portrayal of this imprisonment closely matches the darkened outer portion of the self-circle; namely, **self**, the ungodly aspect of self, which we have repeatedly likened to the unregenerated nature of humankind.

The Importance of Consistency

As we consider those who witness our outward marks of Christian spiritual maturity with their own God-given senses, I would like to make another observation about Christians as lights of the world. As we know, light is diffusive; it has a quality of spreading or scattering in many directions. As a result, light diminishes and becomes less intense or bright as it spreads away from its source. The practical application of this physical phenomenon of light is that those who would best witness the illuminating features of Christian virtues are those who are in closest proximity to others, both in distance and relationally.

Who might these people be? If not unbelievers, most likely they would be family members, relatives, close friends, and associates with whom we work and socialize frequently. Of utmost importance, they are often children who look at their parents or guardians to meet their fundamental needs of love, guidance, sustenance, protection, and acceptance.

Most would agree that a person's belief system within his heritage, whether Christian or not, is rarely if ever observed in isolation, but is lived out before a watching world. Jesus certainly would have agreed with this truth, for He regarded Himself as the Light of the world (John 8:12), and He applied the same role to His disciples. I again ask, "Who watches our lights?" Paul, a seasoned disciple, apostle, and preacher of the gospel, says to those in the church at Philippi that they (the light producers) "appear as lights" to a "crooked and perverse generation" (Philippians 2:15).

We are acutely aware that numerous false lights are emitted from a willful generation in a contrary world. In the eyes of these individuals, what about our lights distinguishes us from the other lights?

Charles Ringma offers one answer to this question.

> What people are looking for is not always self-evident. They are looking for a consistency [of Christians] between our words and our deeds. Thus we are in the arena under the spotlight, not because people are deliberately seeking the light, but because we who claim to live in the light often do so poorly. Their scrutiny calls us to greater consistency and, in their appraisal; they may yet see a glimmer that resonates in our being. (2002, meditation for January 15)

It is this glimmer of the true light in the children of God that may well help diminish the darkness in the lives of others, and perhaps motivate them to seek something in followers of Christ that they do not possess.

But here again, we have to be candidly honest with ourselves and fully admit that the radiations we often emit are sometimes hybrid, a mixture of motives, a distorted cross between our two natures that is unlike the purity of Christ's light. It is a combination of rays coming from both our self-life and from our Christlike life. Could this be the lack of consistency about which Ringma was talking?

Ironically, Jesus, the true Light of the world, is also associated with a cross! Here I do not refer to the cross He carried and died upon, but a cross of His two natures, divine and human. However, instead of contradicting each other, Jesus' natures both were beautifully perfect and complete; they were harmoniously blended together in oneness with His Father to yield the true light of the world and the perfect sacrifice that was required to redeem the incompleteness of humankind.

Like Jesus' paradoxical sayings and commandments that He gave to the disciples (Matthew 16:28; Mark 8:35; Luke 9:23), He, too, had to deny Himself and carry His cross to complete His work on the cross of Calvary. In harmony with Christ's life and His sacrificial atonement, the work of believers is to daily portray His perfect light in the form of the cross He bore and died upon. This is really the meaning of figure 19.3.

In the twenty-first century, are we to shine our lights into the world as Jesus said His righteous followers were to do? Yes. When our lights shine, our true light that mimics and reflects the light of Christ is providentially designed to draw attention to our cross and our Christlikeness. However, at times, in our state of lostness we emit light from our unrepentant selves that has absolutely no connection to a cross of any kind. To be sure, some would say it is light, but it is a false light derived from a false self. Many of those in the world are astute enough to see that these rays quickly blend into the hundreds of other false lights of the world. To those outsiders, the two different types of radiation that may be emitted from professing believers in Christ may well be the very inconsistencies to which Ringma referred.

The Importance of Resolving Life's Dilemmas

When we feel uneasy and our lives seem to lack meaning and purpose, is this really a dilemma of living an inconsistent life? Life is so complex and there are too many factors that come into play to draw any definitive conclusion. However, I believe Christians do not have to continue living with this type of inner conflict. We can simply come to our senses and remember the anguishing question of the apostle Paul: "Who will set me free from the body of this death [from the carnal fleshly sin nature]?" (Romans 7:24).

In the next verse, Paul immediately answers his own question: "Thanks be to God through Jesus Christ our Lord!" (Romans 7:25). In this exclamatory response, Paul realized that alone he was unable to emancipate himself from his indwelling sin nature. He was exuberantly grateful to Christ for liberating him from the control of his fleshly self. With the power of the Holy Spirit, he was delivered from death to life, from deception to truth, from false to true light, from anxiety to contentment, and from inconsistency to consistency.

Revisiting Two Stories

To reverse and resolve any inconsistency in our lives (like the dilemma of Paul), let's take one last peek at the three shoppers in our story and the associated tale of three people who approached Christianity. I am sure you have already singled out and even placed labels on these characters. In fact, you may have cited your own name on one or more of the actors.

We all know it is not a good idea to tag people with letters in the alphabet, so to some extent, we further want to identify these fictitious people in reality and trace their actions as they might progress from a state of lostness to a condition of joyfulness.

- All three have real names. They are just ordinary folks of all ages with no celebrity status or outstanding background. In addition, no one is exactly like another. Each has his or her own unique personality traits and idiosyncrasies that bear no hint of an ethical or moral value.
- The advertisement that informed them of a possible item was not a newspaper, but the good news of the gospel, whether they read it, heard it, or saw it expressed in lives of Christians.

315

- The lostness of the three people was not physical, but either they were without a complete saving knowledge of Jesus Christ or they did not attain the full and complete stature of Christ.
- The clerk who offered assistance and provided guidance was the Holy Spirit.
- The reception of the sought items by two of the individuals varied. One obtained it with sincere acceptance, and the other gave only a half-hearted, insincere response.
- The cashier and owner of the store was God. The payments were not of money. God, speaking through Isaiah, invites everybody to enjoy salvation and all of its benefits, but not to spend money to gain it, for it is a gift (Isaiah 55:1).
- The items turned out to be articles of clothing, a wardrobe of garments that would reflect the quality of the nature of the person wearing them. Some items were beautifully colored and durable, while other garments had little attractiveness and resembled old clothing that should have been discarded long ago.
- The first person significantly matured in the sanctification aspect of his salvation and was glorified.
- The second person did not mature spiritually because he failed to enter abundantly into the wonderments of sanctification.
- Other unidentified people who saw the wearers of these items were impressed to the degree that they either sought to buy the goods or decided not to.
- Regarding the parable of the sowers of seed, those sown on good soil likely are representative of the first person who produced a great harvest. His success may not have been because he was necessarily the most mature in terms of Christlikeness when compared to other maturing believers, but because he was better able to rid his soil of rocks and thorns. The second person may best be likened to those who heard the Word, but because his soil contained unmanageable rocks and thorns, the seed brought no fruit to maturity.

Last, when the Word is stolen by the evil one, there is only unbelief. This would be reminiscent of the third person.

- Regarding the illumination of self, the first person possessed a purer mind and clearer vision when compared to the second. Moreover, the first person experienced joy and manifested character virtues that should not only please God, but also serve the purpose of attracting others to Christ.

These tales are told as analogies for twenty-first-century believers who desire to become more Christlike in their journeys of faith. Based upon the doctrine of salvation derived from the Holy Scriptures, maturing Christians who apply the gospel message in their lives know they will experience peaks and valleys, but that they should anticipate the joy of discovering meaning, purpose, and worth in their lives. I personally attest to the truthfulness of these statements.

The Importance of Growing Spiritually

The importance of maturing spiritually for the sake of Christ involves faithfully losing the phoniness, selfishness, and pride of our old corrupt life. It also causes the shedding our old heritage and claiming our new heritage as adopted sons and daughters in God's family. In concert with the presence of God's Spirit, growing in Christlikeness powerfully renews and regenerates the illumination of our true selves. Followers of Christ have come to realize that expressions of spiritual growth are not only what we do, but who we really are as true selves. In this doing and being we can, in the here and now, envision fulfillment and contentment with God, others, and ourselves.

All Christians are called to become more mature in their journeys of faith. Along with diminishing our self-lives and enhancing our Christlike lives by transformations of our minds, we should realize that these God-ordained life changes can become the attractants to those who are not believers and to the many who identify themselves as Christians but have not progressed in their journeys of faith.

At this concluding juncture, let us briefly reflect on our journey so far. As nonbelievers and Christians, at some level, we all started in a state of lostness. We ended in the process of finding and in a condition of being found. In a reformative and repetitive fashion, we have gone from misguided troubled selves to realms of satisfying wellness. The intertwining threads that connected the limits of lostness and finding were the features of guidance, assessment, and action. In our journey, the specific action on our part to detach the obstacles of spiritual maturity and acquire Christlikeness was one of faithful obedience to Jesus' commands of daily self-denial and cross-carrying. In addition to joyfully discovering the infamous and wonderful *it* stated in Jesus' promise, we have found and will continue to find favor with God.

I trust that I have, at least in part, achieved my goal of helping you to envision a fulfilling life of Christian spirituality.

> "Then Jesus said to His disciples, 'If anyone wishes to come after Me, let him deny himself, and take up his cross and follow Me. For whoever wishes to save his life will lose it; but whoever loses his life for My sake shall find it.'"
> —Matthew 16:24–25

Appendix A

Hyphenated Self-Terms

self-abnegation. The denial of self (a Christian virtue).

self-absorbed. Preoccupied with self; excessively concerned with your own life and interests.

self-abuse. Criticism of self; somebody's deprecation or deliberate misuse of his or her talents and abilities.

self-actualization. Realization of one's full potential.

self-aggrandizement. The act or process of making oneself greater.

self-assertiveness. Outspoken; tending to be aggressively confident in making your views heard and your presence felt.

self-assuredness. Self-confident, sure of oneself.

self-awareness. The realization or perception of one's own personality or individuality.

self-centeredness. Thinking only of self; tending to concentrate selfishly on your own needs and affairs and to show little or no interest in those of others.

self-confessed. According to own admission, admitting freely to having a particular characteristic, quality, or behavior.

self-confident. Behaving in a relaxed manner that displays confidence that your views and abilities are of value.

self-confidence. Having confidence in oneself when considering a capability, or faith in one's own abilities.

319

self-congratulation. Smugness; the frequent mentioning of personal achievements and the displaying of the smug satisfaction taken in them.

self-consciousness. Ill at ease, feeling acutely and uncomfortably aware of your failings and shortcomings when in the company of others and believing others are noticing them too, excessively concerned with appearances; highly conscious of the impression made on others and tending to act in a way that reinforces this impression.

self-containment. Having everything required; possessing all the features and facilities required to function independently or keeping feelings private; able or tending to keep feelings and opinions private or to control feelings and reactions in front of others.

self-control. Restraint; the ability to control your own behavior, especially in terms of reactions and impulse (a Christian virtue).

self-deception or **self-delusion.** The state of being deceived by oneself or the act of deceiving oneself.

self-defense. The act of protecting or defending oneself; or a plea of justification for a given action.

self-denial. Denial of own desires; the setting aside of your own wishes, needs, or interests, whether voluntary, altruistic, or enforced by circumstances (a Christian virtue).

self-destruction. Ruining of one's own life; the ruining of your own life or an aspect of it such as your health, happiness, or career; an act or instance of suicide.

self-determination. Right to decide for self; the ability or right to make your own decisions without interference from others.

self-discipline. Ability to motivate self; the ability to do what is necessary or sensible without needing to be urged by somebody else.

self-divinization. Humankind elevation to demigod; in philosophical terms, the elevation by human beings of humankind to godlike status.

self-esteem. Self-respect; confidence in your own merit as an individual person.

self-effacement. The placing or keeping of oneself in the background.

self-exaltation. Exaltation of oneself, or vainglory, which is excessive pride, especially in one's achievements.

self-examination. Reflection on one's own condition; careful reflection on your own thoughts, beliefs, behavior, and circumstances (a Christian virtue).

self-fulfillment. Personal satisfaction; contentment or happiness as a result of personal work, initiative, or talent (sometimes a Christian virtue).

self-glorification. Boastful behavior; promotion of your own qualities and abilities, especially beyond what is true or appropriate.

self-governing. Using self-control; able to control your own actions and behavior (a Christian virtue).

selfhood. Individuality: the possession of a unique identity, distinct from others or somebody's character or personality; all the qualities and characteristics that make up somebody's character or personality or complete sense of self; or the possession of a fully developed personality.

self-image. Opinion of self; the opinion that you have of your own worth, attractiveness, or intelligence.

self-importance. Arrogance; an unrealistically high evaluation of your own importance or worth.

self-indulgence. Pursuit of own pleasure; lack of self-control in pursuing your own pleasure or satisfaction; something showing no self-control; something that reveals a lack of self-restraint.

self-interest. Selfishness; the placing of your own needs or desires before those of others; one's own needs or desires: somebody's own individual interests and welfare, especially when placed before and over those of other people.

self-introspective. Thoughtful, meditative, pensive, reflective (probably has no place for Christians because self gets in the way).

self-justification. Making of excuses for actions; an attempt to explain your own behavior or actions by making excuses; something done as justification; something somebody does or says in an attempt to explain personal behavior or actions.

self-knowledge. Knowledge of or understanding of one's true capabilities, character, feelings, or motivations (a Christian virtue).

self-love. The love of one's self; desire of personal happiness; tendency to seek one's own benefit or advantage.

self-pride. Self-esteem, pride in oneself.

self-made. Successful as result of work; successful or wealthy through your own efforts, rather than through birth or from the work of others.

self-mortification. Self-administered punishment; often as prescribed by religious precepts, because of some perceived fault or flaw, a term that indicates to mortify (degrade, put down, humble, kill) some aspect of a person (sometimes a Christian virtue).

self-opinionated. Certain of being right; confident of holding the correct opinions, or vain; very conceited.

self-pity. Pity felt for self: the self-indulgent belief that your life is harder and sadder than everyone else's.

self-preservation. Instinct to keep safe; the instinctive need to do what is necessary to survive danger.

self-reliance. Reliance, confidence, or trust in one's own efforts and abilities.

self-realization. Personal completeness; fulfillment of personal potential.

self-regard. Lacking regard for others; self-interest rather than concern for the well-being of others.

self-renunciation. Altruism, magnanimity, self-denial, temperance (sometimes a Christian virtue).

self-respect. Belief in your own worth and dignity.

self-restraint. Control over one's own actions: the ability to restrain the urge to do or say something (a Christian virtue).

self-reliance. Reliance upon one's own efforts and abilities.

self-righteousness. Believing in one's own virtue; sure of the moral superiority of personal beliefs and actions, usually to an irritating degree.

self-right. Natural independence; right to assert and possess natural virtues.

self-sacrifice. Giving up of things for others; the giving up of personal wants and needs, either from a sense of duty or in order to benefit others (a Christian virtue).

self-satisfaction. Usually smug satisfaction with oneself or one's position or achievement.

self-seeking. Selfish; interested only in gaining an advantage over others, not in sharing or cooperating.

self-seeking behavior. Behavior intended to secure an advantage over others.

self-serving. Lacking consideration of others; putting personal concerns and interests before those of others.

self-sufficiency. Not needing things from others; able to provide what is needed, without having to borrow or buy from others; able to manage alone; able to live independently of others.

self-surrender. Surrender of self; a yielding up (as to some influence) of oneself or one's will (a Christian virtue).

self-vindication. Defense or justification of self against denial or censure.

self-will. Stubbornness; stubborn determination to hold to personal views and behavior.

self-worth. Self-image; the perceived or assessment of one's value or quality.

Appendix B

Scripture References to Self-Denial

Definition of self-denial: a denial of one's own desires; the setting aside of one's own wishes, needs, or interests, whether voluntary, altruistic, or enforced by circumstances.

GENERAL REFERENCES

Please note that the following Scripture passages do not necessarily include the term *self-denial* but by themselves or taken in context infer self-denial. Also, bracketed remarks indicate instructional or informative text inserted by the author.

> "I will not offer burnt offerings to the LORD my God which cost me nothing."
>
> —2 Samuel 24:24

> "Surely I will not enter my house, nor lie on my bed; I will not give sleep to my eyes, or slumber to my eyelids; until I find a place for the LORD."
>
> —Psalm 132:3–5

"He who is slow to anger is better than the mighty, and he who rules his spirit, than he who captures a city."

—Proverbs 16:32

"Put a knife to your throat if you are a man of great appetite" (Proverbs 23:2; advice given to restrain one's appetite at all costs in the presence of a ruler at a meal.)

"I did not eat any tasty food, nor did meat or wine enter my mouth, nor did I use any ointment at all, until the entire three weeks were completed."

—Daniel 10:3

"If your right eye makes you stumble [meaning, causes you to fall into sin], tear it out and throw it from you; for it is better for you to lose one of the parts of your body, than for your whole body to be thrown into hell. If your right hand makes you stumble, cut it off and throw it from you; for it is better for you to lose one of the parts of your body, than for your whole body to go into hell."

—Matthew 5:29–30;
see also Matthew 18:8–9; Mark 9:43

"Then a scribe came and said to Him, 'Teacher, I will follow You wherever You go.' Jesus said to him, 'The foxes have holes and the birds of the air have nests, but the Son of Man has nowhere to lay His head.' Another of the disciples said to Him, 'Lord, permit me first to go and bury my father.' But Jesus said to him, 'Follow Me, and allow the dead to bury their own dead.'"

—Matthew 8:19–22; see also Luke 9:57–60

"He who loves father or mother more than Me is not worthy of Me; and he who loves son or daughter more than Me is not worthy of Me. And he who does not take his cross and follow after Me is not worthy of Me. He who has found his life will lose it, and he who has lost his life for My sake shall find it."

—Matthew 10:37–39

"The kingdom of heaven is like a treasure hidden in the field, which a man found and hid again; and from joy over it he goes and sells all that he has and buys that field. Again, the kingdom of heaven is like a merchant seeking fine pearls, and upon finding one pearl of great value, he went and sold all that he had and bought it."

—Matthew 13:44–46

"Then Jesus said to His disciples, 'If anyone wishes to come after Me, he must deny himself, and take up his cross and follow Me. For whoever wishes to save his life will lose it; but whoever loses his life for My sake will find it.'"

—Matthew 16:24–25; see also Mark 8:34–35;
Luke 9:23–24

"For there are eunuchs who were born that way from their mother's womb; and there are eunuchs who were made eunuchs by men; and there are also eunuchs who made themselves eunuchs for the sake of the kingdom of heaven. He who is able to accept this, let him accept it."

—Matthew 19:12

"Jesus said to him, 'If you wish to be complete, go and sell your possessions and give to the poor, and you will have treasure in heaven; and come, follow Me.'"

—Matthew 19:21

"Sell your possessions and give to charity; make yourselves money belts which do not wear out, an unfailing treasure in heaven, where no thief comes near nor moth destroys."

—Luke 12:33

"And when they had brought their boats to land, they left everything and followed Him."

—Luke 5:11

"He [Jesus] said to him [Levi the tax collector], 'Follow Me.' And he left everything behind, and got up and began to follow Him."

—Luke 5:27–28

"If anyone comes to Me, and does not hate his own father and mother and wife and children and brothers and sisters, yes, and even his own life, he cannot be My disciple....For which of you, when he wants to build a tower, does not first sit down and calculate the cost to see if he has enough to complete it? Otherwise, when he has laid a foundation and is not able to finish, all who observe it begin to ridicule him, saying, 'This man began to build and was not able to finish.' Or what king, when he sets out to meet another king in battle, will not first sit down and consider whether he is strong enough with ten thousand men to encounter the one coming against him with twenty thousand? Or else, while the other is still far away, he sends a delegation and asks terms of peace. [Here, Jesus cautions His followers to consider carefully the cost of full commitment to Christ in a life of service.] So then, none of you can be My disciple who does not give up all his own possessions."

—Luke 14:26, 27–33

"He said, 'The things that are impossible with people are possible with God.' Peter said, 'Behold, we have left our own homes and followed You.' And He said to them, 'Truly I say to you, there is no one who has left house or wife or brothers or parents or children, for the sake of the kingdom of God, who will not receive many times as much at this time and in the age to come, eternal life.'"

—Luke 18:27–30;
see also Mark 10:29–30

"And He saw a poor widow putting in two small copper coins. And He said, 'Truly I say to you, this poor widow put in more than all of them; for they all out of their surplus put into the offering; but she out of her poverty put in all that she had to live on."

—Luke 21:2–4; see also Mark 12:43–44

"He who loves his life loses it, and he who hates his life in this world will keep it to life eternal."

—John 12:25

"And now, behold, bound by the Spirit, I [Paul] am on my way to Jerusalem, not knowing what will happen to me there, except that the Holy Spirit solemnly testifies to me in every city, saying that bonds and afflictions await me. But I do not consider my life of any account as dear to myself, so that I may finish my course and the ministry which I received from the Lord Jesus, to testify solemnly of the gospel of the grace of God."

—Acts 20:22–24

"Paul answered, 'What are you doing, weeping and breaking my heart? For I am ready not only to be bound, but even to die at Jerusalem for the name of the Lord Jesus.'"

—Acts 21:13

"Knowing this, that our old self was crucified with Him, in order that our body of sin might be done away with, so that we would no longer be slaves to sin."

—Romans 6:6

"So then, brethren, we are under obligation, not to the flesh, to live according to the flesh—for if you are living according to the flesh, you must die; but if by the Spirit you are putting to death the deeds of the body, you will live."

—Romans 8:12–13

"But put on the Lord Jesus Christ, and make no provision for the flesh in regard to its lusts."

—Romans 13:14

"For not one of us lives for himself, and not one dies for himself; for if we live, we live for the Lord, or if we die, we die for the Lord; therefore whether we live or die, we are the Lord's."

—Romans 14:7–8; verses 1–12
are about not judging other believers

"Now we who are strong ought to bear the weaknesses of those without strength and not just please ourselves. Each of us is to please his neighbor for his good, to his edification. For even

Christ did not please Himself; but as it is written, 'The reproaches of those who reproached You fell on Me.'"

—Romans 15:1–3

"All things are lawful for me, but not all things are profitable. All things are lawful for me, but I will not be mastered by anything."

—1 Corinthians 6:12

"For if someone sees you, who have knowledge, dining in an idol's temple, will not his conscience, if he is weak, be strengthened to eat things sacrificed to idols? For through your knowledge he who is weak is ruined [not eternally, but probably in his spiritual life], the brother for whose sake Christ died. And so, by sinning against the brethren and wounding their conscience when it is weak, you sin against Christ."

—1 Corinthians 8:10–13

"If others share the right over you, do we not more? Nevertheless, we did not use this right, but we endure all things so that we may cause no hindrance to the gospel of Christ."

—1 Corinthians 9:12

"What then is my reward? That, when I [Paul] preach the gospel, I may offer the gospel without charge, so as not to make full use of my right in the gospel. For though I am free from all men, I have made myself a slave to all, so that I may win more."

—1 Corinthians 9:18–19

"I do all things for the sake of the gospel, so that I [Paul] may become a fellow partaker of it."

—1 Corinthians 9:23

"Everyone who competes in the games exercises self-control in all things. They then do it to receive a perishable wreath, but we an imperishable….But I [Paul] discipline my body and make it my slave, so that, after I have preached to others, I myself will not be disqualified."

—1 Corinthians 9:25, 27

"All things are lawful, but not all things are profitable. All things are lawful, but not all things edify. Let no one seek his own good, but that of his neighbor."

—1 Corinthians 10:23–24

"Giving no cause for offense in anything, so that the ministry will not be discredited."

—2 Corinthians 6:3

"I [Paul] have been crucified with Christ; and it is no longer I who live, but Christ lives in me; and the life which I now live in the flesh I live by faith in the Son of God, who loved me and gave Himself up for me."

—Galatians 2:20

"But I say, walk by the Spirit, and you will not carry out the desire of the flesh. For the flesh sets its desire against the Spirit, and the Spirit against the flesh; for these are in opposition to one another, so that you may not do the things that you please."

—Galatians 5:16–17

"Now those who belong to Christ Jesus have crucified the flesh with its passions and desires."

—Galatians 5:24

"Do not merely look out for your own personal interests, but also for the interests of others."

—Philippians 2:4

"Therefore consider the members of your earthly body as dead to immorality, impurity, passion, evil desire, and greed, which amount to idolatry."

—Colossians 3:5

"No soldier in active service entangles himself in the affairs of everyday life, so that he may please the one who enlisted him as a soldier."

—2 Timothy 2:4

"If we endure, we will also reign with Him [Jesus Christ]; if we deny Him, He also will deny us; if we are faithless, He remains faithful, for He cannot deny Himself."

—2 Timothy 2:12–13

"Instructing us to deny ungodliness and worldly desires and to live sensibly, righteously and godly in the present age."

—Titus 2:12

"Through Him then, let us continually offer up a sacrifice of praise to God, that is, the fruit of lips that give thanks to His name. And do not neglect doing good and sharing, for with such sacrifices God is pleased."

—Hebrews 13:15–16

"Submit yourselves for the Lord's sake to every human institution....For such is the will of God." (1 Peter 2:13, 15; in verses 11–16 Peter urges his readers to exercise the grace of God by submission to governing authorities and to be law-abiding citizens, all for the Lord's sake.)

"Therefore, since Christ has suffered in the flesh, arm yourselves also with the same purpose, because he who has suffered in the flesh has ceased from sin, so as to live the rest of the time in the flesh no longer for the lusts of men, but for the will of God."

—1 Peter 4:1–2

"For they [traveling missionaries] went out for the sake of the Name, accepting nothing from the Gentiles."

—3 John 1:7

"And they [the believers] overcame him [Satan] because of the blood of the Lamb and because of the word of their testimony, and they did not love their life even when faced with death."

—Revelation 12:11

Notable Instances of Self-Denial

Abraham willingly gave his son Isaac to the Lord (Genesis 22:1–12); he accorded to Lot, his junior, his preference of the land of Canaan (Genesis 13:9; 17:8).

Moses chose to suffer affliction with the people of God rather than enjoy the pleasures of sin (Hebrews 11:25); he took no compensation from the Israelites for his services (Numbers 16:15).

Samuel administered justice with integrity (1 Samuel 12:3–4).

The widow of Zarephath shared with Elijah the last of her sustenance (1 Kings 17:12–15).

Daniel denied himself the food and drink from King Nebuchadnezzar (Daniel 1:8); he refused rewards from Belshazzar (Daniel 5:16–17).

Esther risked her life for the deliverance of her people (Esther 4:16).

The Rechabites refused to drink wine or strong drink, or even to plant vineyards (Jeremiah 35:6–7).

Peter and other apostles abandoned their vocations to follow Jesus (Matthew 4:20; 9:9; Mark 1:16–20; 2:14; Luke 5:11, 27–28); forsook all to follow Jesus (Matthew 19:27; Mark 10:28).

The widow who cast her all into the temple treasury (Luke 21:4).

The early Christians had everything in common (Acts 2:44–45; 4:34).

Joses (Barnabas) sold his possessions and gave all he received to the apostles (Acts 4:36–37).

Paul did not count even his life dear to himself (Acts 20:24; Philippians 3:7–8); did not covet any man's silver or gold or apparel (Acts 20:33); labored for his own support while he also taught (Acts 20:34–35; 1 Corinthians 4:12; 10:33).

Appendix C

Scriptures Containing Key Words (NASB)

References	Deny	Self	Cross	Life	Follow
Matthew 10:38-39	O	O	X	X	X
Matthew 16:24-25	X	X	X	X	X
Mark 8:34-35	X	X	X	X	X
Luke 9:23-24	X	X	X	X	X
Luke 14:26-27	O	O	X	X	X
Luke 17:33	O	O	O	X	O
John 12:25-26	O	O	O	X	X
Legend: X=presence of word					
0=absence of word					
Note: Some references equate					
'come after' to 'follow'					

Models of Self

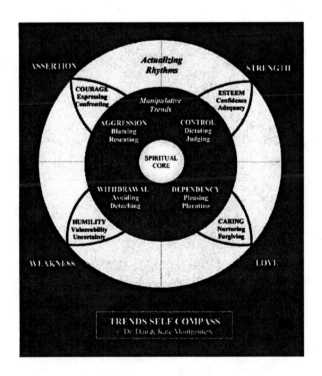

The Trends Self Compass

The central model of the Self Compass is a growth tool, an instrument for personality assessment, healing, and transformation. (From the website, Compass Therapy™ and Compass Psychotheology. Founder Dr. Dan Montgomery)

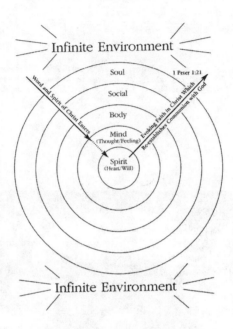

The Human Self

The human self is depicted as a series of concentric circles representing the inner circle of the human spirit, which includes the heart and will of the individual, the mind, the body, the social dimension and lastly the soul which integrates all the smaller circles (Willard 2002, 38.)

Appendix E

Works of the Holy Spirit

In regard to Christian spirituality, maturity, and the transformation of self-life to a Christlike life, we keep talking about the power of the Holy Spirit being as a guiding force with creative power. We need to be perfectly clear about what specific actions the Holy Spirit performs in followers of Christ as a result of these functions. The following features summarize a few of the works of the Holy Spirit with corresponding Scripture references.

The Holy Spirit impregnated Mary. "The Holy Spirit will come upon you [Mary]...the holy offspring shall be called the Son of God" (Luke 1:35).

The Holy Spirit indwells the believer." Do you not know that your body is a temple of the Holy Spirit who is in you, whom you have received from God?" (1 Corinthians 6:19).

The Holy Spirit guides the believer. "For all who are being led by the Spirit of God, these are sons of God" (Romans 8:14).

The Holy Spirit functions in regeneration of the believer. Jesus said, "Truly truly, I say to you, unless one is born of water and the Spirit, he cannot enter into the kingdom of God. That which is born of the flesh is flesh, and that which is born of the Spirit is spirit" (John 3:5–6).

The Holy Spirit works with Christ in salvation and renewal. "He [Jesus Christ] saved us...by the washing of regeneration and renewing by the Holy Spirit" (Titus 3:5).

The Holy Spirit, in the process of regeneration, delivers from death and creates new life in the believer. "By the Spirit you are putting to death the deeds of the body, you will live" (Romans 8:13).

The Holy Spirit creates and preserves life. "You [God] send forth Your Spirit, they [living things] are created" (Psalm 104:30); "The Spirit of God has made me, and the breath of the Almighty gives me life" (Job 33:4).

The Holy Spirit sanctifies the believer. "God has chosen you from the beginning for salvation through sanctification by the Spirit and faith in the truth" (2 Thessalonians 2:13).

Appendix F

What Christians May Know about Themselves

The following scriptures are purposely selected out of many, many more that directly speak to the two questions, "Who am I?" and "What do I now possess?" as they relate to a regenerated believer in Jesus Christ. These verses were also chosen because of their relevance to several issues discussed in this book, such as the aspects of salvation, identification with Christ, deliverances, indwelling of the Holy Spirit, and the newness of becoming like Christ.

I Know Who I am and What I Have Received

I have been justified and redeemed. "Being justified as a gift by His grace through the redemption which is in Christ Jesus" (Romans 3:24).

My old self was crucified with Christ, and I am no longer a slave to sin. "Knowing this, that our old self was crucified with Him, in order that the body of sin might be done away with, so that we would no longer be slaves to sin" (Romans 6:6).

I have been set free from the law of sin and death. "For the law of the Spirit of life in Christ Jesus has set you free from the law of sin and of death" (Romans 8:2).

In Christ Jesus, I have understanding, virtuous morality, am set apart, and emancipation. "But by doing you are in Christ Jesus,

341

who became to us wisdom from God, and righteousness and sanctification, and redemption" (1 Corinthians 1:30).

My body is a temple of the Holy Spirit, who dwells in me. "Do you not know that you are a temple of God and that the Spirit of God dwells in you?" (1 Corinthians 3:16).

I am joined to the Lord and am one spirit with Him. "But the one who joins himself to the Lord is one spirit with Him" (1 Corinthians 6:17).

I am a new creature in Christ. "Therefore, if any man is in Christ, he is a new creature; the old things passed away, behold, new things have come" (2 Corinthians 5:17).

Because of God's mercy and love, I have been made alive with Christ. "But God, being rich in mercy, because of His great love with which He loved us, even when we were dead in our transgressions, made us alive together with Christ (by grace you have been saved)" (Ephesians 2:4–5).

My new self is righteous and holy. "Put on the new self, which in the likeness of God has been created in righteousness and holiness of the truth" (Ephesians 4:24).

I have been raised up with Christ. "If you have been raised up with Christ, keep seeking the things above, where Christ is, seated at the right hand of God" (Colossians 3:1).

There are also many scriptures that speak of the followers of Christ as being totally received by God. The following verses were particularly selected for you who may have some misgivings or doubts about being completely accepted and unconditionally loved by God. In this regard, each one of the following eleven passages of Holy Scripture should provide clarification as to who you are or what you have received as a result of God's acceptance.

I Am Accepted. I Know Who I Am and What I Have Received.

I am complete in Christ. "For in Him [Christ] all the fullness of Deity dwells in bodily form, and in Him you have been made complete, and He is the head over all rule and authority" (Colossians 2:9–10).

I am Christ's friend. "No longer do I [Jesus] call you slaves, for the slave does not know what his master is doing; but I have called you friends, for all things that I have heard from My Father I have made known to you" (John 15:15).

I have been justified. "Therefore having been justified by faith, we have peace with God through our Lord Jesus Christ" (Romans 5:1).

I am a member of Christ's body. "Now you are Christ's body, and individually members of it" (1 Corinthians 12:27).

I have been redeemed and forgiven of all my sins. "For He [God the Father] delivered us from the domain of darkness, and transferred us to the kingdom of His beloved Son, in whom we have redemption, the forgiveness of sins" (Colossians 1:13–14).

I am a saint. "Paul, an apostle of Christ Jesus by the will of God, to the saints who are at Ephesus, and who are faithful in Christ Jesus" (Ephesians 1:1).

I am united with the Lord, and I am one spirit with Him. "But the one who joins himself to the Lord [Christ] is one spirit with Him" (1 Corinthians 6:17).

I have direct access to God through the Holy Spirit. "For through Him [Christ] we both have our access in one Sprit to the Father" (Ephesians 2:18).

I am adopted as God's child. "Just as He [God] chose us in Him before the foundation of the world, that we should be holy and blameless before Him in love He predestined us to adoption as sons through Jesus Christ to Himself, according to the kind intention of His will" (Ephesians 1:4–5).

I have been bought with a price. I belong to God. "Or do you not know that your body is a temple of the Holy Spirit who is in you, whom you have from God, and that you are not your own? For you have been bought with a price: therefore glorify God in your body" (1 Corinthians 6:19–20).

I am God's child. "But as many as received Him [Christ], to them He gave the right to become children of God, even to those who believe in His name" (John 1:12).

List of Commonly Held Virtues

As a further exercise to describe the marks of a spiritual, maturing Christian, the reader may want to compose a list of virtues that are found in this book or in the Bible. Sometimes such a list can be personalized by incorporating values that are not found in Scripture. To assist in this endeavor, see the following list commonly held virtues that have no particular connection to a religious belief or spiritual orientation:

acceptance	charity	detachment
altruism,	chastity	determination
appreciation	cleanliness	diligence
assertiveness	commitment	discernment
attention	courteousness	empathy
autonomy	consideration	encouragement
awareness	contentment	endurance
balance	cooperativeness	enthusiasm
beauty	courage	equanimity
benevolence	courteousness	equity
candor	creativity	excellence
caring	curiosity	fairness
caution	dependability	faithfulness

fidelity
fitness
flexibility
foresight
forgiveness
fortitude
friendliness
generosity
gentleness
happiness
health
helpfulness
honesty
honor
hopefulness
hospitality
humility
humor
idealism

imagination
impartiality
independence
industriousness
innocence
integrity
intuition
inventiveness
justice
kindness
knowledge
lovingness
loyalty
mercy
moderation
modesty
morality
nonviolence
nurturing

obedience
openness
optimism
patience
peacefulness
perseverance
philanthropy
piety
potential
prudence
purity
purposefulness
resilience
remembrance
respectfulness
reverence
responsibility
restraint
self-awareness

Glossary

Because of the wide diversity of background and understanding among people of the Christian community it is essential to identify and briefly clarify a few terms widely held within doctrines of the Christian faith. This approach should be especially helpful while reading this book, as well as the Bible, which may include theological terms that are infrequently used in everyday communications. These listings are presented in abbreviated form and expressed in lay terms as much as possible.

atonement. Reconciliation (at-one-ment) between God and humans brought about by the life and death of Jesus Christ.
born again. See "new birth."
confession. The acknowledgment of sin (specific or general), either before God or people as a condition of forgiveness.
covenant. An agreement; as relating to salvation, those agreements initiated by God and agreed to by a person in which God offers salvation on conditions, and the person accepts the offer and the condition.
Decalogue. The Ten Commandments; God's moral law.
expiation. Atonement for sin through the life and death of Jesus; removal of guilt.

faith. A person's cooperative response of trust and obedience to God; a cooperating commitment to His expressed will as revealed in His Word.

forgiveness. God's pardon for sins and sinfulness.

godliness. Conduct of God reproduced in child of God.

grace. The undeserved benevolent acts and love of God for sinners.

guiltless. The state of being innocent, blameless, and pure.

holiness. When applied to human beings, holiness is the likeness to God in character and freedom from all that is contrary to His character.

humility. The state or quality of being free from pride and selfishness.

imparted righteousness. That righteousness, or acceptable character, that is developed by the Holy Spirit in the cooperative believer. The development of such a character makes individuals fit for heaven.

imputed righteousness. The holy and perfect character of Jesus that God credits to the repentant, believing sinner's account. A person who has this character credited to him or her holds a title to heaven.

incarnation. The act of the second Person of the Trinity becoming human in the person of Christ.

justification. The act of God of declaring a repentant, believing sinner righteous by imputing to him or her the perfect character of Jesus. See "imputed righteousness."

justification by faith. The same act as in "justification" above, obtained only through faith. See "faith."

kingdom of God. That spiritual kingdom over which God is King. This phase often designates the kingdom of grace and its future post-Advent phase, the kingdom of glory.

law. The moral law is summarized in the Ten Commandments. It is a reflection of God's character and shows how we must live if we are to be like God. In Romans and Galatians, law is often used with reference to Jewish laws; some hoped to be saved by keeping these laws.

love. The principle of respect and active concern for another person, as defined in the law and portrayed in the life of Jesus; the principle that impels responsible, unselfish actions.

meditation. The act of thinking reflectively on Bible teachings and spiritual subjects, as they pertain to the meaning of the Christian life.

new birth. A figure of speech describing a sinner's turning to God and God's acceptance of him or her as His child. "Born of God" is a similar description, suggesting that at conversion one begins a totally new life. It highlights the fact that a divine element is introduced, effecting a miraculous change.

new covenant. God's ancient agreement to save humankind, ratified by the death of Jesus. See "covenant."

old man. Preconversion human nature, characterized by a preference for sinfulness over righteousness.

pardon. Forgiveness; the removal of guilt.

perfect. The quality of completeness ascribed to a person's character development wherein there is continuous growth in fulfilling God's will.

perfection. Although never fully attained while on earth, it is the ultimate goal of Christian development believers seek to attain as they reflect the image of Jesus.

quicken. Old English word meaning to make alive, applied in the New Testament to God's act of awakening a person who is "dead" in sin.

reconciliation. The restoration of harmony between humans and God through the death of Jesus. The change occurs in people, not God.

redemption. God's act of retrieving men and women from sin and the bondage of law; reclaimed through the death, burial, resurrection, and intercession of Jesus.

reformation. A correction or improvement in Christian conduct and service.

righteousness. Quality or state of being right, that is, being in harmony with God and His law.

righteousness of Christ. Christ's uprightness as revealed in His perfect character. Christ's righteousness is both imputed and imparted to the believer. (See "imputed righteousness" and "imparted righteousness.") The former act is often described as justification, and the latter as sanctification.

righteousness by faith. A phrase showing that the righteousness of Christ (see above) is received only by faith. (See "faith.") Those who seek it by any other means, such as by works, will not receive it.

repentance. A divinely inspired recognition of, sorrow for, change of mind, and a renunciation of sin. The result is a reformed life, characterized by obedience to God's law.

revival. A resurgence of spiritual life, a returning to faith after a period of spiritual decline; reformation of life is the result of genuine revival.

sanctification. See "imparted righteousness," and "righteousness by faith."

sin. That which is out of harmony with God's law or character; the sinner rejects God as the center of life and retains self as the center.

temptation. Enticement to sin.

transformation. A change, alteration, modification, renewal, or metamorphosis that usually denotes an improvement or betterment. An event that occurs when something or someone passes from one state or phase to another. The change by which a lost person is found and becomes more like God in character.

trust (in God). Confidence that God will make good on His promises; it is one of the elements of faith.

union with Christ. A relationship with Christ that identifies with Him in every regard. One who identifies with Christ in aims, purposes, conduct, and in and with His passion. Identification of a believer with Christ, in His crucifixion and resurrection, provides the means to exchange one's self-life for the life of Christ.

victory. Triumph over Satan's temptations and in achieving the Christian goal of sanctification.

will. The capacity of a person to choose between alternatives and to act upon his or her choice.

works (of a Christian). These are the expressions of love to God and others, resulting from faith in Jesus.

works (of law). Efforts to earn salvation by observing a body of laws apart from faith in Jesus.

yoke. A symbol of service. Christ's yoke being the service He expects His followers to perform.

Resources and Suggested Reading

Adam Clarke's Commentary on the New Testament. 1999. Parsons Technology.

Amplified New Testament. 1958. Grand Rapids, MI: Zondervan.

Boa, Kenneth. 2001. *Conformed to His Image: Biblical and Practical Approaches to Spiritual Formation.* Grand Rapids, MI: Zondervan.

Brownback, Paul. 1987. *The Danger of Self-Love.* Chicago: Moody Bible Institute.

Chambers, Oswald. 1963. *My Utmost for His Highest.* Uhrichsville, OH: Barbour.

Chantry, Walter J. 1981. *The Shadow of the Cross: Studies in Self-Denial.* East Peoria, IL: Versa Press.

Circuit Rider 29, no. 4 (July/August 2005). http://www.umph.org/resources/publications/circuitrider.asp?act=displayissue&cr_issue_id=61.

Crossan, John Dominic, and N.T. Wright. 2006. *The Resurrection of Jesus.* Edited by Robert B. Stewart. Minneapolis: Fortress.

Forbes, Stephanie. 1996. *Help Your Self: Today's Obsession with Satan's Oldest Lie.* Wheaton, IL: Crossway.

Foster, Richard J. 1988. *Celebration of Discipline: The Path to Spiritual Growth.* San Francisco: HarperSanFrancisco.

Hegre, T. A. 1960. *The Cross and Sanctification.* Minneapolis: Bethany.

Ingram, Chip. 2003. *The Miracle of Life Change: How God Transforms His Children*. Chicago: Moody Press.

Interpreter's Bible, Volume VII, General Articles on the New Testament, The Gospel According to Matthew and The Gospel According to Mark. 1951. Nashville: Abingdon.

Lewis, C. S. *The Screwtape Letters* and *Screwtape Proposes a Toast*. 1962. New York: Macmillan.

————. *Mere Christianity*. 1980. San Francisco: HarperSanFrancisco.

Lindsell, Harold, ed. 1971. *Lindsell Study Bible, The Living Bible*. Wheaton, IL: Tyndale House.

Marshall, Catherine. 1991. *The Inspirational Writings of Catherine Marshall: Something More* and *A Closer Walk*. New York: Inspirational Press.

Martin, James. 2006. *Becoming Who You Are: Insights on the True Self from Thomas Merton and Other Saints*. Mahwah, NJ: Paulist.

Milton, John. 2003. *Paradise Lost*. Edited by John Leonard. New York: Penguin.

Morris, Leon. 1992. *The Gospel According to Matthew*. Grand Rapids, MI: Eerdmans.

Mulholland Jr., M. Robert. 2006. *The Deeper Life: The Spirituality of Discovering Your True Self*. Downers Grove, IL: InterVarsity.

Murray, Andrew. 2003. *Absolute Surrender*. Minneapolis: Bethany.

————. 2004. *Humility*. Gainesville, FL: Bridge-Logos.

Neuhaus, Richard John. 2000. *Death on a Friday Afternoon: Meditations on the Last Words of Jesus from the Cross*. New York: Basic Books.

New Interpreter's Bible, Volume VIII, Matthew and Mark. 1995. Nashville: Abingdon.

Newton, Gary C. 2004. *Growing Toward Spiritual Maturity*. Wheaton, IL: Crossway.

Packer, J. I. 1973. *Knowing God*. Downers Grove, IL: InterVarsity.

Pink, Arthur W. 1980. *The Attributes of God*. Grand Rapids, MI: Baker.

Pope Benedict XVI. 2007. *Saved in Hope*. Encyclical Letter, Libreria Editrice Vaticana. San Francisco: Ignatius Press.

Prince, Derek, 2000. *Bought with Blood: The Divine Exchange at the Cross*. Grand Rapids, MI: Chosen Books.

Ringma, Charles. 2002. *Resist the Powers with Jacques Ellul.* Colorado Springs: Piñon Press.

Rolheiser, Ronald. 1999. *The Holy Longing: The Search for a Christian Spirituality.* New York: Doubleday.

Ryrie, Charles Caldwell. 1978. *The Ryrie Study Bible, New American Standard Version.* Chicago: Moody Press.

Schweitzer, Albert. 1998. *Out of My Life and Thought, An Autobiography.* Baltimore: Johns Hopkins University Press.

Sproul, R. C. August 2009. *TableTalk.* Ligonier Ministries.

Thomas, Robert L., ed. 1980. *New American Standard Exhaustive Concordance of the Bible.* Nashville: Holman.

Tolle, Eckhart. 2005. *A New Earth: Awakening to Your Life's Purpose.* New York: Penguin.

Tozer, A. W. 1955. *The Root of the Righteous.* Camp Hill, PA: Christian Publications.

———. 1982. *The Pursuit of God.* Camp Hill, PA: Christian Publications.

———. 2005. *The Radical Cross: Living the Passion of Christ.* Camp Hill, PA: WingSpread.

Unger, Merrill F. 1980. *Unger's Bible Dictionary.* Chicago: Moody Press.

Warren, Rick. 2002. *The Purpose Driven Life: What on Earth Am I Here For?* Grand Rapids, MI: Zondervan.

Webster's New Collegiate Dictionary. 1977. Springfield, MA: G. & C. Merriam.

Whitney, Donald. 2002. *Simplify Your Spiritual Life.* Colorado Springs: Navpress.

Willard, Dallas. 1990. *The Spirit of the Disciples: Understanding How God Changes Lives.* San Francisco: HarperSanFrancisco.

———. 1998. *The Divine Conspiracy: Rediscovering Our Hidden Life in God.* San Francisco: HarperSanFrancisco.

———. 2002. *Renovation of the Heart: Putting on the Character of Christ.* Colorado Springs: Navpress.

WinePressPublishing
Your Book, Defined.
Since 1991.

To order additional copies of this book call:
1-877-421-READ (7323)
or please visit our website at
www.WinePressbooks.com

If you enjoyed this quality custom-published book,
drop by our website for more books and information.

www.winepresspublishing.com
"Your partner in custom publishing."

9 781414 117171